Polity

Polity

Political Culture and the Nature of Politics

Craig L. Carr

ROWMAN & LITTLEFIELD PUBLISHERS, INC.
Lanham • Boulder • New York • Toronto • Plymouth, UK

ROWMAN & LITTLEFIELD PUBLISHERS, INC.

Published in the United States of America
by Rowman & Littlefield Publishers, Inc.
A wholly owned subsidary of The Rowman & Littlefield Publishing Group, Inc.
4501 Forbes Boulevard, Suite 200, Lanham, Maryland 20706
www.rowmanlittlefield.com

Estover Road
Plymouth PL6 7PY
United Kingdom

Copyright © 2007 by Rowman & Littlefield Publishers, Inc.

British Library Cataloguing in Publication Information Available

Library of Congress Cataloging-in-Publication Data:

Carr, Craig L., 1948–
  Polity : an introduction to politics / Craig L. Carr.
    p. cm.
  Includes bibliographical references and index.
  ISBN-13: 978-0-7425-4825-1 (cloth : alk. paper)
  ISBN-10: 0-7425-4825-2 (cloth : alk. paper)
  ISBN-13: 978-0-7425-4826-8 (pbk. : alk. paper)
  ISBN-10: 0-7425-4826-0 (pbk. : alk. paper)
  1. Political culture.   2. Political science.   I. Title.
JA75.7.C36   2007
320.01—dc22   2006039719

Printed in the United States of America

♾ ™ The paper used in this publication meets the minimum requirements of American
National Standard for Information Sciences—Permanence of Paper for Printed Library
Materials, ANSI/NISO Z39.48-1992.

To the memory of
S. L. C., P. M. C., and C. D. C.

Contents

Acknowledgments

This book grew out of the lectures that I developed over the years for a course intended to introduce students to politics. Gary Scott, then chair of the Department of Political Science at Portland State University, asked me to develop a class that would genuinely introduce students to politics and not simply offer them an introductory course on some subfield of the discipline of political science. I have no idea if I ever managed to fulfill his request, or even if it is possible to do so. But Gary's charge inspired me to think about what such a class, and what such a book, might look like. The work that follows is the product of my ruminations on this issue, and I want to thank Gary both for the inspiration to undertake this project and for his support and friendship along the way. I must also thank the innumerable students at Portland State who have passed and suffered through my Introduction to Politics class. Their queries, comments, and concerns are undoubtedly the most significant influences on this work. My efforts also benefited from the wonderful research and classroom support I received from several graduate students, and so special thanks to Stephen Moore, Christian Woldmann, C. J. Gordon, and Chris Cooney. Tony Lott offered many helpful and thoughtful comments on the work, but I should thank him most for the single malt he occasionally brings me from Scotland. My thoughts on politics have also benefited greatly from discussions with my friends and colleagues Birol Yesilada, Dave Kinsella, and Richard Clucas. Finally, I want to thank Dawn, who helped.

Introduction

We do not find boundaries; we draw them.

Ludwig Wittgenstein

This is a book about politics, and for the most part, it is only about politics. It is not, that is to say, a book about current events, the workings of a particular governmental administration, or the political luminaries who happen to govern particular states. This might leave readers wondering what this book could possibly be about, because when people think of politics, they usually think about things like current events and political actors. But this is a mistake, and exposing and detailing this mistake is one of the major goals of the discussion to follow. Put cryptically, it is a mistake to equate politics with current events because there is much more to politics than the daily events of the governmental process and the activities and personalities of politicians. In fact, I want to propose a rather radical idea, or an idea that will seem radical to those who cannot distinguish between politics and current events: It is simply not possible to understand politics satisfactorily if one focuses only on current political events and the politicians associated with them. To understand politics, it is necessary to step back from these particular matters and take a fresh look at the political world. It is necessary, therefore, to think about politics as a subject of interest and concern in its own right and independent of the issues, policies, and programs of a particular government, as well as the activities and actions of political actors. This, then, is the challenge to be undertaken in a book that purports to be about politics and only about politics.

POLITICS AND BOUNDARIES

The best way to begin is by posing a simple question: what is politics? If politics involves something other than, something more than, the activities of

1

some particular government and the actors associated with it, this question cannot be quickly answered by pointing to some specific governmental process. The question, after all, asks about the nature of *politics*, not about, say, the activities of the national government of the United States. There is no reason to think, prior to examination, that politics is synonymous with the process of governing a particular state. This might make the initial question seem more troubling than it would otherwise seem to be, and skeptics will likely notice that there is also no very good reason to suppose, prior to examination, that politics is not about governmental activity.

But the question "what is politics?" remains a simple one, and like many simple questions, it has a simple answer. Nonetheless, this book is undertaken in the belief that few people are able to offer anything approaching a satisfactory answer to it, and this is because they have become overly inclined to stare at the trees without noticing the forest. Not many would say, for example, that politics is about boundaries, about the kinds of things that unite some people and separate them from others. But this is as good an answer to the question "what is politics?" as it is a simple one. In fact, the ancient Greek notion of a *polis*, or polity, derives from the classic Greek root meaning of the word for "wall."[1] Walls enclose and exclude, and this is a good way to understand politics. Politics brings some people together to form a group, and it leaves others outside the group. It brings into being a sense of "we," and by so doing it necessarily also gives rise to a sense of "they."

Unfortunately, putting simple answers to seemingly simple questions often does more to confuse and mystify than to illuminate and edify. This would seem to be the case when it comes to thinking about politics in terms of boundaries. This apparently simple answer to the question about the nature of politics gives rise to a mystery. In order to decide if this is a good answer to the question, it is necessary to have some sense of how politics unites and how it divides. So it is important to know more about the nature of the boundaries that people erect in the course of their political lives and why they matter. Thinking of politics in terms of boundaries, then, is just a beginning. It gives rise to the more complicated, obscure, and troubling questions that must be examined and answered in order to achieve a more adequate and comprehensive understanding of politics.

But an examination of the kinds of boundaries that seem relevant to people as political beings is a good place to begin the job of trying to understand politics. All kinds of things can establish boundaries, but which of them introduce boundaries relevant to the notion of politics? Geographical boundaries might come to mind first, and to be sure, these boundaries have played a significant role in political history. The United States is bounded by two oceans, for example, that separate its citizens from Europe and Asia, and the resultant isolation during the formative years of American political development is important for a satisfactory understanding of American political history. Switzerland is encased in a fortress of mountains, and this has greatly influenced its political development. Australia sits alone in the Pacific Ocean, and so forth. All these things matter when it comes to understanding the political development of the countries involved.

Although geographical boundaries are important for the political histories of a great many states, they are for the most part irrelevant to understanding politics or to understanding what unites a people into a polity and separates them from the rest of the world. And with technological advances, like the capacity for flight and improved transportation and communication capabilities, they become even more irrelevant. People today are not nearly as geographically separated as they were, say, when Hannibal crossed the Alps to attack Rome. Nor for that matter are states always or invariably geographically separate. No distinctive geographical boundaries separate most of the United States from Canada, for example, but there is a boundary between these two states nonetheless.

A second type of boundary that seems relevant to the subject of politics is suggested by the existence of independent legal systems, and there is obviously something to understanding politics in terms of legal boundaries. The Constitution of the United States is in force over a certain identifiable territory, and the territory where it is in force (i.e., where it anchors the law of the land) is the United States and its legal protectorates. Canadians are not subject to the U.S. Constitution. They have their own constitution, and it is in force over a certain territory (which constitutes Canada), thus introducing a boundary that we might think of as the Canadian *state*. So states can be understood as separate legal entities with a (legal) right of self-determination within the territory in which their legal system has force.

States, in other words, have or enjoy a certain status—a type of legal recognition that involves identifying the territory that is theirs and distinguishing it from the territory that is not theirs. The notion of the state derives from the Latin word *status*, which might be translated as either "status" or "standing." States are legal entities that enjoy a legal right of self-determination, and this right is generally recognized and acknowledged by other states of the world as a matter of international law. But the notion of "the state" introduces problems when it comes to thinking about politics. People frequently speak as if the state is a kind of superperson capable of what philosophers like to call agency, that is, the ability to formulate intentions and act upon them in order to bring about desired ends. But it should be obvious that states are not really agents in this sense at all. Technically, states aren't capable of action; only people are capable of action. If we say, "The state did so and so," what we really mean is that certain people did so and so and that they acted in the name of the state, that is, with the authority granted them by the formative law that *constitutes* the state. It seems appropriate to think of these people as the government or as that group of people empowered and authorized to act on behalf of and in the name of the state.

But this conception of the state gives rise to further and perhaps even more troubling questions. How and why is government empowered or authorized to act in the name of the state? Are there any limits to this power or restrictions on the authorization enjoyed by government? Which people in society are members of the government, and how can they be recognized?

One way to explore these difficulties is to refer back to the legal status of the state. In the United States, people might consult the U.S. Constitution in order to answer these questions. The Constitution provides a blueprint for how government can act, and it defines and limits the way the government may act. It is in this sense that the Constitution *constitutes* a state. But it also seems that the U.S. Constitution does not provide much of a blueprint. Although it is reasonably specific on how government can act, the definition of governmental authority—the sphere in which government is authorized to act—is vague, and the limitations it imposes upon governmental action are imprecise. These matters introduce problems of constitutional interpretation, and this raises additional questions. How should the document be interpreted, and who should do the interpreting? Here the document is strangely silent. But even if the document was specific on these matters, Americans might still want to ask why they should be guided by the Constitution. Why should they recognize and respect the Constitution as the authoritative voice on the power and authority of the government? A legal answer to this might note that the Constitution is the supreme law of the land because it says so in the Supremacy Clause (Art. VI, sec. 2). But this doesn't answer the question satisfactorily, for the question asks why anyone should be guided by the Constitution in the first place. This can't be answered by appealing back to the Constitution itself. Suppose a vast majority of Americans decide that it is time for the state to have a new constitution. Suppose that many Americans want to rethink and reconsider the authority of their government. Would they not be able to do so, and if they elected to change the Constitution, would it not make sense to think that the state had simply revised its system of government? If so, then understanding politics in terms of legal boundaries exclusively would begin to break down. While Americans would have adopted a new constitution, they would still be bound together as members of the same state throughout the process. But this means that the state must be something other than the legal entity established by the Constitution.

There are additional problems with thinking that the boundaries relevant

to understanding politics are fundamentally, if not exclusively, legal in character. While the notion of legal territoriality might enable people to spatially
recognize a given state, it doesn't necessarily say much about who belongs
to or is subject to the authority of the state. Of course, this too could be considered a legal matter to be resolved by appeal to a formative legal document
like a constitution. The U.S. Constitution, for example, indicates who is to be
understood as a legal citizen of the state and who is not. A person born within
the legal territory of the United States or naturalized to citizenship is constitutionally understood to be a citizen of the United States according to the Four-
teenth Amendment. Such persons are continuously told that they are
Americans, that is, citizens of the United States. This makes American citizenship largely an accident of birth for those Americans who are born in the
United States. But why should a person accept this description of herself?
Suppose a person wishes to decline the honor. Or suppose some people
decide to secede from the Union, preferring perhaps to live outside the state
that surrounds them, as the group calling themselves the Freemen have
claimed to do. Can a person decline citizenship and elect not to be a member
of the state? A person can do this by leaving the state and denouncing her
citizenship, but can she denounce citizenship and remain within the legal
parameters of the state? Can the law of the state impose citizenship upon
someone who just happens to reside there? More generally, is being an American simply a matter of legal citizenship, or is there more to the description
of a person as an American than just the identification of a certain legal
status? It seems that there should be more to being an American than this,
but if so, it is necessary to look beyond legal boundaries to understand what
this something more happens to be.

There are, to be sure, other kinds of boundaries that unite and divide people. Culture, ethnicity, race, language, and religion also introduce important
boundaries in people's lives. Groups and communities bound together by a
distinctive religion, language, and/or ethnicity establish clear identities for
their members. Frequently, though not always, they are tightly knit social
units, and membership in them constitutes a formative dimension of one's
self-understanding. In a sense, these groups qualify as political units because
they often share in common the kind of normative and conceptual understandings that seem to be basic to political association. Sometimes such communities are also recognized as politically independent states. Sometimes,
these communities also have legal boundaries generally recognized and
acknowledged, say in international law, as formative of a state.

When this is the case, it is commonplace to think of them as *nation-states*.
Reference to a nation indicates a strong sense of communal identity and
social homogeneity; nations are characteristically united by a common lan-

guage, religion, culture, and ethnicity.[2] When such groups also enjoy legal independence from other groups and complete self-sovereignty, they form nation-states. The city-states of ancient Greece and the Italian republics of the Renaissance provide reasonable examples of nation-states, but such things are rare in the modern world. There is no particular logic to the way religious, ethnic, racial, or linguistic groups are present in states. Sometimes ethnic and religious groups form minorities within much larger and diverse states. Sometimes they occupy a territory that spreads over the boundaries of several states. Many of the states with boundaries that incorporate a great deal of territory, like the United States, have a variety of ethnic, religious, cultural, and even linguistic communities within them. These communities might be spread throughout the general population and not occupy any distinct portion of the territory belonging to the state, or they might constitute a geographic subunit within the state itself and attempt to sustain their cultural or religious homogeneity against outside influence. In either case, they are often significant presences in the state and may well introduce some important and troubling problems for political stability and coherence.

States that comprehend several different ethnic, religious, cultural, and/or linguistic groups within their borders are frequently described as *pluralist states*. All states that are not nation-states may in principle be considered pluralist states, but the more diverse a state's population, the more pluralist it is. Ethnic and religious group differences matter greatly to people. Ethnicity, race, religion, and culture are formative and integral dimensions of personal identity; they introduce conceptual and normative influences that shape the way people see and understand the world, as well as the beliefs they hold about how their lives should go. Therefore, they constitute interpersonal boundaries of the greatest importance to people, and these people will try to defend them when and if they think they are threatened. So, these differences are a potential source of intergroup animosity and conflict, and when such conflict erupts, it can create serious problems for pluralist states.

The fact of pluralism and the existence of pluralist states together suggest two additional questions that complicate thinking about politics. How and why do pluralist states hang together? Why do they not decay into a collection of independent nation-states? What is it that binds the racial, ethnic, cultural, and religious diversity present in pluralist states into a single state? It may be reasonable to suppose that the answers to these questions are related. One reason why pluralist states may hang together is because there is something that the groups share in common despite all that separates them. But what is this something that is capable of uniting groups displaying such great social, cultural, and religious diversity into a common state? This "something," whatever it is, will likely reveal much that is important to understanding the nature of politics, if it can be successfully identified.

Yet this way of putting the matter is potentially misleading. There may actually be several reasons why states hang together and why pluralist states can reasonably be considered states, and different states may hang together and qualify as states for different reasons. But the list of reasons that might explain why states hang together and why they qualify as states regardless of the diversity present there is not very long.

For one thing, states might be held together by force of arms. This is hardly unheard of in the history of the world. If some group or coalition of groups possesses sufficient power to force the population of a given territory to respect its commands, this state is held together, albeit crudely, by force and coercion. Saddam Hussein, for example, maintained control in Iraq by suppressing those groups opposed to his rule, and Joseph Stalin is said to have managed to rule the Soviet Union with an iron fist, thereby ensuring its continued identity. Force of arms can be, and historically has often been, an effective way to sustain the existence of the state. Many people, however, think that it is not a very good way to do so. States with a ruling elite that maintain control over a diverse population in this way are typically and historically thought to be tyrannical or despotic. Accordingly, *tyranny* may be understood as the ability of a ruling group or coalition to maintain control of other groups against their will. Tyrannies don't always have an individual tyrant at their head; sometimes they are under the control of ruling elites or a ruling party that maintains its position by means of brute force. Further, individual tyrants are hardly sufficient to make a tyranny; even tyrants rely on the support of others to maintain and sustain their power.

Tyrannical regimes are sometimes considered unstable because if oppressed groups can muster the power to revolt against their rulers, they will likely do so; however, if oppressors are good at defending their power base, they might turn out to be quite stable despite this internal opposition. Still, if force of arms is one way to maintain the state, it is not necessarily a good way. It does not receive much moral support from those who believe that no group is justified in imposing its will on those groups that cannot escape its power. Moreover, coercive might alone does not supply the bonds of identity necessary to unite diverse groups into a unified state. Coercive might can constitute a state only in the minimalist sense associated with international law; that is, the state in question is recognized by others to have sovereign standing in the community of states, but if such a state has standing in the international community, it still lacks the status of a state if it is supposed that this status requires something more in terms of shared identification and mutual acceptance among the citizens of a legitimate state. The rule of thugs over those they manage to oppress constitutes a state only in the most nominal sense.

Tyranny has historically involved a crude form of control: physical oppression and the threat of violence and death. Control is achieved by creating fear in the minds of the oppressed. Some political thinkers, however, have speculated and worried that in modern times, control has begun to be more sophisticated and subtle, and they usually suggest that things are much the worse for this. The control imagined here is realized not by controlling others through fear and physical intimidation but by capturing the minds of those one wants to control. This involves eroding those conceptual and normative boundaries that define specific ethnic and religious groups and replacing them with the conceptual apparatus desired by the ruling elite. The result is a manufactured homogeneity that eliminates the need for physical intimidation and yields a kind of patriotic allegiance to the ruling elite.

This is not necessarily a viable strategy because groups are likely to resist the reconfiguration of their basic belief systems, but it does provide a frightening twist on the specter of tyranny. It also complicates thinking about politics in important yet subtle ways. States need to cultivate loyalty and respect, and they need to educate their citizenry on the standards of proper behavior expected of them, on the things the state stands for, on the values that encourage allegiance and ensure legitimacy, and on the ideals and principles of association that bring the citizenry together. Education for civil association, this is to say, is a crucial dimension of politics; it is the way states prepare individuals to be citizens. Indoctrination, on the other hand, is typically considered unethical and undesirable. To indoctrinate people is to inculcate in them an allegiance to and acceptance of some doctrine. It involves imposing an ideology upon them and controlling them by capturing their minds. This is the type of thing that seems tyrannical. But how exactly does education differ from indoctrination? How can states educate their citizenry and still avoid the charge of indoctrination? How is it possible for a state to achieve stability by shaping those subject to it into good citizens without also engaging in what can reasonably be considered a form of mind control?

One way that states might deal with the problem of pluralism is to appeal to certain features of some dominant group and link those features with the state itself, thus building a sense of patriotism out of the nationalistic identifications of these groups. Hitler's Germany managed to do this rather well by imagining a picture of an archetypal Aryan individual and identifying it with the ideal German whose virtue rested in a supposed genetic superiority. But some groups are inevitably and necessarily left out of this picture and are consequently identified as alien presences in the state. They become the scapegoats that are deliberately excluded from identification with the state in order to guarantee that others are able to identify with the state. Insofar as these states fail to recognize all groups in the state as members of the state and proceed to marginalize or eliminate some groups, they still qualify as tyrannical even though tyrannical control is managed by the cultivation of a prevailing ideology rather than by means of coercive force alone.

It is best, however, to put these matters aside for the moment and consider another reason why states might hang together. Groups may accept the authority of the state because they think it is in their best interest to do so or because they recognize that they have more to gain by accepting state authority than by rejecting it. According to this explanation, prudence recommends acceptance of the state, even if this means that some group activities will be compromised in the process of endorsing state authority. If prudential reasons counsel in favor of accepting state authority, the resultant form of political association can be called a *modus vivendi* arrangement—a method of getting along with others *under the circumstances*. According to the logic of *modus vivendi* arrangements, a group's best bet is to contract together with others in order to provide and defend the social conditions necessary for a group to flourish or at least subsist given the specific conditions that happen to exist in the territory in question.

Modus vivendi arrangements are often criticized by political philosophers because they seem to be quite unstable. Imagine a treaty arrangement among the groups constituting a state; imagine, that is, that a collection of groups accept a treaty with one another that establishes a central government with authority over each group. A treaty might be accepted by groups because, under the circumstances, the treaty is the best way to realize certain interests that matter to the parties to the treaty. But circumstances may change, and the relative power arrangements existing among groups may shift to favor some groups more than others. If they change significantly or in certain directions, some groups may begin to think that they don't need to adhere to the terms of the treaty any longer, and they may elect to defect from the treaty. If the state is based on such a treaty or *modus vivendi* arrangement, changes in the power relations of the groups may cause the state to dissolve or may incline more powerful groups to resort to tyrannical measures to control other groups. So it may seem that *modus vivendi* arrangements are unlikely to hold the state together for very long. They also lack the sense of identification with the state necessary to transform a collection of disparate and perhaps conflicting groups into a unified state.

There is still another reason why states may hang together. Perhaps there are some universal and objective moral truths, that is, moral principles binding on all persons at all times, that recommend or require civil association.

Recognizing and acknowledging these truths would then require groups to accept state authority because this is the morally necessary and proper thing to do. It has been commonly supposed in the Western intellectual tradition that there are certain natural laws—certain basic moral truths—that govern all people at all times. The state is necessary in order to give exact expression to these moral truths and to defend and enforce the basic rights they express. In turn, state authority is circumscribed by these moral truths; the state forfeits its legitimacy and becomes tyrannical in the event that its functionaries act contrary to or deviate from the demands of the moral law. The state, in order words, is an institution required by the fundamental moral scheme that dictates how human beings ought to live together. Tyrannical states are at best a bastard version of the state from this point of view because they fail to realize the moral purpose of the state, but the fact that some states fail to realize their moral purpose does not mean that the notion of the state should itself be abandoned.

This type of thinking has played a crucial role in the American political context, and we shall have occasion to consider it more fully shortly. For present purposes, it is sufficient only to consider the bonding force of this moral viewpoint. In the Declaration of Independence, Thomas Jefferson supposed that there are certain truths that are simply self-evident, namely, "that all men are created equal; that they are endowed by their Creator with certain inalienable rights; that among these are life, liberty, and the pursuit of happiness." Jefferson here is merely echoing the arguments of the British philosopher John Locke, who had claimed that human beings have natural rights nearly a century earlier.[3] Following Locke, Jefferson supposed that reasonable people would consent to join the state in order to establish a government capable of supporting and policing these natural rights. If and when the government itself violates these rights, or fails to enforce them effectively, it loses legitimacy (or acceptance), and the people are then justified in rebelling against it in order to establish another government that will respect these rights.

Historically, the natural law tradition in Western thought has provided some important answers to some of the most crucial questions about political life. It explains why the state is necessary and thus provides groups with reasons to endorse civil association and accept a civil contract to live together amicably. And it establishes reasonably clear limits upon state authority, thus providing a benchmark for determining the proper business of the state and distinguishing appropriate spheres of state control from governmental lapses into tyranny. Because it premises state legitimacy upon moral necessity, it also reinforces the stability of the state by resting civil association upon binding moral principles.

Moral cynics and skeptics may well object to all this on the grounds that there really are no objective and universal moral truths, and therefore no natural laws that can serve as the foundation of political authority. For example, another British philosopher, Jeremy Bentham, insisted that the notion of natural rights is little more than "nonsense on stilts," ironically at about the same time that Jefferson wrote the Declaration of Independence. But there is no need to settle this issue to recognize a problem with natural law explanations about why states manage to hang together. It is necessary only to recall that ethnic and religious pluralism introduces basic normative and ontological disagreements into the state's population. Given the depth and seriousness of these disagreements, is it reasonable to suppose that all groups will acknowledge and respect the same moral laws or agree about their meaning or implementation? The variety of beliefs it is plausible to associate with the fact of ethnic and religious pluralism makes such basic agreement on common standards of natural law unlikely. Historically, even natural lawyers have disagreed among themselves about the meaning and importance of these laws. While natural lawyers suppose reason reflecting upon the human condition can yield infallible insight into the nature of these laws, this often seems an unacceptably ambitious viewpoint. And where disagreement over the requirements of the natural law exists, or where some groups reject claims about a universal and objective morality, the potential for tyranny is again present.

Is it legitimate for some group or coalition of groups to impose its understanding of the natural law upon those others that might happen to disagree with them? Is it permissible for the state to force wayward groups to adhere to the standards of the moral law as the ruling elites happen to understand them? Attempting to do so may destabilize the state once again and send it spiraling toward civil war. Even if there is a natural law binding upon all peoples at all times, not all cultural, ethnic, or religious groups need recognize it or understand it in the same fashion. And where there is disagreement over such matters, there is the possibility of conflict that may tear at the fabric of the state. In the history of humankind, great evil has been done in the name of promoting the good. So when faced with the fact of deep pluralism, the natural law account of how the state can hang together seems inadequate.

Perhaps, however, there is reason to think that the natural law tradition is correct about one thing. If the state is to hang together in spite of the fact of pluralism, there must be something that its citizens share in common, something that provides all citizens with a sense of identity with the state. There must be some common boundaries that unite the disparate groups present in a given region into a common citizenry and transform this collection of otherwise distinct groups into a *polity*—a community of groups and individuals

participating in the common activity of civil association. But if these boundaries cannot be geographic or legal ones, what might they possibly be? If they
are not forged by moral truth, what is their source? As we shall see, it seems
necessary to recognize these boundaries as conceptual and normative in
nature; they reflect the presence of a shared understanding of public life as
well as a shared commitment to the basic principles and ideals that govern
and direct this life. To put the point differently, to say that politics is about
boundaries is to say that it is about the conceptual and normative mechanisms
with which people understand themselves and their association with certain
others. The nature of this understanding is rooted in the historical effort to
define a common identification with these others in a way that explains why
they belong to each other as partners in a common political enterprise. The
crucial boundaries for understanding politics, this is to say, are the conceptualizations and normative visions that have matured into a specific political
culture. But this view of politics will probably be anything but obvious at this
point; it requires the development and explanation that follows in order to
make it understandable. This is the hard part of thinking about politics.

POLITICS AND IDENTITY

If it makes sense to say that politics is about boundaries, then it is also reasonable to say that politics is about identity. Boundaries, once again, unify and
divide, and in doing so they help forge a sense of identity. To illustrate, consider another simple question: Who are you? While the question seems innoc-
uous enough, it is not necessarily an easy one to answer. Any acceptable
response will both integrate and separate, because this, in effect, is what the
question asks one to do. So, by posing this question to oneself, one's response
should reveal much about how the person in question sees herself in relation
to others. Suppose, for example, someone responds to this question by giving
a proper name: "I am Joan Smith." This unites a person with a particular
family (the Smith family, in this instance), and it separates Joan Smith from
other members of this family by specifying which member of the family the
person in question happens to be. Giving one's name is an obvious answer to
the question, Who are you? But it is not a very complete answer, and people
don't learn much about themselves if this is all they have to say in response.
There are a good many Joan Smiths, for example, but they are obviously not
all the same person. But even if there were no other Joan Smiths, it is not
possible to learn much about who a person is merely by discovering her
name. A name tells us very little about a person. It does not tell us about the
loves and fears this person has or the ideals that inspire her, the principles

that regulate her conduct, and so forth. It merely links a person to a family that may remain mysterious and identifies the person in question as a distinct member of that family.

But someone might also answer the question about personal identity by saying that she is one person among others. This is a fairly oblique response to be sure; it indicates only, but perhaps significantly, that the person in question sees herself as a unique member of humanity. Someone who thinks to answer a question about identity in this way sees persons as such and represents herself as one of these. Of course, people might also answer this question by saying that they are a distinct and independent creature, separate from all others, with a unique perspective on the world and a specific set of wants and desires that identify them in their own mind. To see oneself in this way encourages one to see oneself as special and different from all others—a species of one, so to speak. The German philosopher Friedrich Nietzsche might have wanted to answer the question this way.

Both of these responses to the question about identity are unusual perhaps, but hardly unheard of. They mark the extremes on a continuum of identity running from solipsism to human universalism. But if people think seriously about *who* they are, they will probably give a different sort of answer. It seems more likely that people will explain their identity by associating themselves with certain others and thereby distinguishing themselves from a different set of others. That is, they will identify themselves in terms of the boundaries that link them with some persons and distinguish them from different others. To have an identity, after all, is to identify with some people in ways that distinguish them from others. Some of the basic boundaries introduced in the previous section illustrate some of the ways a person might understand her own identity. A person might identify herself by means of a religious affiliation ("I'm Catholic, and therefore I'm *a* Catholic") or by means of an ethnic identification ("I'm Irish, and therefore I'm *an* Irishman"). Religious and ethnic identifications might even go together in order to further specify one's identity ("I'm Catholic, and I'm Irish; therefore, I'm *an* Irish Catholic").

Describing oneself as Irish, of course, is ambivalent in a crucial sense. By describing oneself as Irish (or Italian, French, etc.), one might be describing one's ethnic identification, or one's political identification, or both. Someone who immigrates to Ireland from, say, Sweden (where she was raised in the ethnic traditions of her Swedish family) and achieves Irish citizenship may describe herself as Irish, but if she does, she privileges her new political identification over her ethnic identification. It is probably not too great an exaggeration to say that political affiliation—affiliation with a specific polity—fixes an important feature of one's identification. If asked, for example, there is a good chance that someone born and raised in the United States with an Irish Catholic background would identify herself by proclaiming that she is an American. The use of gendered pronouns also signals an identity, of course, for in the example at hand, it is evident that we are imagining an Irish Catholic female, and this further fixes the identity of the person in question.

It is probably apparent that a thorough answer to the question of identity can be quite complex, for there are many affiliations people have that play a role in shaping and forming their identity. People may also want to claim that they have worked to shape and determine their own identity, and hence their identity can shift through time according to the way a person elects to reconfigure it. A person might say, for example, that she was born and raised in an Irish Catholic family in Boston and is, therefore, an American of Irish Catholic heritage, but she has forsaken her Irish ways and abandoned the Catholic faith and now considers herself one person among others. This is a somewhat common attitude in the United States; Americans often feel with great conviction that their identity is a matter of their own making and that they are free to determine not just how their lives will go but who (and not just what) they will be.

This laissez-faire attitude is often displayed in the American inclination to identify oneself with what one does for a living. So another possible response to the question of identity could make reference to one's work ("I'm a lawyer," rather than "I'm an Irish Catholic American who practices law"). In truth, a person might be all these things—a combination of religious, ethnic, racial, cultural, and political identities, along with those self-descriptors that one has added to one's being and that round out one's identity. But still, none of this does much to account for a person's identity.

To get clearer on the nature of a person's identity, it is necessary to keep in mind that describing oneself as, say, ethnically Irish, is really a shorthand way of introducing a terribly complex vision of the world. This is perhaps clearer in the case of religion. A person's claim to be, say, Catholic tells others much about her world. It tells them, for example, that she accepts Jesus Christ as the son of God, or that she is a Christian, that she believes in the miracle of transubstantiation, that she recognizes the pope as God's vicar on earth, that she adheres (at least to some extent) to the moral responsibilities associated with the Catholic faith, and so forth. To identify a person as Catholic (or Protestant, Muslim, etc.) is to begin to have a sense of who this person is insofar as knowing this enables one to understand something about the way this person understands the world around her. A similar point holds with regard to ethnicity, for a shorthand identification of ethnicity involves a good deal more than a general reference to family history. It is possible to appreciate this heritage by undertaking, among other things, an exploration of this ethnicity, an unpacking of the various characteristics and attributes of, say, the Irish culture.

To proceed reflectively, one will want to pay attention to the way this culture *develops* those who belong to it by enabling them to see the world in a certain way and to think about what matters to them in a certain way. Put more obscurely, one inherits an ontology (a specific understanding of the world and what is in it, and so forth) and a normative framework (a particular way of valuing the things in the world) as one grows into a way of life identifiable in terms of things like ethnic heritage. The world people inhabit is the world they have inherited from certain formative ethnic, cultural, religious, and political identifications (among other things, perhaps), and it is their world in the sense that it is indicative of the human attachments that shape their identity. The ways of seeing and valuing that people have inherited thus shape their identity at a most basic and important level. To say, for example, that one is ethnically Irish is to say that one is a person who sees, understands, and appreciates the world in the fashion on display in Irish culture. This says more than that a person is of Irish descent; it says that the person in question *is* Irish. Sometimes Americans claim to be Irish when they mean, perhaps, that their grandparents came to the United States from Ireland. But these people are not Irish at all; they are Americans of Irish descent. If they have grown up in the United States, they will be American because they see and understand much of the world around them in the fashion of an American.[4]

No doubt many influences work together to shape and determine the identity of specific individuals, and there may be reason to think that this is a good thing. As independent individuals sort through and reflect upon the influences that have shaped who they are, they can sharpen and refine their own identities in a fashion that suits them. Diversity of heritage permits the cultivation of individualism as people place themselves within the context of the various influences that have shaped them. Within the parameters of these general influences, people can configure their own identities and add specificity to the more general expressions of identification that place them within these influences.

It makes sense to say that politics is about identity, then, if political identification also introduces a heritage that has an ontological and normative influence on people and thus helps shape who they are. Political identifications sometimes matter greatly to Americans, and many would surely answer the identity question by noting, perhaps among other things, that they are Americans, that is, citizens of the United States. Does this self-description simply involve a declaration of legal status, or does it carry more important ontological and normative implications? Americans are fond of insisting that

their country stands for certain things that are morally important and should
be respected and treasured. The ideal of freedom receives high praise in the
United States, as does the defense of certain individual rights, human equality, and the standards of democracy—the legacies of Locke and Jefferson, or
more generally the legacies of a period in British history greatly influenced
by Locke and his followers. These notions introduce the American political
heritage, and to define oneself as an American is to say that one's understanding of political life is shaped and influenced greatly by these ideals. But in
order to understand what this means, and thus to get a sense of what it means
to be an American, politically speaking, one must unpack and examine the
elements of this heritage. This will enable us to explain who Americans are
politically, or to recognize the political aspects of an American identity. Insofar as a particular understanding of politics is an inheritance drawn from a
specific political culture, the challenge of understanding politics is necessarily fixed by the culture to which one belongs. And to understand politics is
therefore to understand the realm of the political as it is envisioned and
understood within this culture.

Yet here too there is room for individual refinement and personal development. The conceptual and normative boundaries that shape one's political
heritage are bound to be rather rough around the edges. While Americans
may be agreed upon a certain core meaning of the ideal of freedom, for example, they may (and almost certainly will) disagree over some of the details.
Political heritage, and hence political identity, is not something that can be
discovered lying around somewhere, or something that can be looked up and
definitively identified in a dictionary or textbook on politics. After a fashion,
it is a matter of dispute. Reasonable minds may disagree, for example, on the
most appropriate understanding of the nature of freedom and its relation to
the ideal of equality. (Is someone less free than another if she doesn't have
sufficient money to buy all the opportunities available to someone who is
economically better off?) The boundaries introduced by these concepts and
normative ideals are not fixed and certain. But these are the boundaries that
make politics intelligible; they are, quite literally, the boundaries that forge
one's sense of the political, rough around the edges though this notion might
be. To understand politics, then, necessitates an exploration of these boundaries. This means, in a sense, that to understand politics it is necessary to
acquaint oneself with something that people already know, for as political
beings, people already have some awareness of these boundaries because they
have and use the political concepts that are the building blocks of their sense
of the political. But most Americans spend very little time reflecting on or
ruminating about these building blocks, and consequently their familiarity
with politics remains at a fairly simple and rather skewed level of understand-

ing. This is why it makes some sense to say that Americans may know a great deal about current events and the lives of their political representatives, but very little about politics.

ZOON POLITIKON

It may seem strange to say that politics is about the ontological and normative dimensions of the political culture of a given polity. It may seem even more strange to say that the elements of this culture work like a magical fetish to transform different peoples into a polity, making it a community of fellow citizens and not just a collection of religiously and ethnically distinct groups and individuals held together perhaps only by force of arms or treaty arrangements. This is certainly not the way too many Americans think about politics, and an invitation to think about politics in this way may seem like so much philosophical nonsense. When politics is mentioned, the focus of most Americans goes elsewhere, and it may just seem like this is as it should be.

Suppose someone went into the streets of America's cities and villages, into the urban centers and the rural countryside, and asked the people they came across, What is politics? Many of the people encountered would think this is a simple question, and many would be ready with a simple answer. But it would have nothing to do with boundaries. "Politics," many would probably say, "is what goes on in government. It is what politicians are up to." This rather predictable and fairly popular response hints at two misconceptions about the nature of politics that lurk in the minds of a great many Americans. First, it equates politics with government—the institutions of public policy formulation and implementation, enforcement and compliance, and dispute adjudication. Second, it conflates government with political personalities—the individuals that occupy and operate governmental institutions.

These misperceptions are certainly understandable enough given the way the world of politics is usually presented to Americans by the various media that inform them about political "news." News about politics invariably reduces to news about what individuals holding or seeking public office have been doing lately. In contemporary America, the media-driven obsession with political personalities has turned into something of a spectator sport. Americans are treated to stories about George W. Bush's malapropisms or Bill Clinton's sexual misadventures. The news leaves Americans standing on the political sidelines, so to speak, as various personalities parade in front of them, presented by the media as subjects worthy of respect or targets of ridicule depending upon reporter inclination. Public attention, as a result, is riveted upon those public figures that are presented to them as either celebrities (those individuals that Americans choose to celebrate) or political apostates (those who have strayed from the realm of political propriety).

It is worth remembering, of course, that American politicians are not like British royalty—idle celebrities offering only a cosmetic caricature of the political world. American political figures are the real actors in what gets presented to the public as the great soap opera of American politics. (At the risk of mixing metaphors, if watching politics in America is something of a spectator sport, the show that is presented to Americans does take on the character of a soap opera—reality television at its best.) And American citizens, as dutiful if not always enthusiastic spectators, are the daily audience. Like most audiences, Americans watch their political soap opera rather selectively. Some are riveted on the plot and refuse to miss a day; some tune in selectively when something that matters to them arises; some just catch fleeting glances of the action as they rush off to work; and some catch the action only rarely when the plot really heats up, perhaps for military or economic reasons.

Like most soap operas, the morality play of American politics has its heroes and its villains, but the country typically divides on which is which. The good guys and bad guys of American politics are identified by the inclination of the audience to embrace one end or the other of an imagined "political spectrum" that runs from a so-called conservative view to an allegedly more liberal perspective. But ironically, most Americans are hard pressed to say much about these ideological divisions, even if they are not hard pressed in the least to insist that one side or the other has truth, justice, and the American way on its side—usually because they associate their specific interests, wittingly or otherwise, with one side of this so-called spectrum.

The spectrum is important, to be sure, for the practice of politics in America. It works as an effective shorthand that tells selective elements of the audience who to root for—or in more distinctly political terms, who to vote for. It demarcates the teams at play (still mixing metaphors) and encourages "political involvement" by permitting Americans to decide which side they will associate with. Like sports fans with painted faces rooting for the home team, Americans line up to root for the players on the side of the spectrum with which they happen to identify. And so the show goes on. If a celebrity on one side behaves badly, her or his side is penalized, and the other side gains bragging rights if nothing else. If a celebrity behaves well, appears to be a loyal American, has her or his heart in the right place, seems honest and trustworthy, and manages to represent her or his favored side of the morality play in particularly compelling fashion, he or she is likely to be rewarded with political office, and a new chapter of the play begins. Come election day, Americans stop watching their soap opera for a moment and play a role in the game of politics. But the role they play is invariably highly conditioned by the show they have been watching, as well as by the place on the political spectrum they have decided to occupy for reasons that we needn't explore.

Americans who follow the soap opera religiously will not like the suggestion that few Americans understand politics very well, and they will very likely think that understanding politics in terms of boundaries is unnecessarily obscure, frivolous, and tedious. Americans typically like things simple and straightforward; it is common sense—or what can pass for common sense—and not academic bric-a-brac that works for Americans. It is Harry Truman, and not George McGovern, who resonates with the American consciousness. Sometimes Americans hold on to their ideological views with something that approximates religious zeal. These Americans are convinced that they *know* about politics; they *know* what the state should be doing and what values and ends political actors should embrace and pursue. But all this merely continues to confuse politics with current events and to yield a distorted, primitive, and dangerously inadequate vision of civil association.

Americans have never been forced to think very deeply about politics, at least since the drafting and ratification of the federal Constitution—but perhaps not even then. There have been few crises of political legitimacy in American history. Interests have come into conflict and caused deep fissures in the fabric of the republic, but Americans have rarely lost faith in their form of government, in their Constitution, or in the political ideals they associate with their country. Only during the Civil War did an interstate disagreement fester into a fundamental disagreement on the nature of American ideals so intense that it set brother against brother. But intense though it was, the Civil War is much the exception rather than the rule in the saga of American history. The tremendous stability of American government, and what has been called the "givenness" of American political culture, has left Americans with little practical need to ruminate deeply on politics.[5] There is, needless to say, still reason to think about (and fight about) what government is up to, and what political actors are doing, but not, it might seem, to dwell on the nature of politics. Perhaps, then, there is good reason why Americans would so cavalierly equate current events with politics and feel happy to leave matters at that. Their history has allowed them to leave matters at that. But if Americans are not politically astute, what hope is there that they can make wise and defensible conclusions about the desirability of what their government is doing? How can they hope to assess the morality play that is repeatedly presented to them? Just because there has been no felt need to explore the nature of politics in the past does not mean that there is no need to do so at present or that there will be no need to do so in the future.

The philosopher Aristotle famously defined human beings as *zoon politikon*—as political animals.[6] He noticed that human beings live in the company of others, and to do this successfully, some degree of organization and management is required. But he also noticed that human beings are not "hardwired" to get along with one another. Humans are certainly not the only social animals to be found on the planet. Ants and bees, to name but two obvious examples, also live in one another's company and work to support and sustain their social units. But as near as we can tell, they get along mechanically and naturally because nature has programmed them, so to speak, to perform the functions needed from them by their community. In more directly philosophical jargon, their behavior is determined (again, as near as we can tell); they play their roles like little mobile computers whose behavior has been predetermined for them by forces external to them.

Although it may be the greatest conceit of all, human beings don't think of themselves in this way. In the terms presented in the discussion of identity above, cultural inheritance leads people to think that human beings are different than this. While human beings must live in one another's company, they have not been programmed by some cosmic software writer to get along and perform certain predetermined functions for the community. But get along they must if life is to be the least bit tolerable, and so too must they perform certain functions if the community is to endure. The challenges of social organization and management, however, are left up to them. These challenges are, as Aristotle emphasized, intellectual problems. People need to figure out how to best get along with one another and then apply this knowledge effectively in order to do so. This is what separates political animals from social animals; for political animals, the problems of social life are real challenges that they must resolve for themselves. As political animals, the fate of humanity is in humanity's hands, and the challenge of living together is first and foremost an intellectual one. And as an intellectual problem, the challenge of living together can be managed successfully only if people understand and appreciate the nature of politics—only, that is, if they understand the nature of the cultural inheritance that makes people who they are, politically speaking. Unhappily, this is precisely what seems to be lacking in the American public today. Yet without such an understanding, without such cultural self-awareness, the blind will lead the blind into a confrontation with the problems that await them in the future.

Perhaps, then, there is reason to take a moment to think about politics and try to understand a bit more about ourselves as political beings. This means developing a reasonably sophisticated understanding of politics, and as suggested above, this means exposing, exploring, and analyzing as fully as possible those primary boundaries that fix and present Americans with their vision of politics and that shape (at least a part of) their identity as Americans. This sets the agenda of the journey that follows, and it indicates why this is a book about politics and not a book about current events or politicians.

The connection between politics and political culture means, however, that any inquiry into the nature of politics must be situated within the context of some specific political culture, for it is within the confines of such cultures that the notion of politics has meaning. As should be apparent, the cultural context that informs the following discussion is the political culture of the United States, largely because this work is intended primarily for an American audience. Political cultures vary, and consequently understandings of politics vary as well. But political cultures also often share common histories, even if political practices vary within the context of these cultural influences. It should be no surprise, then, that the understanding of politics to follow may have pertinence in the many modern polities influenced, like the United States, by the liberal tradition of political thought. So, while situated in the American political context, the discussion that follows need not be regarded as restricted entirely to this context.

NOTES

1. See Cynthia Farrer, "Ancient Greek Political Theory as a Response to Democracy," in John Dunn, ed., *Democracy: The Unfinished Journey* (Oxford: Oxford University Press, 1992), 17–40.

2. For a thorough discussion of nationality and its relation to politics, see David Miller, *On Nationality* (Oxford: Clarendon Press, 1995).

3. John Locke, *Second Treatise of Government*, Ch. 2.

4. Cf. Michael Walzer, *What It Means to Be an American* (New York: Marsilio Publishers, 1996).

5. Daniel Boorstin, *The Genius of American Politics* (Chicago: University of Chicago Press, 1953).

6. Aristotle, *Politics*, Bk. I, Ch. 2.

Chapter One

Politics and Power

Power corrupts, and absolute power corrupts absolutely.

Lord Acton

It is not possible to govern without power. It is not possible to sustain and operate the mechanisms of social management and organization without permitting those who control these mechanisms to have the power necessary to do what needs to be done. Governments cannot govern without power; this simple truth may be taken as the first principle of politics. And it introduces one of the most enduring and challenging problems that anyone who thinks seriously about politics must face. If it is conceded that governments need the power to govern, how can people be confident that the government officials who hold this power will not abuse it? This is the problem of political power. James Madison, one of the most notable of American statesmen, understood the problem well. In the *Federalist Papers*, he presented what is perhaps its most succinct and compelling presentation:

> If men were angels, no government would be necessary. If angels were to govern men, neither external nor internal controls on government would be necessary. In framing a government which is to be administered by men over men, the great difficulty lies in this: you must first enable the government to control the governed; and in the next place oblige it to control itself.[1]

In response to this problem, Madison recommended, among other things, a Constitution based upon a system of checks and balances. In this way, he thought that ambition could be made to check ambition. When Americans begin to learn about their form of government and their Constitution, they are often told by teachers who should know better that the constitutional system of checks and balances protects against the possible abuse of political power

23

by government. It would be a happy thing if the problem of political power could be so easily resolved by strategies of constitutional architecture, and no doubt many generations of Americans have found solace in the popular belief that it can be resolved in this fashion. But why should anyone believe that the problem of power can really be overcome in this way? If it is necessary to begin thinking about politics by admitting that power is an essential element of political life, it is also necessary to take the problem of power seriously. And this suggests that it is important to understand the nature and source of this problem and not to underestimate it. This is as good a place as any to begin thinking about politics.

ORWELL'S WORLD

As a prelude to exploring the problem of power, it might be helpful to take a careful look at a relatively famous work of fiction with which readers are hopefully familiar. In 1949, a British writer published a book that was to capture the attention and fuel the anxieties of people for generations to come. The writer was George Orwell, and the book, of course, was *1984*.[2] If it is not altogether charming fiction, *1984* is at least a provocative encounter with politics. The book offers the reader a confrontation with political themes that Orwell imagined to be of the first importance, so important to the author, in fact, that he gave them precedence even over his failing health.[3] Modern readers familiar with his last, if not his finest, novel may consider Orwell something of an alarmist. The year 1984 has come and gone, and few, if any, of the horrible conditions he imagined have come to fruition. Or so it might seem. If *1984* is presumed to be Orwell's guess at what awaited the world, it might seem that he evidently missed the boat, that his projections were well off target. But *1984* was not Orwell's guess about the future. It expressed instead his fears about the problem of political power, and thus understood, the book is timeless.

Orwell is sometimes portrayed as a devoted British subject, with a quirky socialist side to him, who felt a powerful need to make a call to political consciousness as a warning against the evils of totalitarianism, either fascist or communist, that he saw emerging throughout much of the early part of the twentieth century. But this underestimates Orwell as a political thinker. He was committed, to be sure, to a political call to consciousness, and in a sense he worried about emergent totalitarianism. But *1984* is not a warning about the evils of ideology aimed at the politically sensitive, and his warning is no less pertinent today than it was in 1949 simply because the communist movement in eastern Europe has collapsed. Orwell believed that the trend toward totalitarianism was driven by the desire for power, and he understood this to be a desire without specific ideological commitments. Ideology is merely the mask worn by power seekers, a mask chosen specifically to make them look benign and attractive. Ideology, for Orwell, was but a tool in the struggle for and with power, and a frighteningly effective one at that. Orwell's impassioned call to consciousness, then, was inspired by his appreciation for the new and ever more threatening form taken by the problem of power in the twentieth century, and it was directed at the politically naive, even though Orwell seemed in general to doubt that these people would manage to recognize the problem he presented to them or that they would think to do anything about it.

Orwell initially thought to call his story "The Last Man in Europe," but he elected finally to go with the more benign title of *1984*. But "The Last Man in Europe" is perhaps a better name for the story, and at the risk of imposing upon readers already familiar with Orwell's work, it is necessary to review the plot of the novel briefly in order to illustrate the point.

Orwell's story is little more than the tale of an extended struggle between the book's protagonist, Winston Smith, and his tormenter/savior, O'Brien.[4] O'Brien, it turns out, is a privileged member of the ruling party (an inner party member, as Orwell describes it) of the mythical state of Oceania, and Winston is a member of the outer party who toils away under the direction of the mysterious inner party by rewriting history.[5] If we read *1984* not only as an anti-utopian story but also as a tragedy, then Winston can be considered a tragic figure. Tragic figures, of course, have tragic flaws, and Winston has a tragic flaw that gets him into trouble with O'Brien. He thinks too much, and thinking is not good for anyone who lives in Orwell's Oceania. By thinking as he does, Winston commits thoughtcrime—something of a rarity in Oceania. Winston's job in Oceania is to revise (or rewrite) history to make it into what the inner party wants it to be, and it turns out to be a dangerous job. He begins to wonder about the past that has been obliterated by the inner party and wonders what life was like before the inner party emerged and established its dominating control of Oceania.

But before considering Winston's dementia, if dementia it is, it might be a good idea to complete the picture of Oceania's demographics as Orwell imagined it. The inner party, the powerful controllers of Oceania, make up but a small percentage of the population, while the outer party composes about 13 percent of Oceania's citizens. The remaining 85 percent of the population are called the proles, and in many respects, the story is really about them. They are largely uncontrolled by the inner party, at least directly. The thought police, whose job is to search out and identify thought criminals (those poor souls like Winston who take to thinking and thus become danger-

ous), pay scant attention to them—and for good reason. Orwell's account of
them is revealing:

> They were born, they grew up in the gutters, they went to work at twelve, they
> passed through a brief blossoming period of beauty and sexual desire, they married
> at twenty, they were middle-aged at thirty, they died, for the most part, at sixty.
> Heavy physical work, the care of home and children, petty quarrels with neighbors,
> films, football, beer, and above all, gambling filled up the horizons of their minds.
> To keep them in control was not difficult.[6]

The description may sound familiar; there are unsettling similarities
between Orwell's account of the lives lived by the proles and the lives lived
by many contemporary Americans. Orwell's reference to the "horizons of
their minds" introduces a notion for thinking about politics that is worth
developing with a bit more rigor. Consider a fairly obscure question: What is
the breadth and depth of the gaze of one's mind? The question asks about the
things that matter to a person, the things one dwells upon, the focus of one's
life, in effect. Some people fixate only upon themselves and their immediate
future. They think about things they want, and right away, and they don't
dwell too much on the future. The "horizons of their minds" are narrow
indeed, both spatially and temporally. Other people's lives fixate upon family
and friends, and if they are aware of the larger world around them, they pay
little attention to it. It is little more than the background noise that one closes
out as one concentrates on what matters—in this case, family and friends.
Still others see the world differently; the horizons of their mind focus on
larger things or more expansive issues. Imagine someone who worries exclusively about the fate of humanity. Such a person may think about many disparate things: the fate of the ozone layer, the dilemma of nuclear proliferation,
the development of new and exotic diseases, the problem of political power,
and so forth. By comparison with one who thinks exclusively of herself, or
slightly more expansively, of family and friends, the horizons of this person's
mind are expansive indeed. This person's mental gaze is most capacious, and
such a person will focus on varied problems that range well beyond her
immediate life and press into the distant as well as the near future.

Suppose we say that to ask about the breadth and depth of the gaze of one's
mind is to ask about a person's *ontological horizon*—the parameters of the
focus of a person's concern and attention. One's ontological horizon indicates what matters to a person, and it suggests the sphere of interests that
animate her life. Those with a narrow ontological horizon look only toward
things reasonably close to home—like friends, family, or themselves—or
toward those things with which they happen to identify, perhaps their religion
or their favorite sports teams. Those with broader ontological horizons see

themselves as moments in a much larger and more complicated world, and they stretch the focus of their concerns, perhaps both spatially and temporally, to include matters pertaining to the human condition well removed from themselves.

The proles, as Orwell envisions them, have very narrow ontological horizons; they worry about things close to them—doing the wash or whether a half liter of beer is a better ration than a pint. While they are certainly aware of the political world around them, they are not troubled by it. They take it at face value and seem to regard it as something like background noise—constantly present in their lives but rather incidental to the way they live. In some ways, they seem to be primitive characters, and Orwell leaves the distinct impression that he considers them dull witted. While they are certainly aware of politics, they are also insensitive to its features. They don't trouble much about what their government is doing because such matters are far removed from the limits of their ontological horizons. They work hard, ask for little, and take life as it comes. They are the consummate survivors who manage to endure the burdens they carry, apparently oblivious to the drudgery that characterizes their existence.

It is tempting to think they are pathetic, although it is easy to understand why the inner party has no trouble controlling them. They are controllable because they don't think about, and hence don't worry about, the larger world around them. "Proles and animals are free," says O'Brien with the confidence of a prophet. The comparison is appropriate; the proles live brutish lives without any incentive to think beyond the parameters of their little worlds, without any inspiration to stretch their ontological horizons beyond "films, football, beer, and above all, gambling." Their freedom is a condition of their stupidity. They can do as they please because they are no threat to the inner party. They will not exercise their freedom by thinking about politics and beginning to question the inevitability or immutability of their condition.

But we should return to Winston, the last man in Orwell's Europe. Winston rebels against Big Brother, the personification of political authority in Oceania, whose generic face is everywhere. There really is no Big Brother, of course; the great face is but the symbolic image of the state, put to use by the inner party as a mechanism of control and a symbol of political legitimacy. Orwell knew well that political power is most effective when it captures the mind, for then the body comes along automatically; and to capture the mind, one must practice the fine art of the manipulation of salient political symbols. Big Brother is a mechanism of political control. And Oceania, as Orwell imagines it, is a place where political control has been perfected to the point of an art form.

Winston's rebellion is inspired by his curiosity about truth and his conviction that the minions of Big Brother have distorted and tortured the truth. He
wants to know the truth; he wants to recapture the past. He wants to expose
Big Brother and free the people of Oceania from what he considers the tyrannical grip of the inner party. Orwell fully understood that these would be
desirable ends from the readers' perspective and that readers would root for
Winston and expect him to triumph against Big Brother's oppression by the
novel's end. But Orwell builds a curious twist into his story. While readers
invariably expect the tale to include a successful revolution against Big
Brother, like so many similar stories, these expectations are unfulfilled.
O'Brien confronts Winston as a deviant and treats his deviance as an illness
that needs to be cured. Once O'Brien has suitably cultivated Winston's deviance by luring him into ever more thoughtcrime, he takes Winston to the
Ministry of Love, where thought criminals are tortured, and "lovingly" cures
him of his illness. The story ends with Winston willingly embracing the loving visage of Big Brother. Winston is cured; he no longer thinks. Instead, like
a dutiful and obedient pet, he looks upon the powerful and protective face of
Big Brother and admits his dependency. Rebellion was as foolish an idea as
it was unachievable.

Winston's defeat/cure deep in the bowels of the Ministry of Love is complete, both intellectually and emotionally. Winston had thought that Big
Brother couldn't get inside you, that one's thoughts and loves were really
one's own and could not be assailed and altered by external pressure. But he
understood in the end that he was wrong. *They can get inside you!* Sanity
really is statistical, and two plus two really does equal three or five, or whatever Big Brother says it does. The individual mind is utterly defenseless
against the social mind. If *everyone* insists that two plus two equals three,
then that is an end to the matter, and two plus two really *does* equal three.
Anyone who would insist otherwise must be crazy!

And history really is what others say it is. If history texts are changed to
say that Hannibal never crossed the Alps to attack Rome, and if historians
insist (perhaps using doctored evidence) that Hannibal never crossed the Alps
to attack Rome, then Hannibal never did cross the Alps to attack Rome. The
past is exactly as Big Brother describes it if everyone accepts Big Brother's
description. And if there are no voices to the contrary, why should they not
accept Big Brother's description? Even if there are voices to the contrary,
why should these be believed if they lack a commonly accepted authoritative
stature? Individual memories are powerless against accepted belief. The trick,
of course, is to get belief accepted, but this is easy enough, Orwell supposed,
if it is changed frequently enough to incline people to doubt themselves. Anyone who holds out against the collective memory of society and insists that it

is wrong and that they are right must be crazy! So O'Brien's simple theory of control seems frightfully compelling: "He who controls the past controls the present, and he who controls the present controls the future!"

When O'Brien is finished with Winston, and Orwell is finished with his readers, Winston's dementia seems quite real. It now seems easy to appreciate Winston's insignificance in the greater interplay of social and political forces at work in the novel; Winston's defiance of Big Brother seems in the end to be as foolish as it was arrogant. The last man in Europe is powerless against the collective consciousness of his age, and if Big Brother has the power to control this collective consciousness, then his power over the individual is complete. Against such power, the solitary individual has no chance.

Why has Orwell told such an utterly hopeless tale? Why did he feel the need to attack our mythic beliefs about the dignity and integrity of the solitary individual so thoroughly? He has presented his readers with the specter of political control and domination so complete that only the insane are able to recognize the horror of the situation. Sometimes readers respond to Orwell's novel with a type of disbelief accompanied by a familiar form of denial. "Orwell's Oceania is really a horrible place. Anyone can see that," they say, "but it is not like our place. It is not like America; anyone can see that too!" But why is America not exactly like Oceania? How can Americans be so sure that their government does not exercise a similar type of control over the American public? Are the proles so completely different from the vast majority of contemporary Americans? What is it that distinguishes America from Oceania? And most important of all, what did Orwell hope to call to our attention by telling such a frightening story? Is there a moral here that people can learn from, or should people just accept the idea that the future will be little more than "a boot stamping on a human face—forever," as O'Brien describes it to Winston? Should we regard *1984* as a warning of some sort or just as a piece of outdated fiction?

THE ANARCHY ALTERNATIVE

These questions orient and direct the project of thinking about politics. Their careful exploration should do much to develop a more thoughtful and coherent view of political life and expand ontological horizons in the process. Perhaps the best way to approach the problems they introduce is to proceed with a more analytic confrontation with the notion of power. Power over others, in the most general sense, involves the ability to get others to do what one wants them to do regardless of their will. A gunman has the ability to take my wallet from me, even if I hand it over unwillingly. The gun, in this example, is the source of the gunman's power; the gun enables the gunman to exercise the kind of control he needs in order to force me to comply with his demand. Orwell, however, imagines an exercise of power where those in power—the inner party—can control the individual's will by reducing individual thought and belief to a matter of external determination. This is a most thorough and frightening form of power, enabling those who have it to exercise total control over others literally by capturing their will. This is a more thorough form of power than anything the gunman is capable of. It is the type of power Orwell thinks others may be able to exercise if they hold the reins of government. Government is the source of Big Brother's power, for government positions the inner party in a way that enables its members to direct the policy of Oceania, to rewrite history, to declare and end war, to spy upon the people, and to gather the information necessary for the exercise of total control of those individuals they seek and need to control.

Power, it is typically believed, is desirable as a means by which to realize something one wants. People with power can control others in a way that enables them to realize desired ends; people without power are unable to realize desired ends and suffer the fate of being used as tools in the service of the ends of the more powerful. According to this view of the matter, power is of little use if there is no particular end one wants to realize; power must serve a purpose.

Power is also normally considered a relational notion, but this view introduces something of a complication. Taken as a relational notion, power must be regarded as a *dyadic* concept. This means that power involves a relation between two or more subjects, where one subject recognizes and respects another's power. Consider what it means to say that someone with power can get others to do what she wants them to do, willingly or otherwise. Imagine a gunman who issues what can be called a coercive threat; the gunman points his gun at another and says, "Your money or your life." The force of this threat depends not only, or even necessarily at all, upon the presence of the gun. More to the point, the force of this treat depends upon the attitude of the person to whom the threat is issued. Does this person value his life more than his money? Suppose he is dejected and wants to die but hasn't the nerve to commit suicide, though he welcomes being shot to death by the gunman. Can the gunman exercise real power over someone with attitudes of this sort? This seems unlikely because the threat here simply doesn't work as a threat at all.

Understood in dyadic terms, A's power depends upon B's fear of the consequences associated with A's threat coupled with B's understanding that A's threat is credible. If B does not fear these consequences, perhaps because he does not believe A will carry out his threat or because A has misjudged B's fear of A's threat, A has no power over B. But power need not be dyadic or relational in the sense that A's power depends ultimately upon B's will and understanding. The concept of power may also function to describe *monadic* relationships, or relationships in which A can realize the desired control of B regardless of B's will. Consider again the gunman example. The gunman who says, "Your money or your life," is not really expressing things very accurately. What she is really saying is, "Your money or your money and your life." If B does not hand over his wallet to the gunman, the gunman can always shoot him and take the wallet off his body.

Those who insist that power is primarily a dyadic notion can point to the fact that many of the things that people want from others can only be gained by their consent. (Imagine a gunman wanting to coerce an important secret out of her victim.) But this still supposes that A's power holds against B only in physical terms, that is, that A can do X to B (or to someone or something that B treasures) if B does not do what A wants, where X is calculated by A to be less desirable to B than doing what A wants. Orwell, however, imagines a different sort of situation in *1984*. O'Brien's power over Winston is monadic in nature because O'Brien is able to capture or control (or defeat) Winston's will. Winston doesn't believe they can get inside you, but in fact they can, as he eventually learns. That is, O'Brien's power over Winston holds in psychological terms; O'Brien controls Winston by controlling his will. This is why the power displayed in Orwell's story is so unsettling and so complete.[7]

But power is relational in the sense that one person is more powerful than another if she has greater power resources than the other. The gunman's gun, once again, is a power resource, but it isn't much of a resource if everyone has a gun. Sometimes our worries about the power of others are selfish. If others are more powerful than we are, if they have more power resources, we have reason to worry because they can use this power to achieve their desired ends even if their doing so hinders or obstructs our ability to realize our interests. One way to protect against this is to cultivate power, to make sure that we have power resources equal or slightly superior to others. Let us call this a balance of power; no one is very powerful if everyone has roughly the same power resources.

If governments need power to govern, it is because government officials need to have the ability to make sure that others will comply with the commands of government officials. It thus presupposes an extremely unequal distribution of power resources in society. In fact, some thinkers have gone so far as to describe government as that institution occupied by individuals with a monopoly of coercive force in society.[8] Control of government thus implies an extraordinary—perhaps even unmatched—power resource. And this introduces the traditional reason why political power seems problematic. What will prevent people with such power resources from using this power to pursue and achieve their own ends and interests rather than working to promote the public interest? People may feel compelled to put their trust in government because they seem to have no other choice. But given the imbalance of power that control of government brings into being, what reason is there to trust individuals who manage to control government?

But this is not the problem that Orwell imagines; the inner party in Oceania does not seek power in order to get things desired by its members. Power in Oceania is not a means; it is an end in itself! Power, Orwell warns, may have the magical ability to seduce the powerful and transform the desire for power into and end in itself. Power now exists for its own end, and the joy of having power is in exercising it, in controlling others, and not in what one can get with it. If power actually corrupts in this sense, the problem of power in politics is far more sinister than might be originally supposed.

The most pessimistic possible reading of Orwell's novel suggests that human beings have doomed themselves to Orwell's world—to the world he imagines in *1984*—by committing to political power in the first place. Once inequalities of power are introduced by the establishment of government, the transformative force of power will work its magic, and soon the state will be composed only of the controllers and the controlled. Even though the controllers can't manage to amass the power necessary to control the proles should they organize in opposition to Big Brother, the proles are no threat to the inner party, for the proles will control themselves and make the job of the controllers that much easier. The proles potentially have enough power resources, by virtue of strength of numbers, to overthrow the inner party. But they lack the will to do so largely because they lack the reflective capacity to grasp their situation. Their ontological horizons are just too narrow.

If one takes this reading seriously, it might seem that Orwell wanted to warn his readers about the transformative force of political power, and hence about the terrible threat that political power poses to human well-being. Since there can be no government without power, this might seem to reduce to a plea to do away with government and opt for a condition of anarchy. If people should avoid political power at all costs, if public trust in government can never be justified, the only alternative would seem to be anarchy. But is anarchy really a viable form of human association?

Anarchy has appealed to some political thinkers, but not many. Anarchy maintains a rough balance of power in society by eliminating the resource imbalance of power brought into being by government. It checks the corrupting transformative force of power by blocking the possibility of a significantly unequal distribution of power resources. In terms that will be explained more fully in subsequent chapters, anarchy can be described as the most decentralized imaginable form of social life. This does not mean that organization and collective institutions are not permissible under conditions of anarchy, but the authority of any such structures will be tightly circumscribed. In an anarchical condition, all human relationships must be based upon voluntary choice and consent. No person can be forced or coerced to do something against her will; this is a defining condition of anarchy. Under anarchy, people cannot even consent (assuming they would even want to) to social arrangements that would empower some to coercively compel those who have consented to these arrangements to comply with the commands of powerful authorities. So, while people can agree to form managerial organizations, the authority these organizations have under conditions of anarchy depends ultimately upon the continuing willingness of those subject to this authority to continue to consent to it. Where the corrupting force of power is minimized in this way, anarchists contend, human beings can get along quite famously and amicably with one another. Individual industry and initiative can supply society with all it needs, and natural forces will ensure that independent human initiative meets all the needs of the larger community. Human beings only make trouble for themselves by opting for centralized government and by bringing power imbalances into being. If power corrupts, why not do away with relationships based upon power? Why not do away with government, since it is, of necessity, the seat of centralized power?

The anarchist vision is admittedly attractive, but is it realistic? Even people who are desperately suspicious of political power often admit the need to answer this question negatively. One popular reason for rejecting anarchy asserts that anarchists simply don't understand human nature. According to his objection, human beings aren't the friendly, amicable characters that anarchists imagine. They are more brutish than this, and if not opposed by a powerful external force, they will prey upon one another mercilessly. Unless we introduce a force capable of constraining the beast—or controlling the negative elements of the human character—the life of man will be exactly what the seventeenth-century British philosopher Thomas Hobbes imagined it would be, "solitary, poor, nasty, brutish, and short."[9] People need government, in short, to protect them from themselves, and it is only after people admit this that they need worry about how to protect themselves from government.

It would most certainly be foolish to deny that human beings have a tendency to prey upon one another from time to time; the history of humankind and the morning newspaper offer sufficient evidence of this. But are the critics of the anarchist position really justified in claiming some privileged insight into human nature? If so, how did they come by this knowledge? And why do they think that human behavior is so thoroughly and unalterably fixed by nature in the first place? There seems something arrogantly presumptuous about the claim that some people just happen to have privileged access into the nature of human nature. Can anyone really know for sure that human beings have a nature and that one has figured out what it is?

Some philosophers have started to think about politics by beginning in this way and presuming that their science enables them to grasp human nature. Once this vision of persons is in place, it then becomes necessary only to design the social environment that seems most suited to the particular kind of creature that human beings happen to be. But this isn't a very good way to start thinking about politics because claims about human nature, no matter how scientific they might appear to be, are inherently suspicious. What one takes to be human nature might just happen to be the product of social forces and influences. How could anyone hope to control for all these social influences in order to generate some picture of human nature as it really is? Humans seem to be invariably social creatures; people are born into and raised within the company of others. Social influences, in other words, begin to shape human *being* from birth. Is it possible to strip away the layers of social influence that have shaped human consciousness and finally reach natural man? And why should anyone presume, ahead of the investigative process, that humans really have a nature that locks their behavior into some discernible natural pattern? Might it not make more sense to admit that human consciousness is forged significantly, though perhaps not entirely, by social factors and influences? Perhaps people should even question the classic distinction between nature and nurture when it comes to thinking about human nature. Perhaps, that is, there is really no dichotomy recognizable here at all; perhaps what people customarily think of as human nature is simply a complex condition of biological and social factors.

When one looks at what past philosophers have said about human nature, one finds a few wild generalities about how human beings act based upon some nebulous observations of how human beings have acted in the past. And as one might expect, there is also considerable disagreement about how human nature is to be understood. Yet even if one could get clear on human nature, it doesn't seem likely that this would be of much help in addressing the problem of power. Suppose one contends that human beings are naturally disposed to prey upon one another. How does this help us think about politics? "We need the state," a familiar answer goes, "to police predation and make sure that people respect each other's rights." But this just reintroduces the problem of political power with a vengeance. Who will police the policemen if the policemen are also human beings? By giving such power to some, it just becomes that much easier for these people to prey upon others. If humans really are naturally disposed to prey upon one another, Orwell's nightmare world would be our world; if human beings naturally prey upon one another, government cannot stop this. It can only affect the form this predation takes.

But suppose, instead, that human beings are believed to be naturally sociable and benevolent toward one another. This, of course, is the anarchist view. But it is just as suspicious as the more pessimistic view of human nature, and for the very same reason. Why should anyone think that anarchists have a more exact or accurate insight into human nature than anyone else? Moreover, even if human beings are naturally sociable (whatever this might finally be understood to mean), they could still find reasons to come into conflict with one another, and these conflicts might become violent from time to time. Even reasonably amicable individuals may have disagreements that are likely to get out of hand. This may not be sufficient reason to think that civil association is a better arrangement than anarchy, but it is reason to wonder whether anarchy would be such a good bargain in the final analysis. More importantly, it does not follow that civil association is a bad idea simply because human beings happen to be naturally sociable. And if human beings really are naturally sociable and amicable, one might also wonder why power should corrupt this nature. Why should naturally sociable beings not live peaceably with one another amid a condition of civil association, confident that power won't corrupt the powerful because their nature is naturally sociable? Moreover, sociability does not mean that human association might not require institutional and organizational arrangements with the power to meet the many problems and challenges that human beings create for themselves in the process of living together.

Suppose finally (and as a good many philosophers have supposed) that human beings exhibit something that might be called an unsocial sociability by nature.[10] Humans are generally able to get along with one another and to live amicably in one another's company. But sometimes things may take a turn for the worse, and people may behave in a most unsociable manner. Given the saga of human history, this seems a reasonably sensible generalization. But what does it mean for understanding politics? Does it follow from this that civil association is a better idea than anarchy? This would follow only if there were reason to suppose that committing to some degree of centralization, and thus bringing a state (complete with coercive powers) into being, would help to check our unsociable side without encouraging those who enjoy the political power that comes with centralization to abuse this power. This, however, is the very concern that Orwell supposes is altogether unrealistic, and if he is right, there is again reason to conclude that anarchy is a better arrangement than civil association. But such a conclusion hardly seems justified. If one concludes, for whatever reason, that human beings do

exhibit by nature a type of unsocial sociability, there would seem to be no
reason to prefer anarchy to civil association or vice versa. Which is preferable, the frying pan or the fire? Either way, the unsociable side of human
nature is going to cause problems.

The moral of the story should now seem fairly clear. Although many philosophers have begun to think about politics by hypothesizing some vision of
human nature, this does not seem like a very good way to begin. Even if it
were possible to be clear on the nature of human nature (and this seems
unlikely), a particular vision of human nature isn't sufficient to indicate
whether anarchy would be a better arrangement for human beings than civil
association. The anarchists cannot guarantee that things will go swimmingly
if only people would do away with government, although they might convince some people that the possible little evils likely to be suffered at the
hands of others are preferable to the great evil likely to be suffered at the
hands of those holding political power. But any such conclusion is likely to
be purely speculative; there just isn't sufficient information about human
beings to know how to choose a preferable poison or to know if the anarchy
alternative is a good one.

THE PURPOSES OF POLITICS

Given the problem of political power, it seems appropriate to take anarchy
seriously, at least for a moment. But doing so doesn't seem to help much with
the problem of power, because it isn't possible to know whether people have
more to fear from government than they do from their neighbors. But the
discussion thus far has introduced one fundamental reason to opt for government and accept at least a modest form of institutional centralization. Regardless of what one thinks about human nature, one can be fairly confident in
the veracity of one generality about the nature of the human condition.
Human beings are not inevitably and invariably at one another's throats; if
they were, no form of social intercourse would be possible. But disputes
between people do break out from time to time, and for any number of reasons that needn't be catalogued here. When these disputes do break out, they
are likely to become violent and destructive if there is not some effective way
to resolve them. One key reason to concede the need for government, then, is
to have available a referee with the power and authority to resolve disputes
when they arise, and in the process to police the violence that may be associated with these disputes.

This is a good reason to endorse civil association and reject anarchism, but
it has also been suggested that it is not necessarily a very good or compelling

reason. It is still necessary to wonder if it is possible to police the policeman and domesticate the referee. But there are other reasons why it makes sense to endorse civil association, and as these become more evident, the scales of wisdom begin to tilt in favor of accepting civil association, and against the alternative of anarchy.

In order to appreciate these additional reasons for accepting civil association, it is necessary to understand that thinking about politics must invariably take place within the context of some determinate social condition. People inherit the social world as it is, and when they begin to think about politics, they necessarily do so within the context provided by this social condition. People may wish that their social world were different, and if they had the powers that some attribute to a deity, they might elect to create an entirely different kind of social arrangement. But one cannot undo what has been done in the past; it is possible only to think about how best to live with it. Since people cannot recreate their social condition, at least without a monumental effort of all parties involved (and imagine what the chances are of everyone agreeing on what a new social condition should be like), they had best attempt to identify ways to go on within it. Suppose, then, that we look at our social condition as it is and ask ourselves if there are any things that should be managed and organized by a centralized authority. It has already been noticed that dispute resolution (and the mutual defense associated with it) is one reason to centralize, but there are others. It is perhaps worthwhile to list them and then comment on them independently. The list need not be considered exhaustive, although it needs to be relatively suggestive of the types of activities and responsibilities that require centralized management and control if social life is to go well.

1. Manage conflict resolution.
2. Manage property transfers.
3. Manage interstate issues.
4. Provide and manage necessary services that are not market viable.
5. Manage coordination problems.
6. Manage collective action problems.
7. Manage public safety.

Resolve Conflicts. This necessary political function has already been anticipated. Society needs a fair and unbiased method by which people can settle disputes and resolve the problems and misunderstandings that might arise between them. Sometimes conflicts arise between strangers; they do so, for example, if one person happens to have something that another person wants who is willing to try and get it by force if necessary. This is the sort of thing that leads to the problem of human predation. Life goes better for everyone if there is a way to hold in check the general tendency to help oneself to something at the expense of others. But conflicts may well arise between even the friendliest of strangers and the friendliest of friends. Frequently people can manage to work these things out among themselves, and when they do, this is all to the good. But some conflicts are difficult to resolve, and it makes sense to have a central authority capable of reviewing such problems and providing impartial and reasoned remedies. In fact, peaceful and amicable solutions to interpersonal conflicts are often worked out by people for themselves because they know that the state is there ready and willing to resolve the problem if they can't resolve it by themselves. Interpersonal bargaining and cooperation is enhanced by the fact that either party can appeal to the state as a neutral third party in the event that the other party is unwilling to settle matters fairly or quickly. Where there is no central authority to manage conflicts, things may get out of hand and explode into large-scale feuds that endanger social peace and stability.

Managing conflict is particularly important in large, pluralist societies like the United States. When different groups with different cultures come into conflict, more dominant groups will likely attempt to impose their will on their adversaries. Centralized management of these conflicts is important to ensure a basic element of social justice and to guarantee that dominant groups do not tyrannize or terrorize minority groups. This public function can only be achieved, however, if dominant groups do not also control the state—a point that introduces another twist to the problem of political power.

Managing Property Transfers. Politics does not make property possible. Property—that is, ownership of those goods, commodities, or things subject to being owned—is a social convention. Property is a way to distribute and control the things of the world. Some people think it is a good way to do this; others don't. But people need to use the things of the world to sustain themselves. Life's necessities include food, shelter, and clothing, and most of what people own probably fits into one of these categories. If people are to survive and life is to go well, people need access to these things as well as the unhindered opportunity to put them to personal use. Of course, life's luxuries also fit into this category, and in wealthy societies, people claim much more as property than what they need to survive. Things become troublesome when some people manage to own a great deal of the wealth available in a society and others don't have enough of this wealth to supply themselves with life's necessities.

Some people think government serves the interests of the wealthy by protecting their wealth against the poorer elements of society, some of whom may not have sufficient wealth to sustain themselves. Government may at times work this way, but as we shall see, this is a reason to question its just-ness. Within a system of property ownership, government legislates and enforces the rules that control and determine how property is to be distrib-uted. All societies need rules of this sort (i.e., rules regarding the use and transfer of the things needed to support and sustain life) because all societies need to manage the distribution of the resources that people need to sustain themselves. Because the nature of human need changes, all societies also need ways to review and amend these rules when necessary. This typically becomes a job for government, and the importance of this job introduces a reason to think that civil association is a good idea. Many of the disputes, introduced above, that might arise between people are caused by questions about the use or control of property, or of things over which someone has a rightful claim of ownership. But not all disputes between persons need be over property, and the management of property transfers need not always involve a dispute of some sort. Imagine someone making out a will. This person needs to know how to transfer his property upon death, but this is not necessarily a disputatious issue if it is generally accepted in the society in question that one has the right upon death to dispose of one's property as one wishes.

Managing Interstate Relations. Anarchy is problematic if and when exter-nal states exist, for societies may well have (or need to have) relations with these other states. In order for a society to have relations with external states, it is necessary for it to have an official spokesperson—someone who speaks with the authority of the society as a whole and is recognized by external states as the proper contact point when it comes to addressing their dealings with this society. It is commonplace to notice that decentralized social arrangements are at a certain disadvantage when they are surrounded by cen-tralized states. The organization and coordination that centralization allows means that states are able to marshal resources to threaten the security and well-being of decentralized societies. To defend against the threat of external aggression, societies do well to centralize for their own protection. As the notable political scientist E. E. Schattschneider once remarked, states are minority organizations.[11] People organize in order to guarantee that they will be allowed to manage their own affairs and control their own territory free from external aggression.

But in these complicated times, the state does more in the international arena than just provide for national security. It also acts as the advocate for the interests of its citizenry within the international community. It makes interstate travel and commerce a more efficient possibility, and it works with other states to regulate things like the use of airways, waterways, and commu-nication channels. As human life becomes more complex, as technology complicates the social world and endangers the global environment, the efforts of states to identify and manage transboundary issues become that much more important. So, because other states do exist, anarchy is hardly a very desirable social arrangement.

Managing Necessity in Non-market-viable Contexts. The free market typically associated with capitalism is a very decentralized arrangement. In theory at least, all the functions performed by government could be performed by market-driven practices. Where some people recognize a market for a certain service (or a certain good), capitalist theory suggests that they would do well to organize in order to provide the service (or the good) for a profit. Things go well if they make money providing the service because presumably they will then continue to provide it. Evidence of the need for the service is indicated by the fact that people are willing to pay for it. If people aren't willing to pay for it—if the service isn't worth the cost to them—then the market corrects as people abandon the service in search of one that people are willing to pay for. In this way, people get the services they want, and competition within the industry guarantees that people will get wanted services at the most reasonable possible price.

Classic capitalist economic theory approaches a form of anarchism if all market transactions are voluntary and consensual and if market arrangements actually provide all the needed services for a society. A minimal state is necessary, under this theory, only to manage disputes, defend property rights, and protect the state against external aggression. But an overly rigorous capitalism is problematic because there are some services that are not easily or properly left to market providers. Police services and national defense come quickly to mind here. Additionally, market-driven services hardly resolve the problem of political power; instead they complicate matters by introducing the possibility of private centers of power. If some managerial institutions are necessary to provide social services, and if these institutions possess power of some sort as a necessary condition of their ability to provide the required services, then they constitute a threat to others in the society. Nor does it matter whether they call themselves corporations or governments; the problem is still the same. A private protection agency with the power to defend the rights of its subscribers also has the power to hold its subscribers hostage to higher rates of pay and even to drive competition out of business. So, classic capitalist economic theory can't supply an answer to Orwell's problem of political power. Instead, it introduces new things to think about. If it is supposed that a market is a good way to provide certain services, people must decide which services should be provided by market arrangements and which should not. And they must think about how best to sustain an open market in the event that some providers attempt to defend their position in the market by capturing the market itself and controlling a monopoly in the services they provide.

Moreover, while there are some services that it is best not to leave to market arrangements, there are others that cannot be left to market arrangements because it is not cost effective to provide them. Some services cannot be provided at a reasonable price and still prove profitable. Imagine the problem of mail delivery in very rural regions. The cost of mail delivery in such regions is rather high, and it is unlikely that a market-based venture could deliver mail there for a profit and still offer reasonable rates to its constituency. Should people living in such regions forego receiving mail, or should society make some arrangement that subsidizes mail delivery by asking government to provide the service?

Managing Coordination Problems. Decentralized social arrangements are clumsy. If they are small enough, social custom and routinization may suffice to allow people to go about their business without unnecessarily getting in each other's way. People may be able to learn the rules of the road well enough that driving would be possible without centralized management of the activity, and there may be other large-scale social activities that could be managed through custom and habit. But in general it is hard for people to keep from bumping into one another in complex and crowded social settings, and so some centralized management of society seems necessary to coordinate the variety of activities that would be frustrated without such coordination. Two radio stations cannot use the same frequency in close proximity, for example, and the Boston Pops can't hold a concert in the park at the same time and in the same place that the American Nazi Party wants to hold a rally.

Social organization and activity management sometimes seem like needless hassles, but they are necessary hassles if society is to make effective use of the public resources of space and time. These are social resources that need to be managed in order to guarantee that people can plan events and be reasonably certain that things will come off as planned. Once social arrangements reach a certain stage of complexity, once they develop beyond a fairly primitive simplicity, anarchy seems unworkable. There is just too much going on in complex societies, and the channels of communication are just too limited to guarantee the kind of infrastructure coordination necessary for people to conduct their lives and plan their daily activities in harmony with others.

Managing Collective Action Problems. Human actions sometimes have unintended consequences. This possibility is compounded as large numbers of individuals engage in activities that would hardly cause concern if only a few did them. Imagine a neighborhood where people are permitted to burn the leaves that drop in their yards in the fall. Probably nobody would care about this very much if only a few neighbors decided to burn their leaves.

But if all the neighbors began to burn leaves, the smoke from the fires would quickly fill the neighborhood and create environmental problems. There are a number of things the neighbors might do to address the problem. They might limit burning to only a few days a week or assign burning dates in order to limit the number of people who can burn on any given day, thus keeping the smoke problem within acceptable parameters. But there are problems with these strategies. It isn't necessarily clear that burning can be effectively limited in a way that still enables neighbors to get rid of their leaves. And as the neighborhood grows in size, or as more people from adjoining neighborhoods begin to burn, burning opportunities must be further limited to keep the smoke problem under control.

Voluntary arrangements of this sort also give rise to *free rider problems*. Suppose the neighborhood places a limit on acceptable burning days, but Jones decides to burn on a nonburning day, thinking that the small amount of smoke he produces that day won't cause any great harm. If Jones defects from the arrangement, what will keep Smith from doing so as well? But if everyone feels free to defect, the voluntary arrangement quickly fails. The larger some cooperative agreement becomes—that is, the more parties there are to some cooperative agreement—the greater the likelihood that someone will defect. So large cooperative agreements of this sort are decidedly unstable things.

The obvious alternative to reliance upon decentralized cooperative agreements is to empower a central manager to resolve collective action problems and watch for defectors. At some point, the neighborhood is likely to get so large that burning is no longer a viable option for getting rid of the leaves, so an alternative strategy needs to be implemented. Now the problem has grown to such a size that it begins to transcend the ability of neighbors to develop and implement decentralized cooperative strategies for resolving it. Greater expertise and a broader range of jurisdiction are necessary at this point, and this requires a centralized manager.

Managing Public Safety. Societies are now terribly complicated matrices of human activity, which means there is an awful lot that can go wrong and cause harm to people. Additionally, Americans have become little control junkies; most Americans are confident that almost every feature of human life can be controlled and managed in order to guarantee that things go well for them. Americans take public safety for granted, but the public isn't necessarily a very safe place. How do people know that the medicine their doctors prescribe for them is not worse for them than the problem it is intended to cure? How do they know that the elevator that takes them up to the thirtieth floor in their hotel is safe? How can they be sure that a fire that breaks out in a neighbor's house will be contained and will not spread to their house? If there is a natural disaster like an earthquake or hurricane, how can they be certain that someone will come to their aid?

People might rely upon the decentralized goodwill of their neighbors in the event of a natural disaster of some sort, but even if these neighbors are willing to provide the needed assistance, can anyone be assured that they have the skill and knowledge required to effectively help those who need assistance? Similarly, people might trust the pharmaceutical company from which they purchase their medicine to provide them with safe and appropriate goods. But how can they be sure that this company has made sufficient effort to research and understand, say, the long-term consequences of the drugs they market? If people leave these matters to free market initiatives, what protection do they have against price gouging? The price of umbrellas goes up when it rains; the price of snow tires goes up when it snows. This is the nature of market relationships. Should people be willing to live with the prospect that the price of fire protection may go up when a fire breaks out? Are these matters that are best left to free and open markets, or is it preferable to rely upon centralized management in order to guarantee public safety? Once again, it looks like centralized management is a good bet, and so once again there is reason to question the desirability of anarchy.

These are but a few illustrations of the kinds of things that people need or want government to do for them. These examples introduce functions that it is best to allow government to perform. And this suggests a reasonably attractive account of government. Let us say that *government* is a centralized institution charged with performing certain functions and providing certain services that cannot or should not be left to market organizations to provide. This is a functional account of government; it tells us, in general, why government is necessary, although it does not provide a clear insight into all the various things that citizens need government to do for them. It offers a functional account of government without an exhaustive listing of the functions that government ought to perform. It should be clear, however, that in those areas requiring the centralized management provided by government, government needs the power necessary for effective management. Power is necessary if governments are to effectively resolve disputes, control property transfers, defend the state from external aggression, raise the revenue required to provide non-market-viable services, effectively police coordination problems, address collective action problems, and safeguard the public against natural and social disasters. This is why it is not possible to govern without power.

THE MANAGEMENT DILEMMA

Given the functions that government must perform, it seems reasonable to say that today society is unworkable without centralized management. This is reason to abandon the hope that recourse to anarchy will resolve the problem of political power. So it is necessary to find another way to avoid Orwell's world, and this means that it is important to think again about what Orwell could be telling his readers about how best to address the challenges posed by the existence of political power. His warning about the abuse of political power cannot reasonably be interpreted as a recommendation to do away with this power; he understood too well the importance of the very power that troubled him so deeply.

Anarchy might work rather well in a small community of friends where it is possible for the community as a whole to provide for the modest support services it requires. As society grows, however, and people move away from modest social units toward complex social arrangements, the functional support required to make life in this social setting viable requires the introduction of institutions dedicated to providing the necessary functions. Because it falls to government to provide for the effective management of the problems caused by increased size and complexity in society, it seems appropriate to give a functional account of government. The managerial challenges that face government, on the other hand, are going to be significant and complicated, and will increase in significance and complexity as society grows larger and more sophisticated. The managerial responsibility that government faces is thus sure to seem daunting, and government will need to draw upon all the resources at its disposal in society in order to get the job done. And this suggests the need to supplement our functional account of government and to understand *government* as an institution dedicated to coalescing existing social expertise in order to address large-scale social problems—problems that require centralized management in order to keep social life viable. Yet this definition, extensive though it is, isn't quite extensive enough, because government must also manage the social problem of making sure that society is producing the diverse expertise necessary to resolve these social problems; that is, government must make sure that society is producing the kind of expertise it needs to manage its problems effectively.

If the job of government is to manage large-scale social problems within its jurisdiction, it is also reasonable to think of the polity as a mutual support system. Members of the polity—its citizens, in other words—ideally work together to make social life there go well. Government is a part of this process, but it isn't all of the process. Polities can be relatively decentralized if members work independently for each other's well-being. Market incentives provide selfish reasons for people to do just this; in fact, the classic logic of the capitalist market holds that self-interested behavior will promote the public interest by providing everyone with compelling incentives to contribute to the needs of the public. The need for centralization is some testimony to the limitations of this logic, but there may be limits to the logic of centralization as well. Society may go better if all its members work to aid and support the lives of others. Government may be necessary to do part of the job of making social life go well by identifying and resolving certain large-scale social problems. But it may not be a good idea—in fact it may even be a bad idea—to suppose that government should do the whole job of making social life go well. There may still be a role for more decentralized activity in the smooth operation of the polity. Regardless of whether the motive is selfish or not, it may still be a good idea to leave some social services to market forces. But this possibility introduces another tough problem, something that can be called the management dilemma. The conclusion of this inquiry into the viability of anarchy suggests that some centralized social management is necessary for society to go well. But just how much management is necessary or desirable? How extensively should the polity centralize, and to what extent should it rely upon decentralized social arrangements to provide the goods and services people require? Here, then, is the dilemma: Just how much management does a polity need?

These are important questions, and they become more important as societies become ever more complex. Simplicity seems to be a casualty of modernity, and this has important ramifications for thinking about politics. The management dilemma is not the same as the problem of political power, but it is related to it. As centralized management becomes more necessary in society, government will grow bigger and more powerful at the same time. This seems inevitable, but it also exacerbates the problem of political power. As governments become ever more powerful, they dwarf the individuals they presumably serve. Might not an overly zealous government reach a point where it can no longer recognize the need for limitations upon its power? Might it not reach a point where it simply seeks to control social life for the mere sake of doing so? And isn't this exactly what has happened in Orwell's Oceania?

NOTES

1. James Madison, *Federalist*, No. 51.
2. Readers not familiar with Orwell's novel might find it useful to read the work along with the present text.

3. Orwell took up residence in the north of Scotland, and it was there that he wrote the manuscript. But he had long suffered from tuberculosis, and the Scottish climate was not conducive to his health. Yet rather than leave and convalesce in a more hospitable climate, he elected to stay in Scotland to complete the work. The damage to his health proved to be irreversible, and he died of the disease in 1950, only a short time after the work had gone into print.

4. Orwell's character, Winston Smith, is given an identity similar to Orwell's own. The character's first name, Winston, is taken from Britain's great leader during World War II, Winston Churchill, while the character's surname is a commonplace British name. George Orwell, on the other hand, was born Eric Blair; he adopted his pen name by taking a commonplace British first name and a surname taken from the Orwell river which flows through the southern part of England. See Michael Sheldon, *Orwell: The Authorized Biography* (New York: Harper Perennial, 1992), 194–95.

5. The name "Oceania" as a pseudonym for Great Britain was not original with Orwell and was perhaps taken from James Harrington's eighteenth-century work *Oceana*. Orwell's dystopia, *1984*, might thus be read as a counterpoise to Harrington's earlier utopian work.

6. Orwell, *1984* (New York: New American Library, 1961), 61–62.

7. Readers familiar with Orwell's tale may note that this last comment is not quite true to the story. O'Brien defeats Winston as an emotional being by making it evident to Winston that his fear of a horrible death (his fear of death at the hand of rats) is greater than his love for Julia. By controlling this fear, O'Brien finally impresses upon Winston that there is really nothing more sacred to him than avoiding the horrors that O'Brien can inflict upon him.

8. See, for example, John Austin, *The Province of Jurisprudence Determined*, ed. H. L. A. Hart (London: Weidenfeld and Nicolson, 1968).

9. Thomas Hobbes, *Leviathan*, Ch. 13.

10. This view of the matter is explicitly present in the political thought of the great German philosopher Immanuel Kant. See Kant, "Idea for a Universal History with a Cosmopolitan Purpose," in *Kant's Political Writings*, ed. Hans Reiss, 41–53 (Cambridge: Cambridge University Press, 1970).

11. E. E. Schattschneider, *Two Hundred Million Americans in Search of a Government* (Hinsdale, IL: Dryden Press, 1969).

Chapter Two

Liberalism: Politics in the American Mold

The state of society and the Constitution in America are democratic, but there has been no democratic revolution. They were pretty well as they now are when they first arrived in the land.

Alexis de Tocqueville

If Orwell was too sophisticated a political thinker to have recommended anarchy as a solution to the problem of political power, what else could he have been up to? What *is* the moral of his story that mattered so much to him? The most pessimistic and no doubt cruelest reading of *1984* would leave us with a view of Orwell as an embittered cynic who had given up hope, or political hope, for his beloved England and who wanted simply to purge the remnants of idealism from his character by projecting a dreadful future for his native land. But there is no reason to accept this view of him if it is possible to identify a more generous reading of his work, and fortunately, he left several hints that point in the direction of a more positive message.

POLITICS AND CULTURE

There are several clues in *1984* that suggest the book was intended to be an impassioned invitation to think about politics coupled with a stark illustration of the costs that will accompany the failure to do so. The first clue, although not actually in the book at all, is indicated by Orwell's initial thoughts about the proper title for the work, "The Last Man in Europe." This might be taken to imply that Winston is the last thinking individual in Oceania, but this is evidently not the case. O'Brien was certainly a thinking individual and was,

47

for that matter, far better at it than poor Winston. For O'Brien does not just brutalize Winston into submission deep in the Ministry of Love; he actually *reasons* him into submission. Winston's own frailty, both physical *and* intellectual, is exposed to him by O'Brien in a way that leaves little left once O'Brien is done. But this takes us to Orwell's clue. What has Winston lost under O'Brien's torture/tutelage?

One good answer to this question is to say that he has lost his dignity; he has been robbed of his self-respect. In an important sense, he no longer belongs to himself; nothing of him is truly his. They have gotten inside him and totally remade him. His thoughts, his loves, and his ideals are no longer his; they belong to Big Brother. His dependency is complete, and he understands this now. He no longer struggles against it; he no longer thinks there is someone there, in his skin, capable of being independent, self-determining, and self-actualizing. He has been purged of the foolish belief that he was at one point an independent, self-determining being. Now he knows better. He is not an independent *self* but a species being, a construct of forces put into effect and manipulated by Big Brother. Winston has found Big Brother, but he has lost himself. He is now just like the other species beings around him who accept their world as it is presented to them, faithfully, openly, and without quibble or question.

This is a good way to answer the question about what Winston loses in the Ministry of Love, but it also suggests an even better one. In losing his sense of self, Winston has also lost his identity. When O'Brien is done, Winston no longer has an identity of his own; he is the person Big Brother tells him he is. He is only what Big Brother says he is, and it seems that Big Brother can revise his identity at will, or even stamp him out of existence if he so chooses. This is, perhaps, the ultimate exercise of power over another individual. It dwarfs the account of power offered previously. O'Brien does more than just get Winston to do what (and whatever) he wants; he remakes Winston's being in the fashion that suits him. And this awesome exercise of power is made all the more disturbing by the fact that it is entirely reasonable and understandable. O'Brien *does* defeat Winston intellectually as well as physically. Winston is not so much brainwashed by O'Brien as he is educated by him. Like Socrates leading his interlocutors through a Platonic dialogue, O'Brien takes Winston into the light of understanding and reason, and Winston is crushed in the process.

This is a good answer to the question about what Winston loses in the Ministry of Love; he loses his identity, and along with it his individuality, which in a way amounts to the same thing. But it is not complete as things stand, for one can wonder about the identity that Winston has lost. What was it that made him the last man in Europe? Winston's work, readers will recall, involved revising history by changing historical documents to reflect the reading of history desired at the time by the inner party. Unlike the rest of the outer party drones, Winston actually thought about what he was doing, and he did so by wondering what life was like *before* the emergence of Big Brother, before the inner party came to exercise such total control over Oceania. If individual identity is fixed by the culture in which a person is immersed, as was suggested earlier, then by wondering what life was like before the cancer of the inner party took control, Winston was wondering in an important sense about who he was. By searching for a past, by searching for *his* cultural past, Winston was searching for an identity.

If Oceania has no identity of its own—if it has no legacy, no history, no culture, no tradition—then neither does Winston. If Oceania's past is eclipsed by powerful individuals who work to reconstruct it at every turn, then the people of Oceania have no identities either; they are all and only what those with power make them to be. They don't control their own fate, to be sure, but even more to the point, they don't control their own identities. They can't discover themselves because there is nothing left for them to discover. Winston is the last person in Europe not just because of his inclination to think and inquire; he is the last individual who seeks to know who he really is—the last character in the novel searching for what it means to be a person, to have (and have self-consciously) a sense of self.

So it seems that Orwell is inviting readers to consider the importance of the culture and traditions that have been formed in the past and that fix an important aspect of one's personal identity. But there is also another clue that Orwell leaves us about what he was up to. Winston's apparent confidence in the mortality of Big Brother is based upon his (occasional) optimism that the proles will eventually recognize their deplorable condition and rise as one to do something about it. In the jargon of students of Karl Marx, Winston thinks the proles will "come to consciousness." They will manage to educate themselves politically on the way that Oceania works against their true interests, and in the process they will form a clear and collectively understood sense of what their true interests are. And the clearer the proles become about their true interests, the more corrupt the leadership of Oceania will appear to be. Eventually, their greater numbers will be turned to their advantage. They will rebel against the inner party and overthrow them; after all, a small clique of rulers can hardly hope to dominate such a large segment of the population once the latter get a solid grasp of their true political interests.

Winston sounds a lot like modern radicals when he exclaims to O'Brien, almost gleefully and with characteristic Marxist optimism, that the future lies with the proles. But O'Brien shrugs this off as just another illustration of Winston's dementia, insisting in fact that Winston really knows better. "If the future lies with the proles," O'Brien quips, "there is no future." The pro-les will not come to consciousness. They won't manage to educate them-selves. History really has ended for them. The times will change, but their plight will not. To borrow a line from the mule, Benjamin, in Orwell's earlier novel *Animal Farm*, "things will go on," for the proles, "as they always have, that is, badly." But the proles, for their part, will hardly seem to notice.

It is not difficult to see why Orwell felt comfortable in demystifying radical political beliefs about the inevitable transformative power of the proletariat, those hardy, dedicated workers who actually carry the load of productivity in developed societies. Their ontological horizons, the "horizons of their mind," are desperately narrow, and where a person's awareness of what is and what matters is so diminished, so closed and shallow, nothing can force it to expand. The proles find comfort and a dimension of happiness within the confines of their diminished horizons; ignorance may not be bliss, for Orwell, but in the case of the proles, it is no barrier to a crude and simple happiness. The proles may even be admired for their ability to endure the world around them and find a bit of joy in it. Thinking and wondering about who he is becomes a burden for Winston and is a source of anguish far greater than anything O'Brien could impose upon him.

This account of the proles might be taken, rather naively, as yet another appeal by the politically righteous for the people to get politically involved and engaged. But this isn't what Orwell was doing at all, something that becomes clear when one appreciates the fact that the proles really are quite politically engaged. Orwell's Oceania is constantly at war with either Eastasia or Eurasia, or so the inner party says. Oceania's enemies and allies change from day to day, almost with the speed of contemporary international politics in the present day. Of course, there really are no wars with either Eastasia or Eurasia; if Oceania is at war with anyone, it is at war with its own lower classes. But the imagery of war makes for good thought control, and the pro-les are very much aware of the supposed wars. They are even good citizens after a fashion, if by this one means that they are sensitive to Oceania's politi-cal condition as this is presented to them. They pay close attention to the war news and applaud Oceania's latest victories. They display their hatred and contempt for the enemies of Oceania when enemy soldiers are captured and paraded through the streets. They are riveted to the political events of the day and respond to them with the zeal and frenzy of genuine patriots. If elections were held, one suspects they would surely vote—and for Big Brother at that!

The proles, in fact, display a political engagement rather typical of Orwell's time, and interestingly if not ironically, of ours. Politics for the pro-les is a spectator activity, just as it is for many contemporary Americans. The politics of the day orbit around the periphery of their ontological horizons. It is a distant concern that reaches the fringes of their lives but doesn't encourage or receive much studied reflection. The political life of Oceania is out there somewhere for the proles, and they encounter it in the fashion and on the terms dictated by the inner party. But they still encounter it. If they can be described as apolitical, then it is necessary to mean something more by being politically astute than merely being politically engaged and aware of the current events that surround one's daily affairs.

What might this something more be? The answer to this question is important because it points in the direction of what Orwell was encouraging his readers to think about. While the proles are politically aware in the sense that they pay a certain amount of attention to the events of their day, it is also appropriate to describe them as politically naive. They watch, sometimes keenly, the activities of their government, but they don't have much of an understanding of politics. Their ontological horizons simply don't reach these issues; they seem incapable of the thoughtcrime that was Winston's undoing. Because they don't understand politics, they are the easy victims of the abuse of political power without even being aware of it. But, too, they are not alone. Winston, for all his effort at thinking, doesn't understand politics either, and this is why he is an easy target for O'Brien, who ridicules Winston for not being very good at thinking. But even O'Brien, Winston's otherwise shrewd tormentor/tutor, fails to understand politics, as his obsession with power demonstrates. Where an understanding of politics is so thoroughly absent, power will almost certainly become its own end. Under such circumstances, there can be no point to power other than exercising it for its own sake. The purpose of political power, the reason it is important for civil life, is entirely lost. And when it is lost, only tyranny remains. This makes the moral of the story rather easy to see; political power can be domesticated and tyranny avoided only if people understand politics! But this only puts an obscure answer to a troubling problem. Just what exactly does it mean to understand politics?

Suppose we take this to mean that no one in Oceania has any sense of those purposes that make civil association necessary, no appreciation of the fact that civil association involves identifying those aspects of their shared lives that require some centralized management in order for things to go well for them. This is important to be sure, but it introduces only the first part of the field of politics. It is also important to have some sense of what it means for things to go well for the members of society. Some sense of what counts as living a good life within society must be included in the vision of politics, as well as some appreciation of the values and ideals that living a good life calls to mind. These are the values that regulate governmental activities and direct a shared and public understanding of the proper operation of the public realm. Put in somewhat nebulous terms, an adequate understanding of politics

involves a familiarity with the political culture of the polity. It is this culture
that transforms a state into a polity and makes it something more than, or
something other than, a system of oppression and tyranny.

POLITICAL INHERITANCE

Orwell's Oceania is a perfectly horrible place. Orwell evidently intended the
readers of his day to recognize it as such, and it is still an almost perfect
description of what most Americans will continue to recognize as a terribly
oppressive and tyrannical arrangement. Readers familiar with Orwell's tale
might ask themselves why this isn't a happy book. Why assume automatically that it is a dark portrayal of a world gone horribly wrong? Winston was
a thought-criminal. In more prosaic terms, he was a deviant out of step with
the social world around him, and Big Brother came to his aid. He was taken
to the Ministry of Love and carefully cured by O'Brien, and in the end, Winston *loved* Big Brother. He was brought back into the fold, back to the caring
embrace of Big Brother. Ordinarily, tales about the efforts of society to cure
deviance and bring the deviant back into the world around him are happy
ones. Why, then, should we think Oceania a terrible tyranny?

In order to see Oceania as a tyranny, as a political setting gone wrong, it
is necessary to have some sense of what a tyranny is, and correspondingly,
some sense of how political life should go. These are notions that belonged
to the political culture in which Orwell lived and that continue to make up
the political culture of twenty-first-century America. By describing a political
arrangement drastically inconsistent with the values and norms at home in his
native England, Orwell pulls the elements of this culture into the foreground
of a reader's awareness and illustrates their importance. It is this culture that
is missing in Oceania, and it is this culture that separates, say, contemporary
America from Oceania. But it can do so, and continue to do so, only if it
remains a conscious presence in the lives of the citizenry. To understand politics, in other words, is to understand the culture that makes civil association
meaningful and intelligible to people. If it is right to say that Americans don't
understand much about politics, it is because they don't pay much attention
to the culture that fixes and informs the way they think about government and
the proper scope of political power.

Political culture is a historical artifact; it is the product of past political
struggle. So, to understand who they are as political beings, people must
understand their political inheritance. Correspondingly, it is best to think of
polities—civil arrangements bounded by, among other things, distinct political cultures—as things that exist in both space and time. They are spatial in

the sense that they occupy a particular place bounded by the customs, traditions, perceptions, and ideals of a specific political culture. They are temporal, on the other hand, in the sense that they exemplify perceptions and ideals that have emerged through time and have been shaped by the struggles and controversies of previous ages. As the notion implies, political culture needs to be cultivated; it needs to be nurtured and refined as past ideals confront contemporary problems.

A polity's political culture anchors its citizens and establishes their political identity. To be an American (to think again about politics and identity) involves something more than merely having American citizenship. It also means that one's political consciousness is shaped in a particular way. As Americans, the people of this political culture inherit a particular way of seeing themselves and their relations to others, as well as a value system for thinking about how the purposes of civil association should be realized. Americans worry about the abuse of political power—they *can* worry about the abuse of political power—because they have inherited an understanding of politics that emphasizes the need for constraints upon this power in the name of liberty. If they lose this vision of politics, if they fail to keep their political inheritance before them, they have taken a huge step toward becoming Oceania.

But political culture is only a modest anchor, and any polity, including the United States, is always a work in progress. Political culture cannot remain static, because society never remains static. Human activity gives rise to new struggles, and new controversies emerge. Political culture needs to be continuously updated and revised in order to meet the demands of changing times. When political cultures change radically and drastically, as they do from time to time, one can speak of political *revolution*. Revolutions involve something more than an effort to change governments; this is usually the aim of things like a rebellion or coup d'état. Revolutions involve a radical transformation—a revolving of—the basic and fundamental political beliefs and ideals of a particular culture. They are transformations of thought that typically bring with them structural change in government, and when they occur, they are frequently accompanied by unrest and conflict. When political cultures change incrementally, one can speak of political *evolution*. All cultures evolve. Oftentimes this obviates the likelihood of revolution, but sometimes it seems revolution is inevitable.

The people of a polity might reasonably wonder about the control they have over the historical drift and flux of their culture. If control is to be had, if political culture is to be cultivated, a polity must understand its own political vision and appreciate how this vision moderates and informs its ability to manage new problems and resolve new controversies that arise. This too is crucial for an adequate understanding of politics, and it is a topic to which we shall return in the closing chapters.

The French thinker Alexis de Tocqueville visited the United States in the early 1830s in order to study what he considered to be a radical transformation taking place in the political cultures of European states. He believed that this transformation had *evolved* in its purest form in the United States, and he wanted to study it there in order to evaluate the changes it might bring to Europe. When he returned home, he published a magnificent critique of American political culture, one hardly equaled even to this day. In his book, *Democracy in America*, he suggested that Americans are the lucky inheritors of a new political tradition based upon what he called the notion of "equality of conditions."[1] Today, political thinkers refer to the tradition of political discourse that Tocqueville believed Americans inherited as the *liberal* tradition.

Tocqueville felt that for the most part the liberal tradition in American developed and matured largely unopposed by alternative political influences. This view gained such popularity that it seems today to be the prevailing political wisdom, but it is often criticized by thinkers who have noticed, quite correctly, nonliberal influences on the early development of American political culture. It is unnecessary to quibble over this issue here, however, though it is important to acknowledge the obvious: as the injustices suffered by women and minorities in the United States aptly illustrate, American liberalism in practice has not always lived up to what Americans now consider the liberal ideal of equal liberty for all. Nor is it necessary to consider here whether the United States suffers from an offensive hypocrisy when its political reality is measured against the ideals of its political culture, or whether these ideals themselves have changed as modern minds have begun to recognize inequality and injustice where before the demands of equality were thought to be satisfied.[2]

For present purposes, it is sufficient to notice only that American political culture has evolved over the years in the direction of liberalism, and liberalism has evolved over the years in the direction of a more substantial and expansive commitment to the fundamental equality of all persons. If one wants to understand politics in the American setting, then, it is necessary to understand liberalism in the American mold. Liberalism not only introduces the primary political vision of contemporary America; it also provides the central viewpoint from which political life in the United States is customarily understood and critiqued. The sense of what politics *is* is fixed for Americans by this cultural background. Strange as it may sound, the American liberal tradition inspires not only conservative, but also most radical beliefs about political life in America. The most basic conceptions of who Americans are as political beings, what their country stands for, and how they should think about how best to live together are shaped and structured by the understanding made available to them by virtue of their liberal past. So understanding politics in the United States can mean nothing more than coming to grips with this political heritage.

From a historical point of view, liberalism can be considered the product of the political thought of several important thinkers of the seventeenth and eighteenth centuries. Its development was influenced particularly by the political thought of John Locke, whose *Two Treatises of Government*, as we have seen, greatly shaped Thomas Jefferson's writing of the American Declaration of Independence.[3] Locke and the other formative thinkers of the emergent liberal tradition believed that philosophical reflection could discover true principles of civil association that should be implemented to govern the political relations of all persons at all times and in all places. Although these thinkers vary in the details that surround their political views, they are generally held to belong to what contemporary scholars call the tradition of *modern natural law*. In Locke's case, for example, natural law views were reconfigured to place great weight on individual rights to life, liberty, and property, and with this, the notion of *natural rights* came into prominence on the liberal stage.

The natural lawyers of this formative period in the development of Western political thought accepted the view, inherent in Christian doctrine, that the relations of all entities in the world are governed by certain immutable laws. In the case of the physical world, these laws governed the relation of matter and were subject to discovery through observation and rational reflection. The world, it was supposed, worked a particular way, and it was designed to work this way by its Creator. By bestowing the capacity for rational reflection upon human beings, the Creator has enabled them to figure out how the world works and to improve their condition by doing so. Human progress in the sciences was made possible by virtue of humankind's ability to use reason to gain insight into God's design.

Things were thought to be slightly different in the case of the social world, however. While the thinkers of this era believed that here, too, God's immutable law governed the relations between human beings, the laws ordained by God to regulate interpersonal relations were not hardwired into human beings. Instead, God gave human beings the ability to reason and thus to discern these laws for themselves. To live as God intended, human beings had to live according to these laws, but it is up to human reason to figure out what these laws are and to live by them accordingly. Human beings can do otherwise, however; they can break or ignore these laws if they choose to do so. But they *ought not* do so; instead, they *ought* to live by them. Thus those laws that regulate human association were said to hold against human beings *prescriptively*; they prescribe how human beings ought to treat themselves and others.

The natural laws that regulate interpersonal relations were taken to be the foundation of human morality. To act morally was understood to mean adhering to God's law, or perhaps to the dictates of reason (which for present purposes we can suppose amounts to much the same thing). The subset of this system of law that could be externally policed by the state became, in turn, the source and inspiration for the positive law of the land. For Locke, as we have seen, insight into God's law involved recognizing certain fundamental and natural rights that define the relations between persons. Because people have these rights by nature, they also have the right to police the actions of others who might violate them in their own case. But a natural condition where everyone is able to be a judge in his own case is sure to be insecure and will invariably give rise to disagreement and discord. To avoid this, Locke considered it necessary to join with others and establish a civil association in the form of what people now think of as the state.

To understand why Locke thought that civil association was a necessary requirement of reason, it is necessary to delve a bit further into his political philosophy. At the center of Locke's argument is his theory of property. The notion of property implies a legal or juridical relationship between people with regard to some thing. If A is in possession of X, then X is under A's control, but possession is different from property. If X is A's property, then A has a right to X, to its use for example, and others have an obligation to honor A's property right, perhaps by not taking possession of X without A's consent. But how could a person come to have such a right to the exclusive use of something? Locke argued that property came into being when a person put his labor into the creation of something and thereby made it a thing of value.[4] The object produced by this labor, Locke supposed, became the property of the laborer because the labor that produced the increased value belonged to the laborer.

But with the introduction of property comes the possibility of property disputes between people. Imagine that A begins to build a house by chopping down trees and shaping the wood into usable lumber. Suppose A tires from his labor and decides to take a rest, and B comes along, sees the usable lumber lying on the ground, and builds a shelter with it. Who is now the rightful owner of the completed project? Both A and B would seem to have a legitimate claim to what has been produced, and if both are authorized to enforce the natural law on their own behalf, the each will insist upon ownership of the product. In the absence of a common judge to settle such disputes, things might degenerate to a condition of war between A and B. Since this seems like a terribly insecure and unstable situation, reason advises the need for a common judge to manage disputes over the enforcement of natural rights claims. Thus Locke concludes that civil association, which introduces a common judge to police and enforce natural rights, is the appropriate remedy for the inconveniences one will encounter in an anarchic social condition.

The anarchic condition Locke imagined was a relatively simple place, and as it happens, his account of the necessity of civil association is also relatively simple. The primary job of the state is to resolve disputes that arise between people. But the state's authority is also circumscribed, Locke insisted, by the natural rights the state is called upon to police. While the state exists for the purpose of policing natural rights, it must also respect and honor them in the process. Governments that threaten or compromise these rights, and thus abuse their power, lose their legitimacy, and Locke claimed that rebellion against such states was altogether justified. Rebellion was thus defended as the proper response to the abuse of political power. Where or when the state abuses its power, its power could be revoked by the people, who remained sovereign in the sense that they were presumed to retain the power (of rebellion) to address governmental abuses. Winston's faith in the proles can be regarded as an inheritance from Locke, and Orwell's concerns about political power, in turn, can be ascribed to his awareness that Locke's simple approach to the problem of political power is no longer satisfactory.

Locke's legacy for American politics, and the influence of liberal thought that he so powerfully inspired, is rather easy to see. The belief in natural or human rights remains powerful in America, as does the idea of the sanctity of property. That which people earn through their labor is still considered to be rightfully theirs, and it is pervasively believed that neither the government nor anyone else should take it away from them. These basic views are the political inheritance of contemporary Americans, and they continue to shape the basic features of American political culture. But does it still make sense to think that they demonstrate insight into God's law and that they hold with the certainty of objective moral truths? Should Americans think that their political culture is objectively valid in this sense and that the United States is to be praised because its political system reflects the ideal demands of human reason?

The issue between *objectivists* (those who hold that there are certain knowable objective truths of political morality) and *relativists* (those who doubt the existence of any knowable objective truths of political morality) is of great importance for the study of politics. Is there an objective political morality that guides and limits the authority of the state, or is this authority guided and limited by cultural beliefs that are relative to particular political inheritances and that can and do change from time to time? At issue is the nature of politics itself and therefore also the nature of the task of understanding politics.

Does an understanding of politics involve a search for fundamental truths of political morality holding for all persons, or is it simply a matter of trying to understand the political culture of a given state or polity? Is a thorough understanding of politics one that speaks to the human condition, or is it limited to the political vision of a particular polity with the accompanying admission that other polities may have different political cultures that can and should be understood in their own terms?

Crucial as these questions are to the study of politics, it is not possible to put a definitive answer to them here, if in fact it is possible to answer them definitively at all. It is possible for Americans to understand politics, however, by looking into politics in the American mold. It is this cultural dimension of politics that seems important for a complete and satisfactory understanding of politics in the United States, and that needs cultivation and preservation in order to domesticate the problem of political power. Americans do not need to decide whether the perceptions and norms of their culture are objectively true in order to appreciate their practical importance for understanding American politics, for making sense of the political world as Americans understand it. In relativist terms, it is sufficient for Americans to see that these perceptions and norms are true *for them*; they set the context within which the American polity's judgments about justice are understandable and comprehensible.

Readers may reason out for themselves whether they should make more of their political inheritance than this. It is worth adding a note of caution here, however, for it seems that almost all political cultures will want to make claims about the truth of their perceptions and norms. If it is supposed that one's vision of politics is true and immutable in the fashion insisted upon by natural law thinkers, how might anyone hope to convince others of this fact? If the standards by which people measure the truth of their political claims are internal to their own culture, and if the same holds true for alternative cultures, how can anyone hope to settle the question of objective political truth? How can they presume to crawl out of their own skins and judge the matter objectively? These questions are presented not to bolster the case for relativism but to illustrate the problems associated with wanting to make more out of one's political beliefs than may be warranted or justified. In the study of politics, along with the study of many other subjects, there is reason for intellectual modesty.

WHAT IS LIBERALISM?

American political culture has been significantly (if not completely) shaped by the liberal tradition of political discourse. By *liberalism*, I do not mean to refer to the "L-word" that many self-proclaimed conservatives have recently wanted to treat with derision. If de Tocqueville is right and Americans have inherited a political culture that has remained generally stable through time, so-called liberals and so-called conservatives may actually share a good deal more in common than they are inclined to admit. As we shall see, both sides of the political spectrum that sets the parameters of much political debate in the United States owe a considerable debt to the liberal tradition.

The basic Lockean influences that have shaped this tradition have already been introduced. Americans make much of the notion of individual rights, particularly the rights to liberty and property. Whether Americans consider these rights natural or merely conventional elements of their culture, they matter greatly from a political point of view. They introduce the conditions under which Americans think all persons are equal. Locke was not so foolish as to suppose that all persons are equal in the sense of having identical intellectual acumen, physical ability, or artistic talent. They are equal, he supposed, because each person possesses the same basic rights. No one can justifiably enslave another or claim another's property as his own. The suggestion that this basic human equality really matters to many Americans will ring hollow to some, and with good reason. American history is replete with instances of grievous inequalities in the treatment of minorities and women, but it is this very belief that has inspired opposition within the culture to these practices and has helped to push American political reality toward America's own declared ideals.

Yet there is considerably more to American liberalism, to American political culture, than this. The American liberal tradition can be analyzed and understood in terms of a distinctive ontology (an understanding of things that exist in the political world) and an equally distinctive normative scheme (an understanding of how things *ought* to be in the political world) that mirrors this ontology. To appreciate the nature of American liberalism, it is necessary to have some sense of this ontology and some grasp of the accompanying normative scheme.

The Ontology of Liberalism. Imagine sitting in a crowded theater when someone approaches and asks you to pick out all the persons in the room. Such a request would seem ludicrous, or ludicrously easy, even though persons come in many different shapes, sizes, and colors. Some may be tall, some short, some bald, others quite hirsute, and some missing a limb or an eye, but it still seems fair to suppose that most Americans (at the risk of understatement) could go around the room and correctly identify all the persons present, and distinguish them from the other furniture of the room, with perfect accuracy. But would a representative person from all different cultures and histories of the world respond to this question in a way identical to the response that would be given by a twenty-first-century American? Would a Spartan of the fifth century BC answer this question the same way as a contemporary American? What about a thirteenth-century Aztec who had not experienced either white or black persons before (and assuming that both blacks and whites are in the theater)?

Suppose for the moment that anyone from any culture existing on the planet at any point in time would answer this question the same way, that is, that all cultures happen to have and share a similar concept of the person. The concept "person" introduces an important conceptual boundary; it enables people to identify a particular type of thing—a person—and to distinguish things of this sort from the other things also present in one's field of vision. But even if all persons from all cultures would answer this question the same way, it doesn't follow that all persons from all cultures also have the exact same concept "person" that twenty-first-century Americans have. The seeing made possible by the concept "person" and its equivalents in other cultures may still have important differences. To complicate matters, imagine that the representatives of different cultures are asked to identify all the animals, and only the animals, in the theater, and suppose that the only animate creatures in the room are persons. Would a contemporary American consider a person an animal? What about the Spartan or the Aztec?

To continue to play with the problem, suppose that all these cultures also have (or had) the concept of an animal and that all are agreed that persons are animals. Does this mean that all these cultures would now "see" the same thing when they see the persons in the theater? Or is it possible that they would see different animals in the way a contemporary American would if there happened to be both persons and chimpanzees in the theater? It seems possible that there could be agreement among cultures about the persons in the theater and still be disagreement about just what this means, and this is because the concept "person"—assuming that all cultures examined have some such concept—may vary significantly from culture to culture. The ancient Greeks, for example, divided the human kingdom in two; they saw either Greeks or barbarians when they looked at persons, but Americans don't do this.

Contemporary Americans take the notion of a person to identify a particular species rather than a genus, at least until it comes time to think about their evolutionary predecessors. Associated with this is the contemporary view that persons are complete and sufficient entities unto themselves. While it is increasingly the case that Americans look at body parts as replaceable units—things like hearts, kidneys, lungs, and livers can be replaced—they still think of persons as distinct and complete entities as opposed to composites of discrete and irreducible elements. Society, on the other hand, is not considered a complete organic unit; it is seen as a composite of different persons. Americans typically do not think of persons as replaceable parts of a larger whole or as components of an independent social unit that is an entity unto itself.

This perspective of the person is of the first importance for understanding politics in the American mold; it introduces the basic parameters of the liberal ontology. Persons are regarded by Americans as the irreducible atoms of social life because this is the way they are conceptualized in American culture—this is how the concept "person" works in the language that fixes the American vision of the world. This means, among other things, that Americans do not differentiate between persons according to the way they contribute to social life. A person's *being* is understood not by how she contributes to the social whole (by whether the person is a warrior, artisan, lawyer, or mechanic), but by the fact that the person is a person. The American perspective on the person is not (at present, entirely) determined by social roles because the concept "person" doesn't work this way. But what is it about persons, or rather the concept of the person in America, that explains and legitimates this distinctive perspective?

This is not an easy question to answer, but it is increasingly common for thinkers working within the liberal tradition to answer it by accounting for persons as *autonomous* beings. The concept of autonomy is somewhat nebulous; historically it has its origins in the ancient Greek understanding of the polis, which was considered to be a self-governing (and hence complete unto itself) unit. The eighteenth-century German philosopher Immanuel Kant incorporated this notion into his moral philosophy in order to argue that human beings are capable of rational self-determination, of authoring the moral law they impose upon themselves.[5] Today, moral and political thinkers use the concept to describe what they see as the human ability for self-determination and self-control. Human beings, it is supposed, are able to think about and formulate for themselves their own sense of the good life and how they think their lives should go. Persons, this is to say, have the ability to be the architects of their own lives, to develop a plan for how they would like to live their lives, and to implement strategies for the realization of the ends they have set for themselves. Persons are presumed to remain social beings in the sense that there are still social roles that they must play, but they have the ability to reflect upon and select the role or roles they will eventually play from the range of options that the social world presents to them.

The Morality of Liberalism. The understanding of persons as autonomous beings constitutes the ontology of liberalism. This ontology tells us what kind of a thing a person is and how persons differ from other things in the world. It identifies the particular perspective that informs the way liberal cultures understand persons. Although it is tempting to speak about autonomy as an ability that persons have in varying degrees—some seem more attuned to reflecting critically and thoughtfully about how their life should go than others—autonomy is perhaps best regarded as a threshold condition enjoyed by all persons. The severely mentally handicapped are thus typically regarded as tragic souls in need of great care because of their unfortunate condition. But even here it seems possible to search for some sphere of control that these individuals can exercise over their own lives. As persons they are incomplete, and the tragedy of their condition lies in this fact, coupled with the additional recognition that their condition was not of their own making. Liberal ontology, in other words, implies a kind of equality in spite of actual differences in personal talents, abilities, or judgment. To say that a particular being is a person is to say that she is like others in a crucial sense, regardless of the other attributes that may make her quite unique.

The morality of liberalism is linked to the ontology of liberalism like the flip side of a coin. Since people influenced by liberal culture recognize persons as beings capable of being the architects of their own lives, they respect them accordingly by acknowledging that they should be allowed to operate as such. Because persons *are* autonomous beings, they should be allowed to exercise their autonomy. The norm of respect attaches automatically to the liberal perspective on persons. To fail to respect persons in this way, to defeat or obstruct their ability to operate autonomously, is to treat them as if they weren't really persons—that is, autonomous beings—at all. Put somewhat differently, the liberal perspective on persons is valorized; liberal cultures attach moral importance to one's status (or standing) as a person.

But what does it mean to treat a person with the respect due her as an autonomous being? The answer to this question introduces the basic building blocks of liberal morality. If persons are able to build their own lives for themselves, to control how their lives will go, then it seems evident that respecting them as autonomous beings involves permitting them to take control of their lives. This indicates that persons should be allowed the *freedom* from interference that enables them to exercise such control over their own lives. And freedom, or *liberty* (we can suppose here that the two words are synonymous), thus becomes a central value of liberal cultures.

The philosopher Plato argued that persons have distinct and differing natural abilities that enable them to contribute to the social whole—the polis—in various ways. The process of education, as Plato understood it, involves identifying these abilities, cultivating them, and then directing persons into those social roles best suited to their abilities. The citizens of Plato's republic have no choice in the matter; their future is determined for them by their natural abilities. Such external control of one's life seems intolerable from a liberal perspective. If Jones wants to pursue a career in major league baseball and become a relief pitcher for his beloved Red Sox, he should be allowed to try and fulfill his life's ambition, even if it happens to be the case that he has all the attributes necessary for making an exceptional brain surgeon. A social arrangement like the one imagined by Plato has no concern for the ideal of freedom as liberal cultures understand it. As autonomous beings, individual lives should be of one's own making, and freedom matters greatly to cultures with this perspective on the person because it identifies and supports the social condition under which it is possible for persons to make their lives for themselves.

But the liberal notion of freedom is also bounded by other elements of liberal morality. Suppose Jones wants to live the life of a plantation owner in the antebellum south; that is, suppose he wants to manage a plantation, own slaves, and buy and sell persons according to his needs and whims. Can he justifiably complain that his freedom is obstructed if the larger society around him coercively prevents him from operating a plantation and owning slaves? The problem in evidence here is that in this case, Jones's exercise of his freedom is inconsistent with the freedom of others. Jones cannot reasonably claim that the fact of his autonomy means that others should respect his freedom and also insist that this freedom entitles him to render other autonomous beings unfree. Jones has no way to argue convincingly that his autonomy makes him special and entitles him to liberties that other autonomous beings should not have. Instead, if Jones thinks others should respect his freedom because he is autonomous, his argument commits him to respecting the freedom of all other autonomous beings.

So, the liberal ideal of freedom, premised as it is on the status of persons as autonomous beings, is fundamentally egalitarian in nature, and this introduces another fundamental liberal ideal—the fundamental *equality* of persons. This means, at the very least, that all persons are entitled to all the freedom compatible with a like amount of freedom for all others. The status and privilege of previous ages that entitled some persons to liberties and opportunities unavailable to other classes of individuals presumed to have a lesser standing is inconsistent with liberal morality. No person under liberal morality is intrinsically more worthy or deserving in a way that entitles her to greater freedom than anyone else. Since the defense of freedom is a shorthand way of defending the right and opportunity of a person to determine how her life should go, the introduction of the equality condition means that all persons should enjoy the equal right and opportunity to determine how their lives will go.

The equal freedom condition is the fundamental ideal of liberal political cultures, but as we shall see, its practical realization introduces problems and paradoxes that are the source of great conflict and confusion in polities whose political cultures are shaped by the liberal tradition. Ideally, the commitment to equality is easily reconcilable with the ideal of freedom; indeed, it is incoherent without this ideal. Understood theoretically, the concept of equality involves little more than an identity relationship. To say that "A is equal to B" is to say that there is some variable, some X, that is predicable of both A and B and that renders A identical to be B with regard to X. There may be a great number of variables A possesses that B does not, and vice versa, and therefore there are a great number of ways in which A and B are not identical—are not equal. But if X is considered a morally significant variable, then any treatment A receives because A is an X should also be accorded to all others who are also Xs. And to say that X is a morally significant variable is to say that it overrides other, morally less (or non) significant variables that might be grounds for treating persons differently.

As should be apparent, under liberal ontology, the morally significant variable that establishes human equality is provided by the notion of autonomy. And an analysis of the implications that this notion has for how people should treat one another is the best way to get clear on the basic elements of liberal morality. With this in mind, it is easy to provide a reasonable defense of Locke's three basic or natural rights: the right to life, to liberty, and to property ownership. Again, it isn't necessary to worry here about whether it is objectively or cosmically true that human beings have these rights. It is sufficient to see that they are natural in the sense that they flow naturally (or logically) from the liberal ontology that determines the way that people influenced by liberal culture will understand the nature of their social world.

Because liberals see persons as autonomous beings, they are compelled as a matter of logic to respect their freedom, that is, the exercise of their autonomy. And the claim that persons have an equal right to life can also be understood against the background of this commitment. The most direct and immediate way to interfere with a person's autonomy is to kill her, and correspondingly, to respect persons as autonomous beings minimally means that others must not render them nonautonomous by killing them. In effect, others ought not kill them or lobotomize them in a way that renders them incapable of self-determination.

The rights to life and liberty thus follow rather easily from the analysis of an understanding of persons as autonomous beings. But what about property ownership? Does it also follow logically from the need to respect persons as autonomous beings? One might suppose that it derives from the right to freedom if it is supposed that being free involves the opportunity to exercise exclusive control over and use of material objects. But ownership introduces significant complications. What things are properly subject to ownership?

Can one own the air, the entire planet, rivers, the sun, the galaxy, or the universe? If ownership follows from the need to respect freedom, are inequalities of property ownership justifiable? Suppose that everything ownable is already owned, but it happens that Jones doesn't own anything. Can Jones legitimately claim that her right to ownership is violated because there is nothing left for her to own?

This introduces modest reason to think that the relationship between ownership and freedom is not as straightforward or as simple as some might wish it to be. The institution of private property is as old as the hills, but the current understanding of the notion has grown up alongside the liberal tradition. Locke, as we saw previously, thought that ownership had to be earned; a person could claim a portion of God's common bounty as his own only if he labored in a manner that brought greater wealth into being.[6] A person could claim as his own the fruits of his own labor, for the wealth produced by work has been created by the efforts of the laborer and should therefore rightfully belong to him. Whether one agrees with this or not—and the idea now seems rather popular in American culture—Locke's argument provides a theory of original acquisition. Today, however, a theory of original acquisition is probably less important than developing the notion of property by adding theories of transfer, distribution, and power.

A theory of transfer involves working out details about how property may legitimately change hands. The most obvious way to enable property to change hands, consistent with the ideal of freedom, is to rely upon the idea of consent. Property can change hands in the event that the parties to the transfer agree voluntarily to rearrange their legitimate property holdings in a particular way. Mutual agreements are the source of contractual relationships that allow for legitimate property exchanges, the exchange of goods for services, or the exchange of services. But a theory of transfer is only the initial step in developing a full and adequate account of property. A theory of distribution considers the way that all ownable goods, that is, the sum total of the *wealth* present in the polity, ought to be distributed to all members of the polity. If property is necessary for a person to sustain herself, and if a particular person lacks the necessary property to sustain herself and her life is consequently threatened, then her right to life enables her to claim a redistribution of property in order to continue living. In principle, a theory of distribution introduces exceptions to a theory of voluntary transfer. If the property holders in a liberal polity refuse to give voluntarily enough wealth to enable a person to continue living, it is consistent with liberal ideals for government to forcibly redistribute wealth in order to sustain life. This is an extreme example, but one that few people would disagree with, particularly if a person's abject poverty is not a product of her own irresponsibility. But theories of wealth redistribution become contentious, as we shall see, when redistribution is recommended even in non-life-threatening situations.

A theory of power is necessary to flesh out the notion of ownership. A theory of power is necessary for a full understanding of property rights because it introduces concerns about what kinds of things wealth can legitimately buy. It responds to the question, What is the proper power of wealth/property? Some things may be taken off the market because people don't think anyone should be entitled to their exclusive control and use. It would be difficult for anyone to enforce an ownership right to the air people breathe, but more importantly, it is doubtful that too many people would want this to fall into private ownership hands. Most Americans also find it objectionable to think that public offices can be purchased for a price or that parents can buy a place for their children in prestigious colleges. Yet at the same time, most Americans would also object if too many things were taken away from the public market. If Jones wants to spend a good amount of his disposable income to buy an exotic car, he would no doubt think it objectionable if the society at large said cars were not a marketable item and stipulated that everyone should have the same type of car to be distributed on the basis of need alone. A theory of power, then, considers the kinds of things that wealth can buy, and so it also involves placing qualifications on voluntary transfers of wealth and services.

Perhaps, however, we should put these musings aside now and return to our initial question. Does the institution of property ownership follow from the morally significant variable of human autonomy? Shocking though it may seem, there is probably no very compelling reason to think that it does. But current American views about private wealth have grown up with the liberal tradition, and it is probably not an overly ridiculous generalization to say that today the great preponderance of Americans think that ownership is an important element of the opportunity to lead and enjoy a good life. The institution of property, in any event, is one way for human beings to make use of social resources in a reasonably efficient and useful manner, so it seems appropriate to say that there is nothing inherent in the notion of property itself that is logically inconsistent with the obligation to respect persons as autonomous beings.

But the institution of private property can be rendered benign and acceptable, or not inconsistent with the obligation to respect persons as autonomous agents, only if a compelling theory of transfer, distribution, and power is also put in place. Such a theory must be reconcilable with and informed by the standards introduced by liberal morality; it must, that is, constitute an accurate expression and elaboration of the morality of liberalism. The articulation and implementation of such a theory is bound to be a source of considerable theoretical and political controversy, but the process of theory articulation and popular acceptance will no doubt be enhanced in a polity whose citizens have an adequate understanding of politics.

A third fundamental element of liberal morality has quietly surfaced from the discussion of freedom and equality. The moral claims empowered by the concern for human freedom and equality seem naturally to be understandable and presentable in terms of the language of *rights*. Rights define relationships between persons as well as between persons and institutions. They protect people from others in several important ways. For example, rights identify a sphere of personal control into which others may not intrude. This point is sometimes expressed by saying that rights carry with them correlative duties. If A has a right to X, all those against whom the right holds have a duty not to violate A's right. If one thinks of freedom as a right enjoyed by persons to function as fully autonomous beings, then others have a correlative duty to permit them to function in this way. When rights indicate duties based upon morally significant variables, the rights and duties identified hold equally for and against all persons. This gives a more exact meaning to the notion of *equal rights*, where all persons enjoy the same rights as everyone else and thus also must acknowledge the same duties to respect these rights as they apply to others.

But rights also empower people to do certain things or alter existing rights relationships between persons. If Smith owns a car, for example, his ownership right entitles him to prohibit others from using his car if he doesn't want them to. This exemplifies the sense in which rights afford protection to persons; the right of ownership means that Smith can exclude others from the use of his car, and others have a duty not to use the car unless he allows them to do so. But the right also entitles Smith to drive the car when and if he wants to, and provided he adheres to the rules that govern the practice of driving, others may not prevent him from doing so. Smith may even alter the rights relationships that control the use of his property because his right of ownership enables him to do so. He can sell his car if he wishes, for example, and thus divest himself of the right of exclusive use and control of the car. By selling his car, Smith transfers the right of exclusive use and control to the buyer, but only Smith is empowered to do this.[7]

Rights have come to carry a heavy burden in liberal political cultures largely because the morality of liberalism has been developed in a manner that rather comprehensively defines the proper relationships between persons in the polity. Rights ordinarily require an enforcing agent, and in order to guarantee, à la Locke, that persons do not become judges in their own cause, this has become the responsibility of governmental institutions within liberal polities. It is probably good for citizens of liberal polities to ask themselves

just how thoroughly interpersonal relationships in the polity should be structured and defined by rights enforceable by the government. But history leaves
little doubt that government is necessary to assure that some Americans will
not deny basic citizenship rights to others that they enjoy and even insist upon
for themselves. Government, that is, has assumed the responsibility for
defending the *civil rights* of all Americans, that is, the right to be treated as
an equal in the public realm, to enjoy the full protection of the law, and to
participate in the sociopolitical process without prejudice or hindrance. These
are but elements of the freedom to be safeguarded in the name of respecting
others as autonomous beings.

If government is necessary as an enforcing agent to make sure that rights
relationships are honored, to adjudicate disputes about whether A has violated B's right, and to punish rights violations when they occur, it also poses
a threat to these relationships itself. This is another way to think about the
problem of political power. If it is government's job to police individual
rights, who or what will serve as the enforcing agent that assures people that
government does not itself intrude upon these rights? One popular liberal
response (deriving largely from Locke) is to say that the people must ultimately police the government and remain ever vigilant in defense of their
rights. As we shall see, however, it might also make sense to establish specific
limitations on the right of government to intervene in certain spheres of citizen's lives. Such limitations are frequently referred to as *civil liberties*—
freedoms that cannot be transgressed by government, but they might also be
considered rights against government intrusion.

The existence of civil liberties in liberal polities creates some interesting
political and legal difficulties. The First Amendment to the U.S. Constitution
tells us, among other things, that "Congress shall make no law . . ." restricting the right of free speech. But Congress and other governmental institutions
restrict speech (or something like it) all the time. Advertisers cannot tell out-
landish lies about their products, students are not permitted to speak whenever they wish in public schools, people cannot shout "fire!" in crowded
theaters (unless there really is a fire), public officials cannot run down the
street yelling out the sailing times of troop ships in times of war, and so forth.
In one sense, it is commonplace to concede to government the right to restrict
speech in the name of the public welfare and decency, and few people think
to challenge the right of government to do this, on the grounds that government lacks the constitutional authority to do so. Here, too, it must be conceded that governments need the authority to govern, and this may mean, at
times, that government is justified in placing certain limitations upon speech
so that legitimate governmental action is not frustrated.

CONCLUSION

So it seems that the problem of political power is present once again. If government needs the power to govern, it would appear that people should not attempt to limit government's authority by charting out a realm of civil liberties that disempowers government from acting in certain predetermined spheres. Civil liberties, in short, work against the logic of government, but they would also seem to provide important safeguards against the abuse of governmental authority. This builds a tension into liberal political culture that will receive further discussion shortly. For the present, it is sufficient to note that this introduces another reason for people to think about politics. Insofar as Americans inhabit a liberal political culture, the morality of liberalism does much to define the proper relationships between persons and between persons and institutions, especially the institution of government. These relationships are bound to be controversial and rough about the edges, however, and consequently they are sure to become the source of political conflict and disagreement. A polity that worries about the problem of political power—and the morality of liberalism guarantees that the citizens of liberal polities will almost surely worry about this—has reason to rethink and review continuously the nature of the rights relationships that exist there and to balance the ideal construction of these relationships against the realities of social, economic, and political necessity. Political cultures are fluid things; with time, they *will* change. And as Orwell observed, they may, with time, even whither and decay to a point where nothing is left to question and challenge the exercise of political power as its own end.

How political cultures change is significant because the future of the polity is at issue. Citizens cannot hope to hold government accountable unless they cultivate the political morality that determines the nature of governmental accountability, and it is possible to find and comprehend this political morality only by looking to its formation and expression within the political culture. Similarly, the citizens of liberal polities cannot reasonably hope to shape the future unless they engage in an ongoing colloquy about the ideals associated with their political culture and how these ideals inform their thoughts, about the power that government needs to meet new problems and challenges as they emerge, and about how the political culture should inform the governmental confrontation with political necessity and how political necessity should be permitted to shape change. It should now be clear that challenges of this sort can only be met by people who understand politics, and this again illustrates the importance of *thinking* about politics without getting lost while watching the soap opera of government.

NOTES

1. Alexis de Tocqueville, *Democracy in America* (Garden City, NJ: Anchor Books, 1969).

2. Cf. John Pocock, *The Machiavellian Moment* (Princeton, NJ: Princeton University Press, 1975). For a discussion of American political culture that emphasizes hostility to liberal thinking, see John Higham, *Strangers in the Land* (New York: Atheneum, 1971) and Rogers Smith, *Civic Ideals* (New Haven, CT: Yale University Press, 1997).

3. John Locke, *Two Treatises of Government* (Cambridge: Cambridge University Press, 1960).

4. Locke, *Two Treatises of Government*, Sec. 27.

5. See Immanuel Kant, *The Groundwork of the Metaphysics of Morals*, trans. Lewis White Beck (Indianapolis: The Library of Liberal Arts, 1959).

6. Locke, *Two Treatises of Government*, Ch. V.

7. For more on the notion of rights, see W. N. Hohfeld, *Fundamental Legal Conceptions* (New Haven, CT: Yale University Press, 1919) and Richard E. Flathman, *The Practice of Rights* (Cambridge: Cambridge University Press, 1976).

Chapter Three

Liberal Ideals

That government is best which governs least.

Henry David Thoreau

Americans are usually suspicious of government. This is a terribly large generality, and careful thinkers are properly suspicious of generalities like this. But there is something to be said for this one. Generalities, however, often tend to be misleading, and this might be the case here as well. At the risk of trading one generality for another, it might be better to say that Americans are fickle, even inconsistent, when it comes to their views about government. Even though Americans don't particularly like government, they still expect government to provide them with services, protect them from one another, defend the nation's borders, and do all the other things they have become accustomed to having government do. One might say that Americans are like spoiled children when it comes to government. This too is a huge generality, but here there may also be a degree of accuracy in the claim. Americans want all sorts of things from government, but they rarely seem very appreciative of what government does for them.

A quick look at American history suggests that Americans have always been suspicious of government. The rebellion against British rule in colonial America was driven by a widespread anxiety about what George III and the British Parliament were up to, by the nagging suspicion that British leadership was working to usurp the freedoms that rightfully belonged to British subjects, and the colonial rebels would have none of this.[1] Suspicion, of course, is prelude to a distrust that inclines a great many Americans to embrace Thoreau's famous quip that "that government is best which governs least."

Yet the American suspicion of government is also prelude to irony. Despite

71

all this suspicion and distrust, government is everywhere in the United States, and Americans are subject to more government than most other peoples of the world. Americans learn when they are young to accept as intelligible and reasonable the oxymoronic notion that they are subject to dual sovereignty. Both state and federal governments are said to enjoy sovereign political authority over them. Each government, Americans are told, is sovereign in its own sphere, but in the case of overlap, sovereign authority goes to the central government. To make matters worse, Americans must also confront and contend with a variety of lesser governments. They are often subject, for example, to city and municipal governments, county governments, regional governments, and occasional public utility districts—all with independent taxing authority. How is it possible that a polity with so much distrust of government has managed to end up with so much government? It is best to explore this question theoretically—which is to say that it is best to talk around it quite a bit and spin an answer out of an examination of the political ideals that emerge from America's liberal political culture.

LIBERTARIANISM

The existence of all the government that Americans must contend with invites some obvious questions. How much government should the United States have? What should people expect government to do for them, and what should be left for them to do for themselves? How can government be structured and organized in order to guarantee that Americans don't end up with more government than they need? It is probably too much to suppose that one can discover definitive and noncontroversial answers to these questions. So it seems preferable to begin by thinking about the kinds of concerns and issues that need to be considered in the process of formulating even the most tentative of possible answers. Some progress in this direction can be made by recalling the conclusions reached thus far.

First, it is important to keep in mind that society is nothing more than a mutual support system. Few people can live in the isolated manner of a hermit whose life is dedicated only and exclusively to his or her own survival and whose daily routine is untouched by human company. Few people, it seems reasonable to suppose, would want to live this way, even if the opportunity presented itself. Ideally, people live lives of their own choosing and construction, but the options they choose from invariably involve different ways of contributing to the lives of others. People do not necessarily choose to have their lives go a certain way because they want to contribute in this way to the lives of others, of course; sometimes people choose a profession for selfish reasons—because they enjoy doing what it involves or because it pays well. But there needs to be a market for their choice; others must be willing to pay for the services a person decides to provide. If people cannot sustain themselves by living the life, say, of a medieval knight, they will not choose this lifestyle, and it will disappear from the menu of options that people consult when choosing how they want their lives to go. Society, in short, is a condition in which people play dual roles; they are both givers and takers. They provide services for others and receive needed services in return.

Second, it has also been noticed that government involves centralized management; the job of government is to manage large-scale social problems within its jurisdiction. Government exists to meet certain needs that people in society have, needs that can't be left to decentralized human activity. Problems that can be managed at a reasonably local level can be left to local governments; problems that extend beyond local government jurisdictions need to be addressed by larger governments with jurisdictions that comprehend the problem. A reasonably complete and reasonably compelling list of responsibilities requiring centralized management has already been considered, but it is worth recalling that some, and some might think a great many, of these responsibilities could and should be left to the decentralized vicissitudes of market relationships. Questions about the extent of government appropriate for a given polity, then, invite people to think about the kinds of social needs that require centralized management and the kinds that are best supplied by means of decentralized social activity—either market or non-market driven in nature.

The third factor to keep in mind when thinking about the amount of government it is appropriate for the United States to have is the nature of American political culture. This provides some ready-made answers to questions about the proper nature and extent of government. In chapter 2, it was noted that the relations between people in liberal political cultures are configured according to a system of rights that support and enforce the equal freedom of all persons in society. Because these rights require an enforcing agent and an agent to adjudicate disputes that arise around them, liberals of all different viewpoints can be agreed on this simple account of the need for government: government is necessary to manage rights relationships. According to the liberal tradition, this is the first large-scale social problem that government exists to manage. But liberals typically disagree, and disagree violently at times, over precisely what this means. This disagreement describes and comprehends most all political conflict and controversy that surrounds American politics. But this will become apparent only after a thorough exploration of the ambiguity and confusion associated with understanding government as an institution charged with managing rights relationships.

Perhaps the most straightforward way to understand what this means is to say that government exists to police and protect individual rights to freedom and property. These are the primary elements of liberal morality within the American context, and not surprisingly, many Americans think that government should be dedicated to their protection and defense. These rights enable and entitle people to build their lives for themselves by entering mutually advantageous agreements involving exchanges of goods and services. Agreements of this sort are consistent with the exercise of freedom, provided they are not coerced, because they depend upon the voluntary consent of the parties involved. As free agents, people in liberal political cultures are presumed to be the infallible judge of what is best for them, how they want their lives to go, and so forth. Once one reaches the *age of consent* (whatever society imagines this to be), people are on their own and are supposed to assume complete responsibility for their lives unless they suffer from some sort of mental or physical impairment. *Paternalism* (or *parentalism*, as it is now sometimes called)—the practice of identifying a guardian with the authority to make and enforce decisions about what is good for another—is objectionable from this liberal perspective because it constitutes the most immediate and dramatic interference with the basic freedom of the individual. Liberal individuals (i.e., individuals who see and understand civil association in the manner made available to them through the liberal tradition) are therefore immediately suspicious of paternalistic relationships.

This traditional liberal view indicates both why liberals think government is necessary and also what the proper limitations upon government authority happen to be. In the tradition of Locke, government is necessary to police individual rights to freedom and property, but this is presumed to be the only responsibility government has. If government attempts to do more than this, it intrudes upon the freedom of the individual, and this defeats its own purpose for being. Contemporary political theorists refer to this conception of governmental authority, and the concurrent limitations on this authority, as *libertarianism*. Libertarians see civil association as a self-defense pact. They regard freedom as the greatest political value because it is crucial to the ability of independent individuals to live their lives as they wish, free from the interference and meddling of others. But they recognize that some policing agent is necessary to safeguard this freedom for everyone.

Libertarianism is an appealing political theory for a variety of reasons. Its attractive simplicity recommends it to people who are rather frustrated by the complexities of civil life and whose political inheritance inclines them to look past these complexities and rest content with the seventeenth-century vision of civil life on display in classical liberal thought. By learning the basic principles of libertarianism—"A's right to swing his fist stops where B's nose begins," and "Everything goes between consenting adults"—citizens of the polity should also grasp the basic limitations upon governmental authority. Institutional safeguards could then be put in place to police unscrupulous governmental leaders in the event they become seduced by the corruptive force of power, but more importantly, the vigilance of the people, armed with their understanding of the limitations of governmental authority, would stand as the most effective sentinel against the abuse of political power. Orwell's fears would be misplaced in such a political environment, and for reasons Orwell could readily appreciate. The political consciousness of the citizenry would work as a constant check against the abuse of political power by government officials, and government officials would retain a clear understanding of their social roles in the polity, thus assuring citizens that power would not become an end unto itself.

But in the twenty-first century, things are hardly so simple, and a variety of problems have now emerged that make libertarianism a rather antiquated political doctrine, despite the fact that it remains attractive from the standpoint of American political culture. Given this continued attractiveness, the problems that bedevil libertarianism need to be explored in order to manage a satisfactory understanding of politics. The realities of political life need to be kept in plain view if Americans are to be able to update their political culture satisfactorily, for political culture is always in the process of becoming. The difficulties with libertarianism are best presented by focusing upon three central problems with libertarian thought. First, the decentralization that libertarianism supports creates a variety of problems that need centralized management to address and control. Second, libertarianism contains a central and damning weakness: the ideal of freedom that it supports is really incoherent. And third, libertarianism seems unable to accommodate effectively the kinds of diverse nonliberal group presences one finds in large multiethnic states like the United States, despite its strong stand on freedom. Each of these problems needs to be considered carefully in order to assess adequately the failings of libertarianism. It is best to consider them in reverse order because some points will emerge in considering the last two problems that are pertinent to understanding the challenges introduced by the first one.

TOLERATION

Political culture is a formative influence on one's ontological horizons and is consequently the primary determinative factor that controls how people understand politics. But it does not do everything. There may be other cultural forces and influences at play upon at least some individuals that either complicate or reconfigure a person's ontological horizons. The above critique of liberalism will sound familiar and seem consoling for many Americans; this is why libertarianism still captures the imagination of many. Some, however, may disagree with or even reject the ontology and morality of liberalism because their own distinct cultural influences incline them to see the world differently. Others may acknowledge the importance of the ontology and morality of liberalism on their ontological horizons but still insist that these factors do not fully determine these horizons; other cultural factors are present that add additional dimension and texture to these horizons. In some cases, there may even be tensions and inconsistencies within one's ontological horizon, due to competing and mutually exclusive cultural influences, that make one's conceptual vision shift from time to time, much like the operation of a kaleidoscope.

Political culture in the United States sits awkwardly beside a host of additional cultural factors that introduce varieties of perspective into the body politic. Religious and ethnic variety adds considerable cultural variety to the polity and introduces the need to qualify the general claim that the United States has a thoroughly homogenous political culture. These cultural factors introduce differing ontological horizons involving the practice of religious and ethnic ways that may be inconsistent with the morality of liberalism. The United States, this is to say, is best viewed as a pluralist polity; in addition to the common and dominant liberal political culture in evidence in America, one finds further layers of cultural influence that contribute (sometimes considerable) normative and ontological diversity to the polity.

As we noticed at the outset, pluralist polities need to come to grips with the fact of diversity. Differing and competing moral and religious perspectives are a source of possible conflict in any society. If this conflict is to be effectively managed and not allowed to swell out of control and threaten the stability of the polity, some basic agreement needs to be reached about how the various groups that introduce moral and religious diversity into the political setting are going to get along with one another. This is no simple chore; moral and religious convictions matter greatly to people, and people see and recognize others in ways that are filtered through the lens that their normative beliefs present to them. If some members of the polity think that the practices of other members are horribly immoral and objectionable, they will likely want to invoke the power of the state to stop all this immorality. But the members of the group thus imposed upon will consider this an abuse of political power and a tyrannical intrusion into their lives. This is the stuff of considerable political controversy.

Illustrations of the kinds of conflicts generated by normative diversity in pluralist polities are widespread and easy enough to identify, but one instance of this sort provides a particularly troubling and poignant example. There are, in the United States, a number of religious communities that practice a form of faith healing. When members of the community, including children, become ill, the group comes together and prays for their recovery, but under no circumstances will they seek medical treatment for the sufferers. Consequently, members of these communities, again including children, often die when they could be saved if they received medical attention.

How should libertarians respond to situations like this? On the one hand, they might say that adults who decide to forego medical attention when ill may do so if they wish, and regardless of whether they are driven by religious or other concerns; this choice is theirs. But what about their children? They seem from one perspective to be innocents in all this, and since they fail to qualify as consenting adults, there is room for libertarians to worry about their welfare. It could even be argued by libertarians that the state should worry about their welfare even though the behavior of the members of the religious community to which they belong, including their parents, does not seem to qualify as coercive. This makes sense because the children are incipient or potentially self-determining agents, and to stand by and let them die from preventable causes hardly seems to respect these incipiently autonomous beings for what they are; their right to life is simply not being honored. Of course, the members of the religious community will not see things this way. They will see their children as God's creatures whose fate is in God's hands, and they will regard governmental interference with their religious practice as a violation of their basic right to freedom.

So here is the problem. If libertarians allow innocent children to die from preventable causes, it looks as if they have compromised their own moral views about the need to respect persons. Such apparent neglect seems to display a complete disregard for a child's right to life and liberty. And this is the very right that libertarians expect the state to protect and enforce. From this perspective, then, it looks like libertarians should welcome governmental intrusion into these religious practices to guarantee that innocent children do not die. But consider too that faith healing is recognized and accepted by some religions as the proper way to deal with illness, and the members of these religions may be presumed to have the freedom to raise their children according to their own religious beliefs and practices. These look like the voluntary and consensual activities of individuals that libertarians think lie beyond the concerns of government. They would, for example, surely find it objectionable if the government was taken over by Catholics who began to take children away from Protestant families in order to save them from eternal damnation. The free and voluntary arrangements and activities of the Protestant families are clearly and coercively compromised here, and this looks like an intrusion into the realm of personal freedom that libertarians want to condemn. But if they condemn this type of thing in the case of Catholics, must they not then condemn interfering with the religious practices of the faith healers as well?

Libertarians can respond to this difficulty in two possible ways. First, they can say that the rights of children need protection from the state and that these rights penetrate religious as well as family units. Therefore, it is a legitimate exercise of state authority to protect children from the immoral practices of parents. The analogy with a Catholic takeover of government, moreover, doesn't hold, because the Catholics are obviously restricting the freedom of the Protestants without defending any basic right to life, liberty, or property in the process, while governmental intervention into the practices of the faith healers does defend the life and liberty rights of the children involved.

It may sound strange to say that the parents of faith healer families are abridging the life and liberty rights of their children, but libertarians must say something like this if they wish to insist upon this solution to the problem. The reason it sounds strange to say that these parents are abridging the rights of their children is because parents don't normally treat their children horribly; instead, they are usually the first people in society to care about their children and look out for their welfare. And if asked, the faith healer parents would undoubtedly say that they *are* doing what is best for their children, and given their beliefs, they seem altogether justified in this conviction. If asked, the faith healer parents would insist that they are looking out for their children in the best possible way, and they would surely recommend that everyone do as they do. But this is the issue in contention, because the larger society thinks that something else is best for these children. So, the heart of the matter is whether libertarians should hold that the government must protect basic rights as this notion is understood in the dominant culture or that government must protect the basic rights of diverse cultural communities to live their lives and practice their cultural ways as they see fit.

This brings us to the second response that libertarians might make to this situation. They might say that the defense of a right to freedom permits distinct cultural and religious communities to live their lives as they wish. Some cultural groups may disagree with what others are up to and believe that they are engaged in deeply immoral and objectionable practices, but if liberty is to be respected, the members of these groups must tolerate the activities and practices of others whom they have reason to condemn as immoral.

That is, libertarians might say that their position commits them to the political virtue of *toleration* as a natural consequence of their commitment to freedom. So far so good, but toleration is a peculiar political virtue. It presupposes that some people are doing something that others find deeply immoral and unacceptable, and it indicates that these others must put up with such activities despite the fact that they consider them morally repugnant. It is not possible to tolerate things about which one is indifferent; to tolerate something means to put up with it even though it is considered to be terribly immoral. Yet if freedom is taken seriously in pluralist polities, it seems necessary to learn to tolerate diverse cultural, ethnic, and religious practices. For it makes a mockery of the notion of freedom to suppose that to be free means to be able to do those kinds of things that the dominant groups in the polity consider permissible, and that the government can and should prevent people from doing those things that the dominant groups think wrong or immoral. Toleration enables people who happen to have conflicting moral viewpoints to get along with one another despite the fact that these conflicting viewpoints incline each to regard the other as damned or disgusting. For this reason, toleration is considered an important political virtue within the liberal tradition that emerged in a time when religious diversity was a source of tremendous political and social conflict.

So then, what response to this predicament should the libertarian make? On the one hand, it looks like libertarians should champion toleration insofar as they suppose that anything should be allowed to go between consenting adults. This would resolve the issue in favor of toleration if children were not involved. If children also have rights to life and liberty, as libertarians typically insist they do, and if parents are not attentive to these rights, then even libertarians must support governmental intervention. Thus, for example, libertarians can and perhaps should support child labor regulations and child welfare statutes that police abusive or neglectful parents. A child's right to life and liberty is effectively lost if the child must suffer from abusive parents or end up in the workforce at an early age and be denied the educational opportunities necessary to provide her with the ability to make important future choices about how her life will go. But should libertarians also support governmental intervention into the religious activities of discrete communities because from their perspective the rights of children are jeopardized?

To answer this, it is important to think back to the ontological foundation of the right to liberty, and hence to life. Persons possess and enjoy such rights because they must be considered autonomous agents. While children might not be fully autonomous, it makes sense to consider them incipiently autonomous beings, and thus to conclude that they too have a right to liberty, and hence to life. Faith healing might work sometimes, but there are other occasions where innocents die despite community and parental prayers, even though they could have been saved with timely medical attention. If the government exists to police basic rights, and if certain group practices jeopardize these rights in the case of children, it looks like libertarians must conclude that government should intervene in the affairs of these religious groups and enforce the basic rights of the children. Toleration, it could be supposed, just doesn't reach situations of this sort; it is simply intolerable to permit innocents to die. Toleration ends where the abuse of individual rights is involved.

No doubt many readers will think this is the correct answer and suppose that this situation does not pose a problem for the libertarian position after all. But it also commits libertarians, as well as less freedom-loving liberals, to the position of holding that *their* moral beliefs are the ones that government should enforce and that basic rights as *they* understand them are what the polity should honor. Groups whose moral perspective is shaped by non-liberal influences may claim, with some justification, that this has little to do with respecting freedom, and faith healers who are prosecuted for the deaths of their children will certainly think that their religious freedom is being compromised by this outside interference. Liberal morality, in other words, can support only so much in the name of toleration within pluralist polities, and consequently, the ideal of freedom loses much of its significance for the polity as a whole if it is understood to protect only those ways and practices that liberals consider acceptable. This merely replicates the initial problem; libertarians can tolerate only those things consistent with their own moral perspective. So, even libertarian defenses of freedom don't seem sufficient to address the problems introduced by ethnic, religious, and cultural diversity in pluralist polities. If these problems are to be met and the diverse group presences in society reconciled with one another, liberal political thinkers will need to fashion a more appropriate theory of freedom that supports and promotes a more compelling theory of toleration.

Libertarians might not see this as much of a problem, particularly if they think faith healing involves an unacceptable disregard for the rights of children. If this is true, the state would then be justified in policing the situation. But this puts us on a slippery slope that leads away from a defense of freedom and toward a form of paternalism. Faith healing introduces only one rather dramatic situation where cultural views come into conflict, but there are others. Groups whose views are inconsistent with the meaning of a right to life and liberty, *as liberals or libertarians understand these rights*, are subject to invasion by government in order to protect their rights from themselves. Not only is this invasion likely to be unwanted, but groups that suffer such invasions may think the liberal rhetoric about freedom to ring rather hollow. Freedom now begins to mean that groups must live according to the standards championed by dominant cultural influences in society. This begins to make a mockery of the right to freedom and the ideal of toleration. But if the right to life and liberty is to mean something to liberals and libertarians, they must live by the meaning that it has or stand accused of a type of bad moral faith.

THE FREEDOM PARADOX

This brings us to the second problem with libertarianism mentioned above. According to this problem, the notion of freedom to which libertarians are so strongly wedded is deeply and subtly incoherent. The problem is aptly illustrated by something the nineteenth-century British philosopher John Stuart Mill, perhaps the most able and compelling of all the classic liberal thinkers, imagined when he claimed, "It is not freedom to be allowed to alienate . . . freedom."[2] Presumably this should be understood to mean that one ought not sell oneself into slavery, for example, even if one wants to; one cannot be free to give up one's freedom. If libertarians accept this view of the matter, then they will again expect the government to police basic rights by prohibiting people from entering arrangements that constitute the alienation of their freedom.

But if this view of the matter is accepted, it is also necessary to abandon the idea that anything should be allowed to go between consenting adults! Imagine that Smith devoutly wants to live a simple, uncomplicated, highly routine life, as free from all stress-inducing situations and activities as possible. Suppose that Brown is willing to feed, clothe, house, and otherwise care for Smith's needs, provided that Smith agrees to give up all rights that would permit him to leave Brown's employ and provided that Brown is permitted to sell Smith to Jones in the event that he becomes unhappy with Smith's job performance. This, let us say, is just the life Smith has dreamed of, and Brown, for his part, is happy to support Smith in exchange for Smith's help with his domestic chores. This looks like a form of slavery, and if it is understood in these terms, it could be argued that Smith should not be allowed to surrender his freedom in this way. But if the arrangement is acceptable to both Smith and Brown, why should anyone else care about this?

Slavery is generally and rightly regarded as unacceptable because it holds some people in bondage against their will, and slavery of this sort is obviously inconsistent with libertarian (and liberal) morality. But libertarians must say more than this if they want to endorse Mill's position. They must also say, à la Mill, that slavery is unacceptable *even if* it is a voluntary arrangement between willing and satisfied parties. They must say this, it might be argued, because freedom should be understood as a basic right to act autonomously. One cannot give up the right/ability to take one's life in one's own hands and determine how it will go and still remain free. One ought not enter an arrangement that limits one's freedom because one can't transfer one's autonomy to another. By selling the ability to determine his future and change his circumstances to Brown, Smith seems to have attempted such a transfer. But this contradicts his basic right to freedom because this right protects Smith's ability to act autonomously. Since the government is responsible for policing this right, it ought to intervene to prevent Smith from giving it up. Policing the right to freedom, in other words, must involve prohibiting voluntary attempts to abandon the right as well as coercive interferences with its exercise.

But it seems impossible to make sense of this Millian view of freedom. Most of the decisions people make about how their lives will go close the doors to alternative possibilities. Imagine a professional athlete who signs a contract to play for a particular team for some period of time, although the team can trade him if it so desires. Is this consistent with an athlete's right to freedom? Keep in mind that if the athlete doesn't like the terms of the contract, she needn't accept it. Or consider the so-called phenomenon of wage slavery. People become dependent upon their jobs because they need money to sustain themselves. Perhaps they would love to quit their dreary jobs and move to Hawaii to enjoy sun and surf, but they are prisoners of their circumstances. They depend upon their jobs and have no choice but to go to work for the salary they are offered. Who is worse off, the so-called slave who happens to be doing exactly what he wants to do and is happy with his life, or the laborer who hates his job but is unable to change his life for the better? Does it seem strange to say that liberals (including libertarians) should worry about the predicament of the slave but not that of the laborer? Is it reasonable to say that the former is unfree while the latter is really free?

Part of the incoherence in evidence here is a result of the fact that it is difficult to distinguish between the exercise of autonomy and its alienation. In the above example, Smith *chooses* to become Brown's slave, if it makes sense to call him that. Suppose he does this knowingly, deliberately, and after some studied reflection on just how he wants his life to go. Others might think him quite crazy for making such a choice, but if the choice is genuinely his, why should it be questioned? More to the point, why, if the choice is genuinely his, should anyone think his decision compromises his standing as an autonomous being by alienating his right to freedom? Why does it not make more sense to conclude that the choice he makes is really an exercise of autonomy that should thus be respected if his right to freedom is to be honored?

Libertarians can again make either of two possible responses to these questions. First, they can abandon Mill and repeat the mantra that anything goes between consenting adults. This means that the result of any and all voluntary arrangements in society must be considered freedom respecting, no matter how servile or tyrannical they might otherwise seem. Voluntary slavery would thus be consistent with individual freedom, odd as this sounds. If, however, libertarians rest content with this response, they must abandon their cherished belief that "that government is best which governs least," or that governmental authority should be restricted only to the protection of basic rights. If any and all social arrangements are freedom respecting in principle, and actually are so if they are the product of the consent of all involved parties, then citizens are free to ask their government to do whatever the citizens wish it to do for them. If citizens would like their government to practice paternalism and prevent them from doing things they might want to do if these things might bring them harm, then government paternalism would be consistent with the citizens' right to freedom.

This is objectionable to traditional libertarians, of course, because paternalism is generally supposed to be inconsistent with personal freedom, a position powerfully defended by Mill.[3] And this is reason for libertarians to prefer a different response to the above questions. This response requires libertarians to amend their views about anything going between consenting adults in order to protect against the possibility of things like voluntary slavery and paternalism. They might now insist that there are some social arrangements that are hostile to individual freedom *even if* some people might want, for whatever reason, to see them brought about. But this response just takes us back to the problem that inspired some of our previous questions. How can people distinguish social arrangements that are freedom respecting from those that are not?

If libertarians cannot answer this question coherently by saying that anything goes between consenting adults, that arrangements arrived at by means of voluntary consent are freedom respecting, how *can* they answer it without being completely arbitrary? How is it possible to answer this question without dogmatically identifying some social arrangements that libertarians happen to like, and thus consider freedom respecting, and some they dislike and thus consider a limitation upon freedom? The conceptual problem on display here might be called the freedom paradox. If freedom is understood to protect only voluntary choice and consent, all social arrangements are potentially freedom respecting, but this is inconsistent with libertarian views about the limits upon state authority, as well as with the general liberal view about things like slavery. But if people think freedom should be understood to protect some social arrangements and condemn others, it is necessary to explain why decisions about which arrangements are freedom respecting and which are not are not entirely arbitrary.

Perhaps this paradox can be resolved by finding something in the notion of autonomy that offers a clue about which social arrangements are consistent with the right to freedom. Mill believed that there is something to be said here that might resolve the freedom paradox. Although he does not speak explicitly in terms of personal autonomy, he imagines persons to be progressive and talented beings who make themselves better when they do things for themselves. People, in Mill's judgment, should not permit themselves to become passive, docile creatures whose lives and welfare are cared for by dominating forces—like parents, spouses, or Big Brother. They should actively engage life, meet its challenges, and take care of themselves. In short, Mill supposed that people should do for themselves, develop and refine their talents and abilities, and struggle against the chains of custom and conformity to become as independent and unique as possible. This, according to Mill, is the road to human happiness, and it is a road that runs away from indolence, lethargy, and paternalism.

This is powerful stuff, and people smitten by the ethos of individualism that Mill helped inspire, and upon which libertarianism (and liberalism more generally) feeds, will accordingly applaud it. But does it follow in any clear way from the notion of autonomy, or is it just Mill's somewhat romanticized vision of what he would like life to be like? Autonomy, once again, involves the exercise of responsibility for self, of making one's life for oneself. Does this mean that one should abandon the company of others and set off like a wandering Davy Crockett to confront one's own personal frontier? This not only seems unreasonable, but it is also inconsistent with the understanding of society as a mutual support system. Understood as a mutual support system, society requires everyone to contribute to the lives of others in particular ways, and this implies that people must find a way to contribute to the lives of others, because few if any will want to be without the company of others. This implies that choices about how one's life should go involve making decisions about how someone can best find happiness, fulfillment, and satisfaction in contributing to the lives of others. If this choice is to be truly one's own, if each individual must make it for herself, then why is it not consistent with the understanding of persons as autonomous beings to choose to contribute to others by, say, serving one or more of these people in a slavish fashion? Who is Mill, or anyone else, to tell the rest of humankind that this falls short of managing one's life effectively as an autonomous being? Mill may not like such a life, and he is certainly at liberty to encourage his posterity not to like it either. But his posterity may see things differently, and if people are to respect others as autonomous beings, then everyone should be permitted to make this decision for herself and not have it forced upon them by Millian libertarians who want people to live differently. Mill's views on individualism seem idiosyncratic after a fashion, and while they will hit a sympathetic chord with people whose liberal inheritance inclines them to value individualism, they still seem subject to the charge of arbitrariness. Thus the freedom paradox is still with us.

Is there another way that libertarians could try to resolve the freedom paradox? Perhaps they might argue that certain social arrangements are considered freedom respecting and others are inconsistent with freedom because cultural forces and influences dictate that some lifestyles are desirable and others are not. Something like this claim has already been encountered in the above example that considered the case of the faith healers. Libertarians might think that faith healing is inconsistent with the right to life and liberty of children, while faith healers might believe just the opposite. This disagreement could be settled by concluding that freedom basically involves the ability of some ethnic or religious group, or cultural community, to live as its members wish, or according to their traditions, beliefs, and customs. And there is something to be said for this view of the matter. Historically, cultural communities and ethnic groups have complained about a loss of freedom when others intrude into their lives and try to impose new ways upon them.

But libertarians (and many liberals of a slightly different stripe) will not like this idea very much because it is inconsistent with the individualism they treasure. Understood in cultural terms, freedom becomes a predicate of cultural communities, not of distinct individuals, but as liberals from Locke forward have held, freedom is a right associated with individuals, not with cultural communities. To think of freedom as a right enjoyed by cultural communities would seem to give too much power to cultural ways by allowing the community to impose its views upon members who might question community views and want to break from community ways. Put differently, libertarians might think that making sense of freedom by having recourse to a cultural perspective is dangerously conservative.

Conservatism as a political notion is largely misunderstood in American politics. Thanks to the confusion wrought by political rhetoric, many Americans now see conservatives as people who favor modest or limited government; that is, they confuse conservatives with libertarians. Traditionally, however, conservatives think there are cultural elements of social life that lend order and stability to the social fabric and should therefore be *conserved*.[4] They are opposed to radicals who would bring about dramatic and sweeping changes in the culture of the community and would do away with the lessons and wisdom of history in the name of abstract ideals that seem rationally attractive to them. While they concede that change in social life is inevitable, they are committed to the idea that it should occur in an evolutionary and not revolutionary manner. And they invite others to see themselves as beings with histories and cultures that matter because they provide a sense of personal identity and introduce stability and order into human life. Orwell, as he has been presented here, might be regarded as a conservative wanting to conserve the perspectives and ideals of a political culture he thought to be in atrophy.

Neither libertarians nor liberals more generally need to be hostile, in principle, to conservatism; in fact, if libertarians live in a properly libertarian polity, they will qualify as conservatives if they seek to conserve libertarian ways and ideals. Because American political culture is shaped by the liberal tradition (and although we are still trying to understand the ramifications of this point), because this is the American political inheritance, it also makes sense to say that Americans are liberals and also conservative in the sense that they are committed to preserving (or more literally *conserving*) the ideals and institutions of their liberal culture. But libertarians can be expected to view with suspicion at least some cultural limitations upon the freedom and independence of the individual, namely, all limitations inconsistent with libertarian views. And libertarians typically don't like the idea that some activity should be prohibited by government just because it is inconsistent with the cultural views of the community. Prostitution and gambling are but two examples of consensual social activities that are generally frowned upon for moral reasons, and a good many people think these reasons justify requiring government to prohibit them. But this is something to which libertarians wish to object; no one should be imprisoned by the tyranny of popular opinion, or what Mill called the "despotism of custom."[5] Mutually voluntary arrangements should not be prohibited by the state, liberals generally suppose, just because others don't like these arrangements. Of course, the freedom paradox is lurking here as well; if libertarians are willing to tolerate things like prostitution and gambling, they still won't permit things like voluntary slavery.

In any event, the individualism to which libertarians are committed makes it unlikely that they would want to accept an account of freedom as a social construct whose conceptual content is given by cultural viewpoint. For libertarians, people should not be told they cannot do things they would like to do just because others don't approve. But this rejection of the social construction solution to the freedom paradox is perhaps unfortunate. Not only does the social construction solution offer a reason to understand why freedom has historically mattered so greatly to oppressed groups and peoples; it also suggests a resolution to the problems posed by nonliberal groups. If these groups should be allowed to be free in the terms of this notion that are intelligible to them, if, that is, the right to freedom is understood in a cultural context, then a liberal commitment to toleration becomes both necessary and desirable. But liberalism in general (and libertarianism as a specific variant) continues to be powered by an individualist ontology and morality, and neither notion will support a social constructionist account of freedom.

THE CENTRALIZATION PARADOX

This brings us to the third and final problem that troubles libertarianism. In considering this problem, it is necessary to keep in mind the functional account of government. Government exists to manage large-scale social problems—problems that cannot or ought not be dealt with by more decentralized means. Libertarians suppose that the primary large-scale social problem it is appropriate for government to address is the general threat that people pose to the rights of others. While government protects people from each other, libertarians think the citizenry must be ever vigilant in order to protect themselves from government. There are, to be sure, other large-scale social problems for government to manage in addition to the defense of individual rights, and libertarians, sometimes grudgingly, often concede at least some of these. Government needs to protect society from external or international threats and aggression, for example, and should also protect personal rights and individual well-being when citizens travel beyond the borders of their home state. There are still other things that government should do to help maintain social life, most of which were listed in the functional account of government discussed previously. Yet libertarians are naturally suspicious about all this. They will likely think that most, perhaps even all, of these things can and should be left to the natural flow of human affairs as they emerge between free and consenting individuals. Things will go better, from a libertarian viewpoint, if social life is not overly managed by a central authority and if social problems are dealt with in a decentralized fashion by independent, diligent, creative, hard-working, and self-promoting individuals. But does this view of the best way social life will go make any sense?

Before exploring this question, it might be worthwhile to think about where this commitment to a decentralized social arrangement comes from. Like America's liberal political inheritance, the vision of a decentralized social system is again an inheritance from the seventeenth and eighteenth centuries. Increased commercial activity in Europe brought with it increased wealth, and as the economic productivity of states increased, everyone benefited. But this also brought with it increased skepticism about the pursuit of wealth for its own sake, something that was traditionally viewed negatively within the Christian tradition. Although commercial venture might not have been regarded as a virtuous lifestyle in all circles, people soon began to realize that independent commercial activity had the salutary consequence of making everyone's lot in life a bit better. Protestant ideals about the virtue of hard work and individual industry were coupled with the realization that the public good was actually promoted by individual efforts to produce marketable commodities for personal gain.[6]

In an era when thinkers were fond of trying to identify underlying laws that controlled the relations of all things (or in a time when natural law thinking was still operative), there was a certain appeal to concluding that individual industry, driven primarily by self-interested concerns (e.g., the desire for greater wealth), would promote the public good, and that society as a whole would benefit accordingly. But a social arrangement that might have a positive impact on the state at one point does not necessarily continue to have such an impact through time. Even if it is presumed that economic prosperity is identical with the social good, it doesn't follow that this prosperity is best sustained by deferring to the private activities of self-interested actors and forsaking any more direct effort to manage economic relationships. Put more straightforwardly, there is no reason to elevate the belief that the public good is promoted by the independent activities of self-interested economic agents to the status of an immutable truth.

A decentralized social arrangement is one without a centralized managerial system charged with making sure that things are going well for society. The primarily economic faith that private effort and industry will promote social well-being is accordingly hostile to centralized management of the economy and of society more generally. If libertarianism is to have much contemporary appeal, this faith in decentralization must be justified. Are there any reasons that would either support or challenge this eighteenth-century faith in a "hidden hand" that guarantees that decentralized social life will go well?[7]

To begin thinking about this question, it is best to consider first the sheer fact of the size of the United States. At present, there are about three hundred *million* Americans, most of whom are in the country at the same time, and all of whom tend to be up to something most of the time. If this collection of distinct individuals is to qualify as a society, there must be some coordination and organization that enables these people to coexist regardless of what they are up to. But society, it has been suggested, is more than just a social environment where people go about their own business and struggle not to get in each other's way; in the terms employed above, it is a mutual support system. If society is to go well, some services must be made available so that individual needs are met, and depending upon what qualifies as an important personal need, some of these services require a great deal of innate ability, talent, and training.

Put somewhat crudely, this means that one of the most important problems that must be resolved by any society is to determine how the right people get into the rights jobs. How can the polity make sure that the people with the required talent and ability manage to get into the social roles (i.e., the particular jobs) where they are needed? This question is asked against the background presumption that people have different talents and skill levels. Not everyone is going to be just as good at brain surgery, rocket science, relief pitching, or singing opera as anyone else. But, if job descriptions like brain surgeon, rocket scientist, and so forth exist, it would be good for society to make sure that able people are recruited to fill them.

The Greek philosopher Plato has provided one way that society might go about making sure that the able people get into important and demanding social roles. In his *Republic*, he imagined a civil arrangement managed by a ruling elite who naturally inclined toward what he considered a philosophical spirit. Ideally, those individuals capable of philosophical insight should be placed in charge of the polity, and they should see to it that the polity is well managed. People gifted in the arts and crafts should be trained as artisans and allowed to find their place in the marketplace as producers of those commodities that society needs. People gifted in the art of war should be trained as warriors and placed in roles where they can defend the borders of the polity against outsiders. And people gifted with philosophical insight should be trained as philosophers and placed in the role of managing the polity and promoting its well-being.[8] The problem of political power simply didn't exist for Plato in his ideal republic because, in his judgment, individuals possessing true philosophical spirit are incorruptible.

This is centralized social management with a vengeance; all features of social life in Plato's republic are controlled and managed by the ruling elite to assure that everything goes as well as possible there. There is no room here for chance, an invisible hand, or a faith that things will go well without informed managerial oversight. Yet the vast majority of Americans will find Plato's republic a terrible and intolerable place. Chief among the complaints to be expected from contemporary Americans is the challenge that Plato's republic has no room for individual freedom. People are told what they will do in life and what social roles they will occupy; they are not allowed to decide for themselves how their lives will go and how they will contribute to the overall well-being of the polity.

But at least Plato had a way to make sure that the capable people got into the appropriate slots, and if his strategy is rejected on the grounds that it is inconsistent with a liberal inheritance, Americans will still need to figure out how to do this for themselves. One way to do this is to proceed by lot. Suppose the names of all ten-year-old children living in the country are put in one bin and all the needed job descriptions in another. (And suppose that questions about whether there is enough of each to meet the demands of the other are put aside.) All that now needs to be done is to draw out one name and then draw out a job description to go with it. In this way, social roles can be distributed by chance. This is an egalitarian strategy; everyone has an equal chance of getting placed in a desirable slot. But it is also a highly centralized way of proceeding, and it seems likely that most Americans would frown on it for the same reason they would want to reject Plato's strategy. It ignores individual liberty. But it is also objectionable because it is a fairly inefficient way of proceeding. Chance cannot guarantee that able people will get placed in demanding roles.

Another way to get social roles assigned is to have an open competition that invites people to compete for desirable slots and that allows the alternative possibility that people can create new slots for themselves by coming up with new services that others might want. This latter possibility is one way to overcome the problem of knowing beforehand what social roles are necessary or desirable for any given society. Plato thought this too could be determined beforehand and that the polity could then be held constant through time. But unless one is willing to monitor and restrict the population of the state, this is hardly a feasible possibility. If populations grow, the available slots in society must be increased so that the products of population growth have ways to contribute to the well-being of others. The alternative to this is to say that some people in society will have no social roles to fill and must therefore be supported by others, immigrate to other states, or find a way to fend for themselves.

A competitive strategy of this sort can be operated in a decentralized manner. No central authority is necessary to choreograph or dictate who does what in society; instead, people are left to their own devices to develop their talents and abilities as they see fit in order to attain the social roles they happen to desire. This distribution of talent and ability thus resembles a free-for-all where ideally the most capable and gifted end up in the most demanding and important social roles or happen to create new roles that enrich and embellish the lives of their fellow citizens. More tinkering needs to be done if the competitive distribution of social roles is to work, however. Suppose society needs brain surgeons and also building janitors. Let us say that the demands of being a janitor are rather modest while being a brain surgeon is quite demanding. While many people could fill the former role, few are able to fill the latter role. To make matters worse, the training and education required to meet the demands of being a brain surgeon call for exceptional effort and personal sacrifice. If this is known in advance, why should anyone bother to go to the effort of becoming a brain surgeon? To put this question in a more general form, how can society make sure that the competition for social roles is properly competitive? How can society be guaranteed that able

people will want to compete for the more demanding, but perhaps more necessary, social roles?

One way to do this is to cultivate in the polity a sense of social responsibility and link it to the social roles that are generally considered of great social
importance. It looks like this calls for at least some degree of centralization.
Someone must decide which social roles are the most necessary, and structures must be put in place to guarantee that people develop the right sense of
social responsibility. This sense of responsibility would require people to say
at some point in their lives, "In determining how my life will go, I need to
decide how I can best promote social well-being and then develop my talents
as fully as possible in order to win the requisite social role for myself." This
procedure still demands a large amount of centralization, for educational
mechanisms must be put in place and monitored in order to guarantee that
the required social conscience is cultivated in the population.

Another way to do this is to link rewards to effort and enterprise. The trick
here is to tie personal visions of one's self-interest to the requirements of
social service, understood in a fairly expansive sense. The trick, that is, is to
get people to say, "I want as much of X as possible," and then to link getting
X with doing Y, where Y is some socially useful enterprise. The more important Y is to social well-being, the larger the reward of X attached to it. Consequently, a large element of the population will be inclined to pursue and
compete for Y, because this is the best way for them to get X. Social needs are
met, not by means of social management, but by letting free and independent
individuals make their own personal choices about how their lives will go.
This returns us to a decentralized form of social life that should work rather
well to get able people into important social roles, provided that the link
between personal self-interest and social service can be effectively sustained
by decentralized means.

Needless to say, this latter strategy for meeting the public welfare is pres-
ently widely popular in the United States, and it is certainly one that libertarians are willing to endorse. Still, this decentralized method of proceeding has
its problems, as we shall soon discover. But one problem requires immediate
comment. Who decides which social roles are important to the public welfare
for the purpose of attracting able people? Suppose society needs the same
number of janitors as brain surgeons. Who decides which (if either) of these
job descriptions is so important to social well-being that a considerable
reward should be attached to it? A completely decentralized social system
will leave this to the general public, and the inclinations of the public will be
left to market forces. If there is a constituency willing to pay a great deal for
brain surgery, the job description will become competitive; if brain surgery

has a low market appeal, few people will bother to assume the training required to become brain surgeons.

The logic of decentralization thus leaves matters to market arrangements to determine the things society needs. If there is a great social demand for, say, athletic entertainment, the market for sports franchises will flourish, and enterprising individuals who sense the opportunity to realize their personal interests will enter the market to exploit it. As a result, society will get more professional athletes and professional sports franchises until the market is finally saturated. If people would like to prolong their lives, the market for doctors (assuming it is widely believed that doctors are best able to prolong life) and medical research will blossom, and people will rush to fill it. Not everyone who tries to enter this line of work will likely succeed, of course; the market has its limitations. But this merely means that the market here is competitive, and this is how it should be if society is to be assured that able people will fill these job descriptions. When a market dries up, the slots will disappear because there is no longer a public demand for them. The activity in question will fade into history. There is not much need for people who make wooden tennis rackets these days. This merely reflects the popular will of the people and perhaps the inevitable march of technological development. If people no longer value, say, medical doctors, and stop frequenting them, the medical profession will be in trouble. But there is nothing wrong with this, libertarians will insist, for ultimately the people decide what is in the social welfare, and their decisions are reflected in the market.

Yet perhaps there actually is something wrong with this. Why should one conclude that social well-being is met by means of market relationships simply because the market (ideally) guarantees that people will get what they want and not get something they don't want? That is, why suppose that the general expression of social wants reflected in the market is equal to, or identical with, the well-being (the social needs) of society? Libertarians, it would seem, must respond to this by claiming that this is just what one means by social welfare. The people decide upon their own welfare, and their decisions are mirrored in the market. What else could anyone mean by social welfare? Could such a thing exist independently of the interests and desires of the discrete individuals who make up society?

But it is becoming increasingly difficult to find much merit in this view of the matter. Its logic, of course, is linked to political inheritance—to the now traditional view that people (as autonomous agents) are their own best judges of their own interests. At one level of reflection, this seems an unassailable notion, and so it is tempting to move too easily from this apparent truism to the conclusion that people should have considerable, if not determinative, control over decisions affecting their lives. But it is nearly impossible to defend this move in the modern world. As one explores the layers of interests people might have, one encounters the need for information, and it is not always easy to get this information. Nor is it readily apparent when and if people have all the information they need. In a technical and complicated society, knowledge becomes an important commodity. Particular individuals cannot hope to have all the knowledge they need in order to realize or even adequately understand their interests in all facets of their lives. Consequently, people become dependent upon the knowledge of others. Consider health care issues by way of illustration. Suppose people want to live long and healthy lives (and never mind where this desire comes from). What is the best way to achieve this goal? Most people probably cannot answer this question for themselves—at least fully. So to answer it, people must consult someone who already has gained the needed knowledge.

Under a decentralized social arrangement, it can be supposed that the market will supply society with people who have the information/knowledge they need, and it surely will. But it will likely do more than this. People will likely find all kinds of people in the market willing to give them, for a price, all kinds of help and advice on how to live a long and healthy life. Which of these should people believe? The traditional market response to this is *caveat emptor*—let the buyer beware. You pay your money and you take your chances. But this is hardly a helpful response in a world that has grown horribly complex and technical. People might have the ability to decide what kind of medical care is best for them by studying hard and learning enough of the medical profession to make solid decisions for themselves; in a highly sophisticated age, knowledge is the only road to self-sufficiency. But few people will be willing—let alone able!—to learn enough about all the issues associated with the pursuit of their wants and desires to be confident that they really can be self-sufficient. And if such an effort is required of everyone, few people would have time for much of anything else. Many of the things people might otherwise want to do will have to go undone because of the constant challenge of amassing the information needed to make informed decisions for themselves. This is simply untenable; even if people wanted to make their own informed decisions and dedicated themselves to doing so, they would still need the help and support of others to show them the way. And no doubt few people want to assume the burden of becoming experts in all those areas touched by their lives.

This is why it makes sense to think of society as a mutual support system. People do not need to be self-sufficient in this way because they can rely upon the aid and support of others. Each individual can develop some information, talent, or ability that helps others, and in turn, each will rely upon the information, talent, or ability of others in many areas of life. A person needn't become a doctor to heal herself; she need only go to a doctor. A person needn't become an automobile mechanic to fix his car; he needs only to take it to a mechanic.

But this merely reissues the problem of trust. People *should* be able to rely upon the information, talent, and ability of others when they need it and provided they can meet the market price. But why should anyone trust those who bring their wares to the market? Finding an answer to this question is made more difficult by the fact that a decentralized social arrangement that depends upon competition to get the capable people in the demanding slots must cultivate in the citizenry certain wants and desires. People are inclined to want to do or pursue Y because doing so is a good way to get X. But if getting X becomes an end in itself, people will look for ways to get it regardless of whether they contribute much of anything to the lives of others. A social arrangement that buys people's talents and abilities is going to have a problem with fraud.

Therefore, it is also going to need some mechanism for protecting against fraud. This now becomes a social need that must be met in order for society to be confident that things are going well. If society lets market forces deal with the fraud problem, how can people be certain that those market agencies that advertise a fraud protection service are not engaged in a fraudulent practice themselves? The best way to defend against this is to pursue a strategy of centralization and establish a central authority with the responsibility to police the market and make sure the public can distinguish between legitimate doctors and snake oil salesmen. This is a necessary service, but it is just not market viable.

Of course centralization is not an immediate fix to the problem of fraud. One might still worry about why the centralized authority should be trusted, but it might prove easier in the long run to address this problem than to leave matters to the market. If, for example, the centralized authority is answerable to the people in some fashion, and if rewards are attached to this job in a way that makes it desirable, then the fear of being replaced may motivate centralized managers to do a good job.

There are other problems with unmanaged markets that press further in the direction of centralization. As a case in point, think about what might be called insurance problems. The problem of unintended consequences has already been encountered. There really are a lot of Americans, and most all of them really are up to something. Why should society be confident that their activities don't have unforeseen and unintended consequences that endanger society or humankind more generally? This question directly challenges the operative assumption of decentralized social arrangements that independent and self-interested action conduces to the general welfare. When faced with the realistic possibility of unintended consequences, this assumption looks increasingly naive. And the problem here is really twofold. First, if some cooperative activity that some element of the population has engaged upon does have dangerous but unintended consequences, the problem will need to be fixed. But it first needs to be discovered. And who is out there looking for it? Second, it would be naive to think that all unintended social problems can be fixed, or fixed at a reasonable cost, without doing some damage that it would be best for society to protect against. This means that someone should be looking for unintended consequences *before* they happen. Somebody needs to be patrolling the social environment to make sure that unregulated social activity doesn't have future unintended but deleterious consequences.

Perhaps, however, these problems can be left to the market. Perhaps some enterprising sort will go into the unintended consequence insurance business and sell protection against unintended consequence problems. But how many people would be willing to pay for such a service? If some group's activities really have no unintended consequences, why should they want to take out insurance of this sort? They might be more inclined to gamble that their actions will not have unintended consequences. Further, a single group's activities might not have any deleterious consequences, but when this activity is proliferated through the activities of many distinct and independent groups, none of which need necessarily be aware of the others, bad things might result. Of course, companies that insure against unintended consequences will need to do more than compensate people whose actions have unintended consequences; they will also need to do their best to prevent unintended consequences from happening. But this will take a lot of study and scrutiny, and how many people will be willing to pay the price for all this if the choice is left to the market?

Situations of this sort are also going to give rise to *free rider* problems. Free rider problems surface around what can be called *collective social goods*. A collective good is something that is a good for everyone in a given society. A clean and healthy environment is important if people are to live long and healthy lives. So this is something that matters to the whole of society, and in this sense it is a collective good—a good recognized and shared by everyone in common. As it happens, a clean environment is also an indivisible good. If society A has a clean, healthy environment, then everyone in A benefits, and no one can be denied the benefit. Might it not be reasonable under these circumstances to see to it that all the citizens of A help pay to sustain their clean environment? Suppose, however, that Jones knows that all his neighbors like a clean environment and are willing to pay the Environmental Insurance Company (EIC) (a market enterprise selling the maintenance of a clean, healthy environment in A) in order to maintain it. Jones knows that if he doesn't pay his share of the bill sent to him by the EIC, things will go on as before. His neighbors will cover the cost of EIC, and he will continue to enjoy a clean environment but without the accompanying cost. If Jones is a rational and self-interested agent—just the sort of character imagined by a market arrangement—then he would elect to take a free ride. Since it isn't possible for the EIC to erect a little smog bank over Jones's house alone, he gets something for nothing. But if it is reasonable for Jones to take a free ride, it is reasonable for everyone else in A to do so as well. The EIC is now in jeopardy of going out of business, and the clean environment is jeopardized as a result.

There are other problems with relying exclusively on markets to guarantee social welfare, but perhaps enough has been said to establish a crucial point. Social welfare is something everyone wants but few are willing to pay for directly. Of course, social welfare really *is* promoted in many and important ways by means of decentralized individual effort and industry. Market activity really *is* a key aspect of the social welfare of the United States. It would be foolish to deny that market practices play a pivotal role in the mutual support system that is American society. It is difficult to imagine a society of over 300 million people working as a mutual support system without relying on market relationships. But decentralization introduces or creates additional problems of its own—problems of unintended consequences, trust and credible market practices, free riding, and so forth—that threaten social welfare in their own right. Consequently, one encounters another paradox that is crucial to political life. *It is the fact of decentralization that makes centralization necessary.* The more a society engages in decentralized social practices, *the more centralization becomes necessary.* And, *the greater the decentralization in a complex society, the more centralization is required to deal with the problems it creates.* This identifies a problem that can be called the *centralization paradox.*

CONCLUSION: BEYOND LIBERTARIANISM

Centralization is the enemy of libertarianism. The more a society needs centralized control and management, the further it moves away from the simple libertarian state charged only with policing individual rights and defending national borders. And ironically, the more decentralized it is, the more it needs centralized control. Libertarian logic is no doubt best suited to small and relatively simple social arrangements where the problems of size and technological complexity have yet to materialize. But modern states are not like this. The United States, for example, is so complex and so decentralized (think again about what all those Americans are up to at any point in time) that centralization is an inevitable aspect of its political landscape. If America's liberal inheritance makes libertarianism a sympathetic political doctrine, the social condition that has developed under the influence of this inheritance makes it a practically impossible one. There is, to be sure, irony here too—irony to which we shall return. In politics, cultures can turn themselves inside out as cultural ideals inspire a social life that begins to transcend and thus endanger these very ideals.

One must confront, then, some questions that are central to a thorough understanding of politics: How much centralization is necessary in any given polity? What things should be controlled by centralized management and what things should be left to the decentralized mechanism of the market? This, of course, is just another way of asking how much government the polity should have—the very question introduced at the beginning of this chapter. The centralization paradox, however, introduces additional complications to the effort to answer questions of this sort. Further, the discussion of this chapter introduces additional questions that matter and that are inspired by questions about how much centralization is necessary in a given polity. As political reality demands accommodation, what happens to the political ideals and values associated with cultural inheritance? According to the centralization paradox, the larger a polity becomes, the more centralization is going to be needed to deal with the problems caused by decentralization. Inevitably, this means that people will begin to wonder if their freedom is not an increasing casualty of an ever growing and ever more powerful state. There is probably no way to defeat the centralization paradox, so it is up to polities that value freedom to learn to live with it. And following Orwell yet again, this is possible only in a polity that understands politics.

NOTES

1. See Bernard Bailyn, *The Ideological Origins of the American Revolution* (Cambridge, MA: Harvard University Press, 1967).

2. John Stuart Mill, *On Liberty*, in *Utilitarianism, Liberty, and Representative Government* (New York: E. P. Dutton & Co., 1951), 213.

3. Ibid.

4. Conservatism is historically associated with the thought of Edmund Burke. Cf. Burke, *Reflections on the Revolution in France* (New York: Penguin Books, 1970).

5. Mill, *On Liberty*, 171.

6. These two notions come together in the work of the Scottish moralist Adam Smith, in particular, whose book, *The Wealth of Nations*, was the first systematic defense of a decentralized market system. But Bernard Mandeville is the thinker most responsible for defending the view that private initiative in self-interested pursuits will yield the public

good. Cf. Bernard Mandeville, *The Fable of the Bees*, Vols. 1 and 2 (Indianapolis: Liberty Fund, 1988).

7. The phrase, of course, belongs to Adam Smith. See Smith, *The Wealth of Nations* (Chicago: University of Chicago Press, 1976), 477.

8. Plato, *Republic*, Bk. II.

Chapter Four

Social Justice

We must have regard for justice even towards the humblest.

Cicero

Justice is the first virtue of social institutions, as truth is of systems of thought.

John Rawls

The implications of the centralization paradox may seem sobering to many readers. Freedom, that most important of all liberal ideals, recommends a decentralized social environment. But decentralization breeds centralization, and centralization can be managed only at the price of freedom. Thus the challenge of the centralization paradox: the more decentralized a social environment is, the greater the need for centralization—and so much the worse for the ideal of freedom.

There will be occasion later to return to the centralization paradox and the problems it poses for the liberal polity, but first it is necessary to give some attention to a concern of importance that follows from the liberal commitment to freedom. As noted above, the freedom at home within the liberal tradition promotes and supports the equal freedom of everyone in the polity. Although freedom is predicated almost exclusively of individuals in the liberal tradition, it is still important to consider the general level of freedom on display in the polity itself, and for the polity to be free, in any significant sense, it must protect and defend everyone's freedom equally. No one's freedom should be gained or vouchsafed by the loss of another's freedom. Since the freedom of some cannot justifiably be achieved at the price of a loss of freedom for others, it makes some sense to suppose that a polity is only as free as its least free member. It follows, perhaps ironically, that the freedom of each person in the polity is permissibly limited in order to guarantee that all persons in the polity enjoy an equal amount of freedom. And it is worth pondering what this means in practice. It is one thing to champion equal freedom with rhetorical flourish, but it is quite another to bring this ideal to life within the context of the polity. What would a polity that commits itself to the ideal of equal freedom look like? Does the ideal of equal freedom necessitate the maximally decentralized polity defended by libertarians, or does it require more centralized state management to realize this end? These are the questions to be taken up in this chapter.

WHAT IS JUSTICE?

The questions posed above introduce the issue of *social justice*. People worry about the justness of their society if and only if their political culture requires them to. Liberal ideals set moral ends that inform and direct public thinking about what the polity should be like, and beliefs about the justness of the polity must be critiqued by studied reflection on how successfully the polity realizes and promotes these ends. If Americans did not have these ideals, or if they were not generally agreed upon, they would lack the common moral standard required to measure the way their polity works against the ideal vision of how they think it ought to work. But of course Americans do have these ideals; they are an integral feature of American political culture.[1] Consequently, Americans can measure their political reality against the largely shared ends of liberal morality. Correspondingly, if Americans did not think their polity measured up to these political ideals rather well, they could not consider their polity to be very just, and they would have important grounds for criticizing the way things are going—grounds that others who share this political culture would need to acknowledge and take seriously. If, on the other hand, Americans think their polity reflects their liberal ideals reasonably well, they may conclude that their polity is reasonably just.

Social justice matters greatly to people; there is perhaps no more significant way to condemn some civil arrangement than to say that it is unjust. A state might be just without also being good, of course; the goodness of a state goes to what is in the hearts and minds of its citizenry. A state is good if and only if its citizens are also good—if they are beneficent, kind, loving, thoughtful, and virtuous. A state can be just, however, even if its citizens are rogues. All that matters from the standpoint of justice is that the citizenry live up to the ideals of its political culture for whatever reason—that is, that the citizenry get along with one another according the ideals its member's share as a polity. Social justice does not require citizens to love one another; in fact, they might very well hate one another. But it does require that all citizens honor the ideals of the polity in their treatment of others, even those they may happen to hate.

The subject of social justice also returns us to questions about the objective validity of the moral norms that ground social reflection on the justness of any given polity. Recall again that according to the natural law tradition, all human relations must be held to be governed by a set of immutable laws. These laws tell individuals how they ought to treat one another (and themselves), and in this sense they speak to all persons at all times and in all places. At least some of these laws, however, can be used as a basis for the positive law of the state, and when written into positive law, they organize social relations—they in effect regulate the polity—throughout the body politic. When positive law is an accurate and appropriate interpretation of natural law for a given state, the state would qualify as just. If positive law is inconsistent with the demands of natural law, the state must be considered unjust. So, according to this view of the matter, it is reasonable to conclude that evaluations about the justness of any state are a matter of rational reflection on the human condition and not simply a matter of political inheritance.

If, however, one decides to reject the idea that there are certain natural laws that govern all human relations, the justness of a given state must be measured against the normative standards that the state has as a matter of political inheritance. Places like Orwell's Oceania that have lost all sense of a political inheritance cannot then be internally critiqued as just or unjust; they simply lack the normative basis for making such judgments possible. (They can still be evaluated by outsiders, however, if the outsiders apply the norms of their own political culture to states of this sort.) In the absence of anything like natural law thinking, it is hard to know what to say about such states. While they cannot qualify as just (at least according to the internal standards of the citizenry), they also lack the standards necessary to consider them unjust. If one abandons the notion of natural law, it is perhaps best to think of places like Orwell's Oceania as tragic; they are tragic precisely because they lack the independent standards necessary for their citizenry to reflect upon their own political condition. Polities are distinguishable from such tragic regimes by virtue of the fact that their citizenry share some common understanding of how things should go politically. There is agreement at the level of the political ideal, this is to say, about what matters when it comes to civil life. At a time and in a place where natural law thinking has begun to wane, political inheritance begins to matter all the more. In such a place and at such a time, only political inheritance can protect a polity from the tragic condition imagined by Orwell.

This, in any event, seems to be the moral of Orwell's story—or so I have suggested. If so, then social justice must matter to Americans because their liberal ideals matter to them, and consequently, they expect their polity to live up to these ideals. This is reason not to lose sight of these ideals, but perhaps more importantly, it is also reason to work to understand what they mean in practice. And this can now be seen as the need to clarify and develop the sense of social justice that properly belongs to a liberal polity like the United States.

At least since the philosopher Aristotle began thinking about social justice, it has been fashionable to divide the realm of social justice into two separate issues: *retributive* justice and *distributive* justice.[2] The former involves attention to the kind of treatment appropriate for particular individuals because of something they have done wrong; the latter involves making sure that everyone in the polity gets treated properly and that no one is allowed to benefit at another's expense. As a prelude to thinking about social justice, it is appropriate to take a closer look at these two senses of justice.

Retributive Justice. As the notion implies, retributive justice is concerned with retribution, that is, with getting even with someone for something he or she has done. Retribution implies some form of punishment. It is customary to think that people who harm others should be punished for the harm caused, and it is unjust to let wrongdoers go unpunished. But of course it is also supposed that people who have done nothing wrong should not be punished, and it is perhaps an even greater injustice to punish the innocent than to let the guilty go unpunished.

This sense of retributive justice inspires a move toward centralization that even libertarians applaud. If people have rights to life and liberty, it is wrong for anyone to violate them. Violations call for retribution; wrongdoers should be punished for the wrong done. Sometimes it is argued that punishment is important because of its deterrent effect; if wrongdoers are faithfully punished, then others won't be so willing in the future to do wrong. No doubt deterrence provides an important reason why punishment is a good idea, but it does not control much commonplace thinking about the nature of punishment. Few people would recommend punishing an innocent person, for example, for the deterrent effect it might have if the state could make the innocent person look guilty. Further, the severity of the punishment has a great deal to do with its deterrent effect; the more severe the punishment, the greater the deterrence. But most people still think the punishment should fit the crime— speeding on the highway should not be punished with the death penalty. So, even if the liberal sense of justice cannot explain why people think punishing wrongdoing is a good idea (or even if they think some appeal to deterrence must be made on this score), it still controls public thinking about how the polity should punish, as well as who should be punished.

It would, however, be awkward to permit those who are wronged to themselves punish those who they think have wronged them. Rights violations, as we have seen, can be controversial; consequently, it helps to have a common judge to determine whether a wrong really has been done, and a neutral party to decide what kind of punishment is appropriate for any wrong that has been done. Since all members of society have an interest in making sure that rights violations are fairly and effectively policed, it makes sense to put this responsibility in the hands of a centralized authority dedicated to doing this job well. This is something Americans expect from their government.

Retributive justice looks to the treatment of specific individuals who have done something to deserve to be treated in a certain way, viz, to be punished. But concern about the type of treatment people deserve—that is, concern about the just treatment of others—ranges beyond the notion of retribution. So there is reason to expand the notion of retributive justice to provide a more comprehensive account of the type of treatment specific persons might deserve.

Justice in this expanded sense—let us call it *personal justice*—looks to specific individuals and signals an obligation to give them what they deserve. A student who receives a perfect score on an examination deserves an A. An athlete who wins the competition she has entered deserves the prize for first place. The student deserves the A because she has *earned* it; her hard work and effort, perhaps along with her natural ability, establish the grounds of her desert. Similarly, the athlete also deserves the first-place prize because she too has earned it by demonstrating superiority in the skill the competition tests. It would be wrong, because unjust, to give the student with the perfect score on the examination any grade other than an A, and similarly, it would be wrong, because unjust, to give the first-place prize to a competitor who finished fourth.

So far, so good, but how can one know what kind of treatment people deserve? What are the grounds that determine when a person is deserving and when she is not? Competitions, like academic tests and athletic events, make this rather easy in particular circumstances, but these circumstances also seem to be rather uninteresting from a moral and political point of view. Are there any morally pertinent foundations of personal desert? Similarly, is there any treatment or concern that people deserve simply because they are people and that would result in an injustice if denied them? Or are all foundations of personal desert based upon some kind of personal achievement or accomplishment? (Retributive justice, of course, looks the other way toward some failure to perform as expected or to fulfill one's obligations, and in this sense, there is a distinction of some importance between retributive and personal justice.)

Given the nature of liberal morality already discussed, it seems plausible to insist that people deserve to have their basic rights to life, freedom, and property respected, and the failure to respect these rights works an injustice. If this makes sense, there is further reason to think that a just society, according to the liberal tradition, is one that respects the basic rights of its citizens and allows them to exercise these rights as they see fit. But it is crucial to ask what it means to respect these basic rights. What kinds of things should people be permitted to do under the protection afforded them by their basic rights? The answer to this question is tied—and importantly so—to the general strategy followed in the United States for getting capable people in demanding jobs.

In a decentralized social arrangement, people might be encouraged to develop their talents and abilities and to use them to contributed to social well-being by rewarding demanding social positions with greater amounts of those things considered desirable: wealth and money, power and influence, or prestige and esteem. These are things that people in the United States learn to want subtly and by encountering prevalent images of a life that is well stocked with these things. By attaching desired goods to social roles, society generates a competition for them; people compete for these roles because they want the rewards attached to them. This is hardly a planned system of role distribution; instead, it is completely decentralized and governed by market relationships. Built into this process is an implicit but important normative element that might be summarized by saying that people deserve the fruits of their labor and that they have earned the largesse that follows from the satisfactory performance of the social roles they have elected to play and have succeeded in achieving.

Social need (however this is determined!), linked with market forces, dictates the amount of social goods that will be attached to social roles and/or offices, that is, to the work people decide to do. The more important the role is to society, the greater the compensation that the market attaches to it. Of course, some people may work to achieve and occupy certain roles because they find such work intrinsically interesting, challenging, or socially useful; it is something of an exaggeration (and perhaps an unnecessarily cynical one) to insist that everyone elects to pursue a certain social role in life for self-interested reasons. But social processes can't depend upon this sort of individualistic decision making because it is rather inefficient to leave role selection to chance in this manner. Perhaps more often than not people decide to pursue a certain career (or acceptable menu of careers) because of the social rewards attached to it. Social roles are desirable because of the lifestyle they make available, not (necessarily) because of the intrinsic nature of the roles themselves. In fact, it is difficult to know how to attach importance to social roles if this is not left to the market.

This social *modus operandi* has its dark side, to be sure. The number of highly rewarding slots in society is rather small in comparison with the overall population, and most everyone (regardless of social standing) typically learns to want to improve their condition in life by gaining the greatest amount of social goods possible—or maximizing their overall social goods as balanced against their desire to work, basic interests, and so forth. Lots of people in society want to be, for example, doctors and lawyers; few want to be mailroom clerks or night watchmen. But, the market being what it is, many of the people who wanted at one time to be doctors or lawyers will end up being mailroom clerks or night watchmen. And as a result, many people may very well live sad, unfulfilled, and tragic lives because they are burdened by the realization that they haven't managed to do very much with their lives. The social cost associated with this phenomenon is rather large, for it is not just wealth that is denied those who fail to achieve their personal goals as a result of social competition. The social basis of self-respect and self-esteem are also compromised, and people whose grand ambitions have come crashing down around them may live out their days in bitterness and disappointment—a point to which we shall return later.

From this brief sketch, it is possible to put together a quick description of a just society according to the prevailing standards of personal justice in America. It seems fair to say that a just society, as derived from the ethic of social contribution and reward in America, is one where people are free to improve their lot in life by working and competing for well-compensated social roles and offices. It follows that these roles and offices should be open and available to everyone in society; no one should be excluded for reasons irrelevant to the criteria that determine potential excellence in the role or office. Roles and offices, that is to say, should be won by exhibiting the abilities and talents appropriate to their performance. It would be unjust to deny a student who merits admission to medical school the desired admission because the admission's director prefers to have her golf partner's daughter admitted. Similarly, it would also be unjust to deny those individuals who have worked hard to achieve desirable social roles the compensation tied to them if they perform well once in these roles. They deserve the fruits of their labor, just as they deserve the advertised or expected compensation for their social contribution that attracted them to these roles in the first place. This looks like a requirement of personal justice.

Distributive Justice. A vision of social justice derived from an exclusive focus on personal justice is terribly incomplete in certain crucial respects. In particular, it begs an important question: how should social goods, offices, and opportunities be distributed throughout society? Or, more specifically, should market mechanisms be the only or even the primary method for dis-

tributing social goods, offices, and opportunities in a just society? These
more general questions introduce the subject of distributive justice. All societies need rules that govern the way social resources are to be distributed and
that correspondingly determine what counts as a social resource in need of
distributional control in the first place. The defense and enforcement of these
rules requires an element of centralization, but the distributional rules themselves do not necessarily require centralization. If, for example, distribution
is to be determined according to market relationships, the rules governing
distribution dictate a decentralized method of operation, with centralization
required only to guarantee that market rules are followed. Thus, according to
market rules, contractual exchanges of goods and services are permissible as
the appropriate way to redistribute wealth, while nonvoluntary exchanges
(e.g., theft) are not. Distributive concerns become more centralized, on the
other hand, if it is supposed that everyone needs or deserves some portion of
the available social resources regardless of the status quo brought into existence by market transactions.

The issue of distributive justice involves two fundamental questions: (1)
What things qualify as social resources requiring rules to govern their distribution to the members of the polity? and (2) What rules should govern the
distribution of these social resources? The first question asks about those
goods and services to be considered a social resource for distributional purposes. Distributional concerns usually arise when the general social desire for
something exceeds the available supply. People don't worry about distribut-
ing air, for example, because air is abundant. Once upon a time, water was
abundant in some regions of the country also, but those times are largely
gone. Most areas of America no longer have abundant and inexhaustible
water reserves, and therefore the distribution of water becomes important.
When demand exceeds supply, a resource becomes scarce, and scarce
resources are the things that polities must figure out how to distribute.

But scarce resources are not the only things that may need social distribution. Some social services may also fall into this category. Educational
opportunity might need distribution as well in order to guarantee that everyone has viable access to it. Similarly, a society will need to consider rules for
the distribution of effective law enforcement and medical care. Some goods
and services may be considered so important that cultural standards dictate
that everyone should have reasonable access to them, and no one should be
denied access simply because they can't afford them. Such goods are considered so important for living a worthwhile life that it is inappropriate to leave
them to the vicissitudes of the market. They are owed to every member of
society in a strict sense, and no one should be denied them just because they
cannot afford, without undo hardship, to purchase them on the open market.

The second question about proper distributional rules raises some challenging problems, but a hint about how it might be answered can be derived from the discussion of personal justice. All societies continue to face the ticklish problem of managing to get capable people into socially important roles, but a free society leaves choices to individuals themselves about how their lives will go and what they will do with their lives, constrained only by the realities of market competition. Thus polities that value freedom tend to rely upon market relationships to get capable people in important slots by effectively buying their talents and abilities. Money functions as an important resource in this regard because it has a virtually universal exchange value. Money is not the least bit valuable in its own right, but with money one can purchase almost everything that one could possibly want, because in market societies almost everything has a price. Socially important social roles attract talented people by offering them high salaries, and with the money they earn they can proceed to buy whatever it might be that they happen to want. From the standpoint of personal justice, this is all to the good. People acculturated to the logic of market transactions by virtue of their political inheritance typically subscribe to the ethical maxim that they are entitled to the fruits of their labor, and the amount of fruit one earns depends upon market demand.

But there are still questions to ask about this distributional strategy. Are there some things that people generally think money ought not be permitted to buy? Are there some things that should be distributed to people independently of their ability to purchase them? Many Americans will want to answer both these questions affirmatively. Prostitution is typically frowned upon, for example, even though it remains a thriving underground industry. People also tend to think that money ought not buy things such as admission to college, important social roles and offices, leisure time, or friendships and good companionship. These are either not considered market commodities or they are regarded as resources that should be earned in the appropriate way rather than bought.

These issues complicate the way the concerns of distributive justice should be addressed in a society dedicated to social justice. A society is just, let us say, not only if standards of personal justice are met, but also if the distributional rules in society guarantee the proper and appropriate distribution of distributable social resources to all members of society. If this is right, then the notion of social justice would seem to involve two key components: a society is just if (1) everyone in the society receives what he or she deserves, and (2) the overall distribution of distributable social resources meets the ideal distribution of these resources as determined by the moral standards of the society's political culture. If this view is endorsed, however, there are problems that must be faced by polities with liberal political cultures because it is not difficult to see that these two standards of social justice often work at cross-purposes.

EQUAL FREEDOM

Libertarians, once again, think that the commitment to basic rights means that the government should police and protect these rights for everyone. This is typically understood to mean that government should permit and not regulate free and consensual exchanges between persons. Market factors should control and determine the distribution of distributable social resources, with government's responsibility confined to the defense of standards of personal justice and the right of free exchange.

It has been noted already, however, that there is reason to be suspicious about the "invisible hand" conviction that often accompanies libertarian thought. While deregulated market activity may and likely will promote overall social well-being in several ways, it cannot guarantee this well-being by itself. A variety of problems invariably emerge that require centralized management by government in order to guarantee that the market continues to function effectively. Enough has been said about these already, but the concerns of social justice raise a somewhat different, and perhaps even more troubling, problem with libertarian views.

There is an obvious case to be made for the integrity of free and voluntary exchanges. If both A and B think that their respective well-being will be improved by engaging in an exchange of services or goods, then making the exchange will improve their well-being, and the new distribution of goods brought about by the exchange should be considered preferable to the status quo prior to the exchange. But this is a fairly idealized picture of the exchange process. Consider a situation where A confronts B with a gun and tells B that unless B gives him, say, fifty dollars, A will shoot him with the intent to kill. Let us suppose that B is convinced that A has the ability to kill him and will do so if he does not hand over the fifty dollars. Now, B might think this a good bargain; it seems probable that most people would be willing to pay fifty dollars in order to save their lives.

Even libertarians will think there is something wrong with this way of looking at things. While the anticipated exchange between A and B looks good from both sides, B still has reason to object to this situation. A's actions are coercive; A cannot legitimately threaten to intrude upon B's basic rights and then indicate that he will avoid doing so for a price—or so B might think. Let's concede that A's actions are coercive, and let's suppose that coercion is the kind of thing that government should protect people against. How might one support and defend this supposition?

Since libertarians think that government is permitted only to police basic rights, they must argue either that coercion of this sort is an impermissible form of resource redistribution or that coercion violates a basic right. It is tempting to think that A's threat is not itself a violation of a basic right, and therefore the threat is legitimate; in the terms popularized by Hollywood, it would seem that A merely makes B an offer B cannot refuse. Why should A's threat/offer be construed as a violation of B's right to life, liberty, or property? *If* A carries through on his threat and kills B, the state could do something to address the wrong done (the infringement upon B's right to life), but of course this will do B little good. If B is confronted by A under these circumstances, he would most likely prefer to pay up rather than have his right to life violated, and knowing this, it seems well worth A's while to make the coercive threat. To defend against this situation, it is necessary to say that the threat itself is something the government can police; so libertarians must insist that the threat itself violates a basic right. This argument can be made if one claims that the threat itself violates B's right to freedom. The threat puts B in a position of having to make a choice he would prefer not to make; it costs him an important element of control over his own life and how things will go for him. It imposes upon him in a fashion he does not wish to be imposed upon, and this diminishes his ability to pursue desirable activities, associations, and life plans. If this makes sense, if the threat itself can be understood to restrict B's freedom, then A has violated a basic right of B's, and government is justified in policing this sort of thing.

The argument would seem to have a degree of merit, but if one accepts it, libertarianism is again imperiled. Acceptance of the argument places libertarians upon a slippery slope that threatens to carry them some distance from their preferred decentralized method of resource distribution. To appreciate this point, consider the circumstances surrounding the rather infamous Supreme Court decision of 1905, *Lochner v. New York*.[3] Lochner owned and operated a bakery in New York City under what people would today consider "sweat shop" conditions. Lochner's employees worked long hours for desperately low wages in horribly hot and austere conditions. The state of New York, thinking that the situation threatened the welfare of the employees as well as the health of the consumers of the product they made, introduced wage and work-time regulations to control the hourly wages of the employees and to limit the number of hours they could be required to work during the week. This looks like just the sort of thing libertarians should oppose. After all, any contractual relationship between Lochner and his employees would seem to be based upon the free and voluntary consent of the parties, and therefore the government ought not interfere with this exchange of goods and services.

But the story can be embellished by introducing some additional facts that complicate matters. In New York during this period, there was a tremendous oversupply of labor that dramatically skewed the labor market in favor of employers. People need certain basic resources to live and care for their dependents. In market relationships, people can manage to get the needed resources only by entering distributional arrangements in which goods and/ or services are exchanged. Ideally, both parties should be happy with the outcome and think it preferable to the status quo, but the outcome can be preferable to the status quo without both parties being happy. If jobs are scarce and the supply of labor great, employers have no particular reason to pay prospective employees well or to worry about the hours they must work or the conditions in which they will find themselves. At some point this situation begins to look much like the coercive relationship discussed above; that is, at some point it seems that an employee's right to freedom is compromised. Employees have no real choice but to submit to the contractual terms offered by the employer even though they may not like the situation and would certainly prefer to have better possibilities.

Is there reason here to think that an employee's right to freedom has been compromised in a way that requires governmental intervention? The situation is unlike the coercive threat that A delivers to B in one crucial way. Lochner has not coercively threatened his employees the way A threatened B. But this might not matter much if one supposes that the problem B faces is produced not by the fact that he is threatened but by the nature of the threat. Suppose A tells B that he has heard that C is looking for B with plans to kill him (and B thinks this is true), but A will protect B from C if B agrees to pay him fifty dollars. This isn't coercive any longer, but B should still not have to pay A protection money; B should not have to worry about the possible violations of his rights to life and freedom. It is the job of government, acting in the name of everyone's good, to protect and police these rights. That is, the job of policing these rights has been removed from market relationships in order to guarantee that everyone's right to life and liberty is protected, *even if* some citizens are unable to pay for this right. Everyone pays for government in order to assure that everyone enjoys the equal protection of these rights, although some are likely to have to pay more in the event that not everyone can pay enough to have these rights secured for themselves. This is the point behind thinking that the protection of these rights is a public right that ought to be safeguarded for all citizens regardless of their wealth or social status. If people have these rights, it is up to the polity to safeguard them for everyone.

If B's right to freedom is violated because A places him in a situation in

which he loses the ability to control how his life will go and to make meaningful choices about his future, then society has an obligation, following from
B's right, to intervene on B's behalf. In the circumstances surrounding the
Lochner decision, Lochner's employees found themselves in essentially this
very situation. Even though Lochner didn't threaten his employees, their situation seemed coercive nonetheless. They had no practical alternative but to
take the job according to Lochner's terms, and Lochner was able to profit
from the social circumstances that worked to his advantage. If A's coercive
threat against B means that B's right to freedom is compromised even though
B might be willing to give A the fifty dollars asked for to prevent being killed,
it would also seem that the right to freedom of Lochner's employees was
compromised by facing a situation where they had to either work long hours
for horrible wages or starve. This is not a choice that entitles them to exercise
much control over their lives; instead, they are forced to sign on as wage
slaves.

Viewed in this light, Lochner's offer of employment begins to look rather
coercive. While Lochner did not directly threaten to violate his employees'
right to life or liberty, he exploited a terrible situation to his advantage without regard for these rights. Imagine that A has fallen into a lake and is in
danger of drowning when B happens along in his rowboat. Suppose B recognizes A's predicament and informs him that he will be happy to pull him out
of the water for a tidy sum of money. If A has the money, he will most likely
pay up, but there seems something rather sordid about thinking that this is
just good business on B's part. If B has an obligation to respect A's right to
life, it would seem that he has a Samaritan duty to come to A's aid if he can
reasonably do so, without making a coercive "offer" in order to take advantage of A's predicament. By extension, a government charged with defending
and policing individual rights should prohibit this sort of thing from taking
place. Perhaps government ought not punish B if he fails to come to A's res-
cue—there is no need to debate this matter here—but the government can
reasonably police these rights in a manner that prohibits B from exploiting
A's situation when these rights are endangered. By way of defending these
rights in the *Lochner* case, the government could intervene in the relationship
between Lochner and his employees in a way that protects the employees
from exploitation. This is exactly what the state of New York attempted to
do, an action that was finally struck down by the U.S. Supreme Court in what
is often considered one of the most tragic decisions in American constitutional law.

If this makes sense, it seems safe to conclude that under some socioeconomic circumstances, centralized management of employer-employee relations is consistent with the liberal ideal of freedom and not a compromise of

this ideal as libertarians sometimes suppose. But it would be a mistake to rush to a conclusion of this sort. It was, after all, Lochner who filed suit against the state of New York and who finally won before the Supreme Court for reasons we need not consider.[4] He alleged that *his* freedom was violated by the New York wage and hour regulations because *his* ability and opportunity to enter contractual relations freely was blocked by the state by virtue of the restrictions placed upon him as an employer. If one concedes, as perhaps one should, that social circumstances can become coercive at times and threaten the individual right to freedom, it might still be asked why the state should intervene in this situation and defend the right of freedom of some by compromising the freedom of others. Why should Lochner suffer a violation of his right to freedom just because social circumstances limit the freedom of others? From the standpoint of personal justice, this seems wrong; Lochner doesn't deserve to have his freedom restricted in order to promote the freedom of others.

It may indeed be true that Lochner doesn't deserve this kind of treatment, but he doesn't deserve to get rich off the misfortune of others either. Some might say that this is just a matter of fate, but this is surely mistaken. The social circumstances in New York around the time of the *Lochner* decision reflect conscious choices the polity had made about how to distribute resources, choices that emphasized free market transactions and decentralized distributional strategies. But a majority of the New York legislature had begun to rethink the desirability of these strategies, even if the Supreme Court seemed reluctant at the time to do so. The problem raised by *Lochner* is a classic issue of social justice. Should one remain committed to decentralized distributional strategies even if the freedom of some is compromised by virtue of the socioeconomic conditions that may happen to arise, or should one ask the government to intervene and defend the freedom of those who suffer under these conditions even if it means restricting the freedom of certain others? This is a crucial dilemma that liberal polities need to address when social circumstances reach a certain point. How does the liberal polity most effectively and adequately support and promote its moral ideals?

By way of exploring how to best answer this question, it should be recalled that liberal morality is fundamentally egalitarian in character. Liberals want to defend the basic rights of everyone, and this means, when it comes to the right to freedom, that they should defend and promote everyone's freedom *equally*. Nobody can claim that her freedom is more precious than anyone else's. To put the point in rather familiar terms, each person's freedom is limited only to the extent required to guarantee an equal amount of freedom for everyone else. But what does this mean in practice?

In one fairly obvious sense, Lochner's employees were as free as Lochner and everyone else under the decentralized market conditions that prevailed in New York at the dawn of the twentieth century. This becomes apparent if it is supposed that the only barriers to individual freedom are those imposed by the government through the initiation of laws that constrain action. Lochner's employees were free to contract or not contract with Lochner, just as Lochner was free to contract or not contract with them. But New York's wage and hour regulations changed all that, and from this perspective, it limited the freedom of *both* Lochner and his employees. Since equal freedom would thus be maximized without these regulations, liberal morality might seem to require the conclusion that they should go. This is the position libertarians are inclined to take, and it is close to the one the Supreme Court actually adopted at the time.

But it is an obvious mistake to think that government-created laws are the only things that can limit or constrain freedom. If this were the case, then liberal morality would support anarchy since this condition would establish the maximum amount of equal freedom. Government, however, is necessary to protect basic rights, including the right to freedom, because others might violate these rights. And the problems posed by the *Lochner* case raise another possibility: socioeconomic conditions might also limit or constrain one's ability to exercise these rights. These conditions may become coercive, in a sense, in their own right and thus skew the equality of the freedom enjoyed by the citizens of the polity. This looks like the condition Lochner's employees were in; given the socioeconomic conditions of the time, Lochner was able, in effect, to hold a gun to their heads. One can suppose that his prospective employees didn't like the circumstances they were in, and if these circumstances were otherwise, they would have been unwilling to accept the contract offer from Lochner that they felt they had to accept under the circumstances. For a choice to be viable, and hence freedom respecting, it must be meaningful; that is, the opportunity to choose otherwise must be present. If this opportunity is not realistically present, the choice situation begins to look coercive. So there is reason to think that governmental intrusion into the deliberation process between Lochner and his employees enhanced the freedom of the latter by balancing the scales of the choice equation. The freedom of the employees was more equally balanced against Lochner's freedom thanks to governmental regulation.

It is important, however, not to take this argument to extremes and conclude that government should police the distribution of social resources in a manner that assures the basic economic equality of all persons. The argument still sits upon a social condition in which market forces control distributive processes, and this once again is necessary to make sure that capable people get into important social roles. New York intervened in employer/employee transactions in order to protect against a particularly abusive situation; it did not act to revise the way individual talents and abilities are purchased by society as a whole. In a society dedicated to the ideal of equal freedom, this is best accomplished by having competitions for desirable slots, and important slots are made desirable by attaching desired rewards to them.

In a market system, money as a universal medium of exchange is obviously a desirable reward. If goods tend naturally to be scarce in society and if money is able to buy a great many other distributable goods, then people will seek money as the primary means for the realization of those ends they might desire that can be purchased with money (and society will encourage people to want things that can be purchased with money in order to get them to want it if it is used as the primary desired reward). This means that winners of the competition for important slots in society will be able to amass greater wealth than others and buy more of the purchasable distributable goods than others. So social resources will tend to fall into the hands of the winners of the competition for desirable slots, and inequalities in the holdings of desirable distributable social resources will result.

WELFARE LIBERALISM

The resultant inequalities of *wealth* (i.e., of desirable distributable social resources) are not necessarily problematic in their own right; they are the logical consequence of a free society's commitment to purchasing the talents and abilities of its members in order to assure that things go well. They are also the inevitable result of a decentralized social resource distributional system. But they may become problematic, and will likely become so if inequalities of wealth enable some people to have an advantage in the competition by means of which desirable slots in society are allocated. Ideally, desirable slots (i.e., well-rewarded slots) need to be open and available to everyone, and the competition for them should be decided by appeal to the relevant merits of the competitors. If some social roles are closed to some members of society at the outset, their freedom is abridged, and the equal freedom standard central to liberal morality is not met. Further, the initial closing of social roles to some members of society is dysfunctional because the members excluded from these roles may be the people whose talents and abilities make them best suited for these roles. Their exclusion would then mean that society will not function as well as it might, because the best people are unable to win these slots.

So then, do inequalities of wealth distort and compromise the competition for desirable slots and stunt the development of a citizenry able and inclined to use individual initiative and effort to make things go better for everyone? Before exploring this question, it is necessary to add to the equation the natural parental tendency to want to see things go as well as possible for one's children. If this is a natural tendency, however, it is not a particularly necessary one; parents might elect to ignore their children or to spend very little on them, preferring perhaps to spend their money on themselves rather than on their children. In general, liberal morality leaves parents free to make their own decisions about the percentage of their wealth they will spend on their children; the care and upbringing of children, liberals traditionally suppose, is none of the government's business.

But there are apparent limits to this conviction. Children are not just future citizens of the polity; they are also incipient adults who possess basic rights and who will one day take control of their own lives as autonomous individuals and chart the direction their lives will take. The polity has an interest in having capable and decent citizens—individuals who understand the principles of the political morality of the polity and who live by them accordingly. But liberal polities also have reason to ensure that children are able to develop the talents and abilities they have and must use when deciding upon a direction in life. Liberal morality requires that children be allowed to develop in a manner that will enable them to fulfill their potential as autonomous beings, and this makes some governmental involvement in child development both appropriate and necessary.[5] Here, then, is another place where centralized governmental management is necessary and where decentralized arrangements are inconsistent with liberal morality.

This introduces a complicated issue that is an appropriate topic of discussion within liberal polities: How extensive should governmental regulation of child welfare be? The question, moreover, needs to be considered against the background of ethnic, religious, and cultural differences within the polity itself, differences that will invariably have significant implications for parental views on how best to raise children. It is best to put this issue aside for present purposes, however, and stick to thinking about the implications of wealth distribution for liberal standards of social justice. Suppose we rest content, then, with thinking that the government can at least require child education to a certain level and assume a responsibility for child welfare, provided that the resultant policies are consistent with the religious and cultural views of the various distinct communities that make up the polity.[6]

Once minimum educational and welfare conditions are established, parents will be expected to meet them on behalf of their children. What should the polity do, however, if parents lack the necessary resources? What should it do if meeting these conditions requires about all the resources parents have so that if they meet these conditions, or are required by the government to meet them, they will have virtually nothing left to meet their own needs? It seems reasonably easy to answer the first question. *If* the polity requires that certain educational and welfare standards be met for its future citizens and for incipient autonomous individuals, and if parents are unable to meet these standards, it seems incumbent upon government to find a way to meet them. The standards are in place because, according to liberal morality, all members of the polity deserve the opportunity to develop themselves as autonomous individuals. A child who has not received the kind of education that will enable her to direct how her life will go lacks the background conditions that allow the right to freedom to matter. And a child who has not had this kind of education, which is required to compete for social roles and the resources that accompany them, will be severely disadvantaged in competition with others who have had the necessary education.

If social roles and offices are legally open and available to all, both the well educated and those who have been deprived of an education are free to compete for them. But the equal freedom requirement here is satisfied in name only; in actual practice, those individuals without the necessary education will not win their competitions with the well educated. Equal freedom must mean something more than this. One would hardly think a state has satisfied the equal freedom condition if it has created a perpetual underclass, lacking the economic resources to meet the needs of their children and thus condemning those who belong to this class to low-paying and unfulfilling jobs, along with a privileged class with the resources to enable their children to compete for the more desirable slots in the polity. So, here equal freedom demands that government find a way to provide the necessary resources to needy parents and thus enable them to meet their children's educational and welfare needs. This, however, requires a degree of centralized management along with an element of resource redistribution—both conditions that again move us further from the libertarian ideal and toward what is now often called *welfare liberalism*, viz, governmental management of the general economic well-being of all citizens of the polity.

The other question about what to do when parental resources are so low that they cannot both meet their children's educational and welfare needs and still care for themselves is slightly more complicated. Suppose certain parents could meet the needs of two children effectively but elect to have ten children. Suppose parents have made poor economic choices in the past, perhaps spending their resources indulgently upon themselves, and are now unable to sustain themselves if they are to meet the needs of their children. Poor parental decisions, one might say, are things the parents themselves must live with, and the polity ought not subsidize their bad judgment. Such subsidies will invariably involve taking some of the hard-earned resources from other citizens and giving them to selfish and indulgent parents. If one believes that people are entitled to the wealth they earn, this would seem to make little sense from the standpoint of personal justice. If so, then government should see to it that their remaining resources are spent on their children and that they take what comes.

But what comes to them might not be good for their children either. Moreover, if the polity tells the parents that they *must* spend their meager resources on their children, it effectively does precisely what it seems unjust to do; it denies the parents the right and opportunity to decide what to do with their own resources, thereby effectively taking these resources from them. Since it is the welfare of the children that matters to the polity, and not the immaturity or selfishness of the parents, the proper end of social policy here would seem to be to meet the needs of the children and not to punish the parents. If it works an unmanageable hardship on parents to meet the educational and welfare needs of their children, then it would seem to be the responsibility of the polity to take on this responsibility in the most cost-effective manner possible. If parents cavalierly squander their resources with the expectation that the polity will see to the needs of their children, there may be reason to hold them accountable, for this looks like a form of stealing from the public treasury. Otherwise, social justice seems to require centralized management to see that the rights of children are protected in situations of this sort.

But imagine a different kind of scenario where parents genuinely care for their children and want to do what they can to make life go well for them. This is the natural tendency mentioned earlier, and it raises different, but equally troubling, questions of social justice. If parents are permitted to spend their personal resources as they see fit, many will no doubt decide to spend on their children in order to buy from the market the kind of education and training that will enable them to compete favorably for desirable slots. Those parents with greater resources will be able to spend more on their children than parents with more modest resources. They will, in effect, be able to pay for more and better schooling. Correspondingly, the ability of the children of the wealthy to develop the talents and abilities necessary to compete favorably for desirable slots will exceed the ability of children from less well-off families. If the respective efforts that children make remain roughly the same, the advantage will go to those children who have enjoyed the opportunity of better educational facilities and opportunities.

Social roles that bring large rewards in terms of desirable social goods should ideally go to those individuals best able to perform them. The ability being measured depends upon both natural talent and individual effort and initiative in refining and developing this talent. If natural talent is held equal, the competition for desirable slots should be won by those most successful in developing this talent. But given the impact that wealth has on the ability of children to develop their talents, the competition will default in favor of the wealthy. In fact, it is likely to default in favor of the wealthy even if natural talent is on the side of the less wealthy. This may result if the parents of the talented lack sufficient resources to provide their children with better and more sophisticated educational and training opportunities.

This situation is potentially dysfunctional and will actually be so if it happens that the children of the wealthy lack sufficient natural talent to meet the challenges of the social roles they win as effectively as the children of the less wealthy, in spite of the education and training they receive. If natural talent is roughly equal, for the most part, between socioeconomic classes, this might not be much of a problem. But questions of social justice still remain. In practice, the children of the less wealthy are unable to compete favorably for desirable slots. The prevailing socioeconomic conditions generate a situation where the more desirable slots will go to the children of the more wealthy, provided that the wealthy spend a sufficient amount of their resources to see to it that their children have educational and training advantages. The likely result is a class system in which the wealthy manage, for the most part, to retain their wealth while the poor, again for the most part, face little hope of social improvement.[7]

People wedded to the idea of letting decentralized market relations determine the distribution of social resources may dismiss this situation as unproblematic. Human beings cannot adjust completely for the consequences of fate and fortune; everyone is subject to the luck of the draw in certain ways. People do not choose their parents; nor can they choose their natural talents or the socioeconomic circumstances they are born into. Therefore, it might be supposed that everyone had best learn to live with a system of unequal wealth distribution that happens to favor the life prospects of the children of the wealthy. And of course there will always be some interclass movement. The particularly talented, able, and industrious of the less wealthy elements of society can, with hard work and effort, achieve desirable social slots or demonstrate effective initiative to gain considerable wealth, and some members of the wealthy class will squander their wealth rather than lavish it upon their children. Since no one is officially prohibited from competing for desirable slots or exercising the type of creativity and industry that will be rewarded in the market, decentralized market arrangements, it may be argued, remain proper and effective ways to distribute social roles and resources. That is, this method of resource distribution remains the most freedom respecting of all possibilities, and this should be the guide in a political culture that champions basic rights to life, liberty, and property.

Still, this view of the matter will not satisfy anyone who thinks that any competition for social resources that is weighted heavily in favor of the wealthy is objectionable on the grounds that it fails to meet the liberal standard of *equal* freedom. If the less wealthy are unable to compete effectively for all social roles and resources available in society, they will be irredeemably left behind in the struggle to achieve some measure of success, and thus satisfaction, in life. Given the advantages wealth commands, the wealthy are almost sure to get wealthier, and the poor are sure to continue to struggle. This does not mean, to be sure, that some of those belonging to the poorer classes in society will not manage to amass a great fortune in life through effort and industry; nor does it mean that all those who are wealthy will prevail in the struggle for still more wealth. But occasional exceptions to the inevitable trend do not negate the problem. The chances of the poor to achieve those things that people are taught to want in society will continue to decline and will continue to fall substantially below the chances of the wealthier members of society. And at some point, the ideal of equal freedom becomes something of a fraud in practice.

In one sense, there does not seem to be much reason for concern in any of this. Consider an analogy with athletic competitions. Athletes work to make their competitions as unequal as possible. Athletes practice, train, and work out in order to have an advantage over their opponents, and competitions are (ideally) won by participants with superior talents and abilities. At the moment, Roger Federer seems clearly to be the finest male tennis player in the world. He does not win all the matches he plays, of course, but he wins most of them. This is testimony to his natural athletic ability, but it also evidences the tremendous effort and hard work he has put into developing and refining his ability. There may be other players with equal or even superior ability, but if they fail to work as hard as Federer to make the most of their skill, they will probably not be able to beat him. And this is as it should be; this is why athletes train hard, work hard, and practice long hours. Athletes don't work hard so that they will have an equal chance of winning against their competition; they work hard so that they will have a better chance of winning than their competitors have. To put this another way, competitions test for inequalities, and they reward those with superior talents and abilities. From the standpoint of personal justice, this is as it should be. So, why should this view not control thinking about how social resources should be distributed as well?

The answer to this question has been anticipated by the previous reflections on the kind of inequality of opportunity brought about by the unequal distribution of social resources. Someone who thinks that considerations of personal justice alone should control the process by which social goods are distributed effectively asks others in the polity to close their eyes to the fact that unequal resources advantage some and disadvantage others when it comes to the opportunities people have to develop whatever ability they are born with. The development of an athlete, for example, requires training and coaching. Parents that can afford (and are willing) to purchase lessons and quality coaching for their children provide their children with a better opportunity for success than is available to parents who simply cannot afford similar training and coaching for their children. People don't usually worry about this sort of thing when an athletic competition begins, but it makes some sense to do so once one appreciates that social life in decentralized polities is a competitive event and that the general distribution of social goods depends upon success in this competition. Resource inequalities matter because they affect equality of opportunity, and equality of opportunity matters because those with less opportunity have less of a chance to do what they would like to do with their lives. In practice, those with diminished opportunity are simply less free to make of their lives what they would like to make of them, and this is inconsistent with the liberal ideal of equal freedom. Moreover, it is also socially dysfunctional, for reasons already encountered. There is simply no reason to suppose that the children of the wealthy are naturally more capable when it comes to filling important social roles than are the children of the poor.

The remedy to this problem is to find ways to redistribute social resources in order to balance the freedom of each against the freedom of all. There are a variety of ways this might be done, but all will seem objectionable to libertarian spirits. Government could mandate that parents can only spend so much on their children but that they must spend this much, or government could make educational and training facilities open and available to the less wealthy and spread the cost of these facilities across the entire citizenry. Government could subsidize less wealthy families by providing them with vouchers usable only for the education and training of their children, and so forth. It is hardly necessary to canvass here all the redistributive strategies government might employ to bring the equal freedom requirement into proper balance. What matters for present purposes is to note that the demands of social justice, that is, the need to make the equal freedom requirement a practical reality in the polity, press in the direction of increased governmental management—in the direction of greater political centralization.

LIBERALS AND CONSERVATIVES

The concerns of social justice again demonstrate the centralization paradox at work. Decentralized market methods of social resource distribution generate social injustices by compromising the equal freedom condition. Centralized management thus becomes necessary in order to guarantee that the demands of social justice can still be met in the face of market distortion. The more the market leads to inequalities of wealth that threaten the equal freedom condition, the more centralized management is required in order to provide the necessary correction. As society grows, as greater social wealth in distributable goods is generated, and as economic relations become more complex, the more complicated and demanding the job of managing resource distribution in the name of equal freedom becomes. Government grows as a necessary and inevitable response to social and economic growth.

This explains why the requirements of social justice are controversial within polities with liberal political cultures. Intuitively, freedom seems to demand decentralized distributive strategies. The requirements of personal justice also dictate that one is entitled to the fruits of one's own labor, and it is an intrusion upon the basic rights to freedom and property (and hence an injustice) to coercively take the wealth of some and redistribute it to others who have not earned it. Additionally, decentralized distributive strategies seem to be the most effective way to encourage human effort and initiative within the polity, and hence to get people to contribute to the well-being of the polity as a whole, either by seeking highly rewarded slots or by exercising initiative and creativity to provide the citizenry with desirable goods and services. Seen from this perspective, the centralized management of resource distribution is both unjust and inefficient.

But there is obviously another perspective. The concerns of liberal morality are put poorly if they are pressed entirely in terms of personal justice, for at some point liberal morality demands that attention be given to the equal freedom of all individuals in the polity. It is tempting to understand this to mean that the requirements of personal justice simply come into conflict with the demands of distributive justice at some point and that the conflict should be resolved in favor of the concerns associated with distributive justice. Libertarian spirits might find here reason to press an objection, for it might seem that preferring distributive to personal justice is a purely arbitrary move. But the temptation to understand the issue in terms of a conflict between personal and distributive justice should be avoided. In practice, the ideal of personal justice actually works against a background condition of *social* justice. Imagine a competition of some sort that tests certain talents and abilities, and suppose that some participants are permitted to train, practice, and work to refine the required talents and develop the abilities being tested but that others are not. It is not difficult to see which group the winners will likely emerge from, but can one then conclude that the winner deserves the award that goes with winning, on the grounds that this is what is required by personal justice? The problem with this conclusion is that there is no real competition here at all; some participants have been advantaged from the outset and others disadvantaged. What sense does it make, then, to say that the winner deserves an award for winning because she has demonstrated superior talent and ability. She has done this, to be sure, but everyone knew that she would prevail in the competition going into the event because of her tremendous advantage. There really is no true competition here because the game has been rigged, so to speak; some participants didn't have a chance, and due to no fault of their own. The competition can be made viable, and hence the demands of personal justice can only make sense, when competitors are not artificially disadvantaged from the outset. This is just another way to assert the importance of equal freedom, and this, in turn, indicates why standards of personal justice make sense only against a background condition of social justice.

To put the ideal of social justice into practice, it is necessary to do more than just remove legal barriers to the roles and opportunities available in society. Legal barriers, it turns out, are not the only artificial barriers to equal freedom; the barriers erected by unequal distributions of social resources constrain and limit the life opportunities of certain elements of the polity just as forcefully as legal barriers. These barriers result from the vicissitudes of market methods of resource distribution and constitute an injustice insofar as they compromise the equal freedom standard. One can eliminate these barriers in two ways: abandon market distribution strategies in favor of governmentally mandated patterns of distribution—let us imagine this as a form of socialism—or supplement market distribution strategies with centralized management policies intended to preserve market relationships *and* redistribute social resources in a manner that controls for artificial inequalities that disadvantage the life chances of some and advantage the life chances of others.

The second option is perhaps the most appropriate choice for liberal polities to make; it provides a meaningful place for the concerns of individual freedom and personal justice without compromising the standards of equal freedom and equal opportunity so crucial to liberal morality. But it also means that some form of welfare liberalism will be necessary in a polity with a political morality that is informed by liberal political culture. For the most part, this is the choice that has prevailed in the United States—and so much the worse for libertarianism. But if this is the choice that drives American public policy, it is also one that drives a good deal of debate and disgruntlement throughout American society. In fact, it is the source of a basic conflict within domestic American politics, a conflict that works colloquially to separate so-called *conservatives* from so-called *liberals*. These are classic terms of political thought that have taken on distinctive and rather unique meanings within the context of American politics. The liberal-conservative distinction comprehends a crucial battleground in contemporary American politics that now interjects an unproductive acrimony into the American political arena. Missed amid all this acrimony, ironically, is the fact that there is very little ideological difference between these two groups.

Imagine a spectrum running from one extreme of libertarianism (decentralized resource distribution) to the other extreme of socialism (thoroughly managed equal freedom). The political conservatives and liberals of American politics fall somewhere close to the middle of this spectrum, with conservatives tending toward the side of decentralization and liberals tending toward the side of centralized management. The difference, however, is one of degree, not of kind. Conservatives understand and respect the need for some management of resource distribution, and liberals concede the importance of relying upon decentralized strategies of resource distribution supported by redistributive strategies driven by the demands of social justice. Conservatives, or economic conservatives, are not libertarians, and liberals are not thoroughgoing socialists. They disagree over both the amount of centralization needed to balance the ideal of social justice with the ends of personal justice and the kinds of policies appropriate to this end, but not about the need for some form of welfare liberalism to redistribute social resources in the name of equal freedom.

This is the stuff of domestic politics in America. As should be apparent, it is driven by the tensions internal to America's liberal political morality. Liberal morality is not easily refined into a perfect picture of what social justice involves or of what the ideally just polity requires in the name of equal freedom. According to liberal morality, people should be the masters of their own lives, should be able to enjoy the fruits of their own labor, and should not be subject to coercive (unwanted) interference from others. But these concerns sit awkwardly beside one another in practice. If everyone is to enjoy the fruits of his or her own labor under market conditions, then some will eventually be less the masters of their own lives than others. Since the polity cannot rely upon goodwill and voluntary philanthropy to relieve this injustice, centralized government management is necessary to assure a modicum of equal freedom, and this often seems coercive.

To make matters worse, legitimate theoretical disagreement over the particular demands of social justice are often subverted by selfish and personal concerns. The wealthy typically do not want to surrender their wealth and don't like the idea that some of it should be redistributed to people that they don't think are very interested in hard work and personal development. Personal and class biases perhaps inevitably sneak into the debate over the most just distribution of social goods.

It might be good if people were less driven to acquire money and wealth, just as it might be good if there were fewer distributable social resources that money could buy. But it seems unlikely that either condition will ever be realized in the United States. America gets capable people in important social slots by buying their talents and abilities. For this to work, the polity needs to make the rewards attractive enough to the people to make them willing to work for them. Aside from the fact that capitalism is a growth economy that demands consumption, the desire to consume must underlie the desire for wealth. This is the final attraction that sends Americans in pursuit of wealth. It is, so to speak, the dark side of emphasizing the freedom of the individual to determine how her or his life will go, for the polity needs a way to get free people to decide to pursue socially important slots. If freedom of the individual is to be honored, it seems necessary to make people into personal self-aggrandizers, and because Americans have been so successful at this, it is also necessary to rely upon governmental management of resource distribution in the name of social justice. Short of a revolutionary transformation in America's liberal political culture, disputes between conservatives and liberals are sure to continue.

But it would be good to recognize that these disputes are not really over competing perceptions of the personal interests that individuals happen to champion, but over the nature of social justice itself. If it is understood and explored in this light, disputes between conservatives and liberals may have a more positive impact on American politics, and the debate may be properly focused upon issues that matter, and matter equally, to all Americans as fellow citizens of a common polity, and not just as individuals with personal interests in competition. Theoretical inquiry, freed from personal bias and class prejudice, can begin to offer insights into how liberal morality can be put into practice and into what a properly just polity should be like in practice according to the ideals associated with this morality. But it is also likely that this will always remain a work in progress, for as society changes and social resources change in value and significance, theoretical visions will need to be reconsidered. One thing seems certain, however; as liberal polities become larger and more complex, the demands of social justice will become both more demanding and more important to the well-being of the polity. The centralization paradox will continue apace, and redistributive strategies will gain in importance. Freed from its customary acrimony, the debate over the nature of social justice can begin to help shape a clearer sense of what justice requires of the polity. Transformed into a vital national seminar, it will permit the American polity to formulate a better vision of how social justice can be put into practice.

There is no perfect picture of an ideally just polity lying around somewhere in the cosmos waiting to be discovered and reproduced by some clever and pioneering political theorist. Any such picture must be forged by public reflection and discourse on what liberal morality demands of those citizens whose efforts support one another within the boundaries that define the liberal polity. Political theory can sharpen and direct public discourse, but it cannot replace it if the ideals of social justice are to become a concrete reality and not just a source of social division and conflict.

NOTES

1. While it is important to appreciate this point, it is also important to recall the qualifications previously introduced about the texture of cultural variety in pluralist polities. Liberal polities need not be homogeneous polities as well, and the ontology and normativity of liberal political culture will likely sit beside alternative cultural perspectives for some (and perhaps a great many) members of the polity.

2. Aristotle, *Nicomachean Ethics*, Bk. V. Aristotle actually uses the term "rectificatory justice," which differs slightly from the more modern notion of retributive justice, but for present purposes it seems appropriate to consider these notions as largely equivalent.

3. *Lochner v. New York*, 198 U.S. 45 (1905).

4. Ibid.

5. There is again reason to qualify this general statement in order to accommodate the realities of pluralism in liberal polities. The claim, for example, might be subject to important cultural exclusions, as the case of religious communities committed to faith healing, discussed previously, may illustrate.

6. These issues have raised some ticklish problems regarding the free exercise of religion that have been addressed by the U.S. Supreme Court. See, in particular, *Wisconsin v. Yoder*, 406 U.S. 205 (1972).

7. Cf. James Fishkin, *Justice, Equal Opportunity, and the Family* (New Haven, CT: Yale University Press, 1983).

Chapter Five

Liberal Institutions

> To inquire into the best form of government in the abstract (as it is called) is not a chimerical but a highly practical employment of scientific intellect.
>
> John Stuart Mill

So far it has been suggested that government is necessary, according to liberal political morality, to police and defend basic rights, to resolve a variety of large-scale social problems that might happen to arise, and to promote the ends of social justice. Liberal polities are stuck with government whether their citizens like it or not, and since government involves necessary limitations upon freedom, it is all but certain that citizens in a liberal polity will not like it. So, a certain ambivalence about government seems inevitable in polities where political consciousness is shaped by liberal morality.

Because liberal polities are stuck with government, it is important to explore the kind of government that is appropriate for a liberal political culture. This challenge introduces some additional questions that need to be examined when it comes to thinking about politics. How should government be structured? What kind of governmental institutions are appropriate? How should they be staffed? What kind of governmental division of labor, if any, is both efficient and appropriate? Given the need for and importance of government within liberal polities, these become crucial questions in need of answers.

POLITICS, POWER, AND AUTHORITY

Governments considered legitimate by those subject to them may be said to be *authorized* by the citizenry to police basic rights, address the demands of

127

social justice, and manage large-scale social problems. This requires a degree of knowledge and expertise. The individuals who come to occupy positions in government must be able to do the job expected of them. Therefore, polities will need to be able to attract talented and capable people to public service and be confident that the people they attract will have the training and skill necessary to meet the challenges and resolve the problems that government must address. This is crucial if citizens are to feel confident about authorizing the government to perform those functions expected of it. Governmental actions and decisions need to be considered *authoritative* by those subject to governmental authority. If the people do not think their government is authoritative, if they do not believe it has attracted individuals with the talent, knowledge, and ability to do the jobs expected of it, there is little reason for them to authorize government to exercise the power needed to meet these challenges.

If the first law of politics is that government needs the power to govern, the second law would seem to be that government must possess the authority required to govern well. To be in authority is to enjoy a right to command others, as well as the corresponding expectation of obedience from those subject to this authority. This implies that the legitimate exercise of authority is premised upon the public's assurance that those issuing commands are authorities on the subjects they have charge of.[1] A doctor cannot order her patient to stop smoking. But if a doctor tells her patient that he should stop smoking or risk suffering poor health and possibly death, the patient has reason to suppose that this warning is credible. Such credibility plays an important role in government, for if people do not think the commands and policies issued by governmental officials are credible or authoritative, they have little reason to endorse and follow them. Regardless of the form government takes, political authoritativeness is fundamental to the legitimacy of the government.

Knowledge is thus a key feature of government, but the nature and extent of the knowledge that government must have depends upon the problems it is called upon to manage. Imagine the simple libertarian vision of government: government protects basic rights and also defends the state against external threats. To perform these functions, government must have an understanding of the basic rights it is asked to police and the notion of social justice that evolves from these basic rights, along with some ability to fight wars in order to defend the state's borders. But the successful performance of these functions requires more than knowledge alone. To succeed in these functions, government needs to be able to raise armies and perhaps float navies and to maintain a monopoly of force within the polity in the event that some citizens attempt to amass sufficient power to abuse the basic rights of others without being stopped by government. It would make little sense to authorize government to perform these functions but deny it the power to get the job done. This is why it is necessary to admit that governments need the power to govern, and power, like knowledge, becomes an integral aspect of the authoritativeness of government.

Traditionally, the commingling of power and authority in governmental institutions is conceptualized in terms of the *sovereignty* of the state. Those individuals holding political power need to be recognized as *sovereign*, or as the supreme power in the state answerable to no other more powerful authority. Sovereignty is the logical consequence of admitting the need for government. If some group or individual is charged with performing certain necessary social functions for the state, its word must be final, and its decisions need to be binding. If some other group can exercise the final say in the matter despite what government officials have said, that group is the true sovereign. Final decision-making authority in government must rest somewhere, and if government is to manage to do the job people expect of it, the ultimate power to make these decisions binding must rest somewhere as well. Taken together, these two abilities designate sovereign power.

Authoritativeness is a basic component of sovereignty. If the great bulk of the citizenry doesn't think governmental officials know what they are doing, or if they think these officials are deliberately policing basic rights in a biased or inefficient fashion, they may decide there is no longer sufficient reason to obey the decisions and commands of government, and they may elect to change their government, either by revolution or by more peaceful means. A government with the brute power to prevent this may be able to maintain political control, but it will now function as a tyranny void of any justifiable claims to sovereign authority. But government does require the power to make sure that its authoritative decisions and commands are obeyed in the event that some citizens challenge this authoritativeness.

So once again the paradox of power manifests itself. But the power associated with state sovereignty should no longer seem so terribly paradoxical. The threat of the abuse of power from government can be effectively checked and constrained if it is understood and exercised against the background supplied by the polity's political culture. This culture informs the polity on the nature and source of political authority in the polity, as well as on the nature and character of the constraints upon the power of government. In liberal polities, government must police basic rights, but it must also respect them, and it is important for all elements of the polity to recognize and acknowledge this. This includes those individuals who serve the public in governmental institutions as well as those who remain subject to the authority of these institutions.

These comments are a prelude to thinking about governmental structure. They suggest that the problem of power cannot be resolved by means of institutional architecture alone. If power corrupts, as Lord Acton supposed, it will corrupt those who have it regardless of governmental structure. If ambition is made to check ambition, as Madison supposed it should be, it is difficult to see how government will be able to govern, or how governmental institutions can avoid a deadlock that jeopardizes their effectiveness. When it comes to designing the government of a liberal polity, it is necessary to consider the requirements of the political culture as well as the kinds of functions government is expected to perform and the practical problems it is required to resolve. The polity must be able to attract to public service individuals with the talents and abilities required to get the job of governing done, and the institutions of government must be structured in a fashion that enables government to work in a suitable and efficient manner. But these needs must also be met in a fashion consistent with the requirements of liberal morality; governmental institutions must be put together and must operate in a fashion that respects the basic rights of all citizens in the polity.

FORMS OF GOVERNMENT

Historically, forms of government have been distinguished from one another by looking to the place where sovereign power resides in the state—a view of the matter as old as the philosopher Aristotle.[2] Ancient philosophers writing on politics identified three ideal or pure structural possibilities for government. Monarchy (kingship) exists when sovereign authority is in the hands of a single individual. Monarchy is an easily recognizable form of government, but it introduces some troubling problems of succession. When the monarch dies, who takes over? Monarchies typically resolve this problem by identifying a ruling family with a right of inheritance to the throne of political power, but of course this works best if there is a readily discernible heir to the throne. Since the rightful heir to sovereign power might be a matter of dispute, *succession*—the transference of political power—tends to be a source of political instability in monarchies. (Graft, corruption, and palace intrigue were historically sources of political instability in monarchies also, but this is true of other forms of government as well and need not be a problem for monarchies with political cultures that encourage a high degree of loyalty to the royal family.)

A second form of government, popularly known as aristocracy, lodges sovereign authority in a ruling elite, usually a collection of the most wealthy and established members of the state. If sovereign power is lodged in an aristocracy identifiable by social position and wealth, aristocracy, like monarchy, offers no guarantee that the individuals holding sovereign power will actually have the knowledge required to govern. If the aristocracy lacks the required knowledge, it is hardly a desirable form of government. It can be transformed into an adequate form of government, on the other hand, if the ruling elite (classically the *aristos*) is trained and educated to be authorities on the functions government is to perform. This would transform aristocracy into a *meritocracy*—a system of government in which sovereign power is lodged in the hands of those individuals best educated and trained to perform the functions of government. If aristocracy is not transformed into a meritocracy, it is not a terribly desirable form of government, unless the *aristos* is willing to listen to experts on the functions of government and follow their advice.

Democracy is the third form of government identified by ancient thinkers. It involves placing sovereign power in the hands of the *demos*—the people who enjoy the status of citizen. On its face, democracy looks like a terribly foolish form of government. For one thing, there are questions about who should be a citizen and have the right to participate in the governmental process. No democracies permit everyone living within their borders to be citizens. In the United States, a self-proclaimed democracy, resident aliens and children are not permitted to vote in public elections. And voting is about the only public act asked or expected of American citizens. Moreover, suffrage rights have been hard won by many Americans, including minorities and women, long denied the right to participate in the political process. These denials, however, did not stop Americans historically from thinking of their form of government as democratic. Whether or not this is an accurate description of American government, even with greatly expanded (if not comprehensive) suffrage rights, remains to be seen.

For another thing, democracies also suffer from the problem of knowledge. States are going to be in trouble if no one in society possesses the knowledge required for effective government, but it is surely not the case that *everyone* possesses this knowledge. By placing sovereign power in the hands of many who may well be politically incompetent, it looks like democracies make the horrific mistake of letting the inmates run the asylum.

It is possible to defend against this by educating and training the people in the information relevant to the functions of government. But this seems as impossible as it does pointless, particularly if the state in question is of any size. This would defeat the social division of labor of which government is a part. If everyone were educated sufficiently to participate effectively in government, there would be little time left to train people to perform other necessary social functions. Ideally, democracy permits all persons likely to be affected by a governmental decision to have some input into the decision process. Since just about all citizens would likely be affected by governmental actions, all citizens should be involved in the decision process. This form of government is usually called *direct* democracy. Under direct democracy, the people introduce policy options, discuss them, and then vote on them, with some form of majority rule (either simple majority or super majority) carrying the day.

Direct democracy obviously exacerbates the problem of knowledge and expertise. It rests on the idea that people ultimately are the best judge of their interests, and therefore they should be allowed to determine collectively what policies the government will adopt and implement.[3] But it is unlikely that all persons in the polity will have a comprehensive and accurate grasp of their best interests. Further, direct democracy looks rather unattractive from the standpoint of liberal morality. Even if it were possible to be confident that citizens generally have the education and expertise to know how best to address political problems, the logistics of direct democracy are simply imponderable if the polity is very large. Citizens would spend virtually all their time governing themselves and would thus become slaves to the governmental process.

If initially the job of government did not take much time, people would be free to pursue their own independent enterprises. But these freely undertaken enterprises would quickly create additional problems (e.g., collective action problems, problems of unintended consequences, etc.) that require government to manage. With increased demands upon government would come increased demands upon the time of the people, and soon they would be unable to pursue their independent interests because they have become overwhelmed with the responsibilities of self-government. The centralization paradox guarantees that the job of government will become more complex and time consuming as society grows larger and more complicated. But the more time people spend attending to government the less time they have to do as they please. And this undermines the commitment to liberty central to liberal morality. Ironically, one of the chief virtues of government as an institution in liberal cultures is that it takes the job of government off the backs of the people, but this is exactly where direct democracy puts it. So liberal political cultures have reason not to care terribly for direct democracy.[4]

It seems, then, that none of the classic forms of government are without their problems. Perhaps, however, at least some of these problems can be surmounted and some form of government made to appear more acceptable than initially seems to be the case. This, in any event, is a possibility that needs to be explored. One way to begin is to contend that governmental form should contribute in some way to the domestication of the problem of political power. Monarchy is objectionable, some might wish to argue, because it gives complete sovereign power to a single individual who will then be tempted to abuse this power and advantage himself to the corresponding disadvantage of the rest of the citizenry. Aristocracy is no remedy for this since the ruling elite may elect to govern in a way that works to their advantage and to the disadvantage of the remainder of the citizenry. The likely result of an aristocratic form of government, particularly in the absence of a shared political culture, is tyranny of the minority; aristocracy is vulnerable to decay into *oligarchy*—something the philosopher Aristotle defined as the rule of an elite in its own interest and to the detriment of the rest of the polity.[5]

Democracy may seem attractive as an alternative to forms of government where the abuse of political power is likely and where institutional constraints necessary to prohibit this possibility are lacking. But democracy admits a form of tyranny as well—tyranny of the *majority*. If democracy runs upon the standard of majority rule (and we can put aside for the moment what is to count as a satisfactory majority), then majorities can always carry the day, and minorities will always lose. Since there is no reason to suppose that majorities will know the best direction for the state to take, this situation looks no better than what might be encountered under conditions of minority tyranny.

Perhaps it is wrong to make too much of majority tyranny. It could be argued, for example, that there really are no entrenched majorities and minorities in society; instead, social demographics might be such that people move between the majority and minority depending upon the way general public sentiment lines up on distinct policy issues.[6] Jones might happen to hold a view that is in the majority on energy policy and a view that happens to be in the minority with regard to campaign finance spending, and so forth. This is certainly a possibility, but it does not offer much solace if social demographics are culturally, religiously, ideologically, and ethnically diverse. Practitioners of faith healing are in a decided minority in the United States, and if the public voted on whether the children of groups whose members practice faith healing should receive medical treatment when they become deadly ill, the medical requirement would most likely pass. Telling those Pentecostal communities that practice faith healing that they may hold majority views with regard to campaign finance reform will not likely offer them much solace. From where they stand, a vote of this sort would deny them their religious freedom and would constitute an intrusion into their basic rights—the sort of injustice that people in liberal cultures think deserves the name of tyranny when the shoe is on the other foot.

The most promising way to avoid the problem of majority tyranny is to adopt a constitutional form of government. Constitutions are the formative documents of government; they *constitute* the government when their terms are understood and accepted by the members of the polity they form. They introduce the legal boundaries of the polity, but they must also correspond to and express the political culture of the polity. Not just any old constitution can be grafted onto a given society. The constitution must fit the society by being an adequate expression of the society's political culture. If the jurisdiction to be covered by a given constitution lacks a common and generally shared political culture, the state established by the constitution is likely to be unstable no matter how wise and compelling the constitution might happen to be.

There is, in all of this, a clue about how people sharing a political culture shaped by standards of liberal morality can begin to develop governmental institutions. The first thing to keep in mind here is that freedom matters in liberal political cultures, and where these political cultures are also characterized by exceptional religious, ethnic, and ideological diversity, the protection of freedom involves guaranteeing that majorities will not impose their will upon minorities. To achieve this, a constitution may be in order.

CONSTITUTIONALISM

What should a constitution designed to fit a liberal political culture do? What should it look like? Should it be a complete and developed legal system, or should it be a formative document that tells those subject to it what things have the status of law and what things do not? Should the constitution be considered fixed, immutable, and unalterable, or should it be possible to introduce constitutional amendments when and if necessary? If one decides to allow for amendments, what kind of amendment process seems to be in order? These are questions that must be answered in order to make constitutional government intelligible. If they cannot be answered satisfactorily, it is hard to know what kind of governmental structure will work for societies with liberal political cultures.

Constitutions are established to endure through time. It would do little good to write a constitution that will be outdated in, say, twenty years. Constitutions must also be considered legal documents; they form and structure a legal system that governs both government and citizenry alike. That is, they initiate a *rule of law* that controls and constrains the actions of both public and private citizens. Constitutions are to be followed and not ignored; if people ignore them, they are no good. If public officials ignore them, they subvert the political process they are presumably committed to serve. Constitutions, then, should be considered fundamental law. They are, as the U.S. Constitution declares, "the supreme law of the land," the foundation of the rule of law within the polity.[7] In states with constitutions that serve as fundamental law, it is correct to say that no person is above the law. Everyone must follow and abide by the law established and inspired by the constitution.

But times change. New problems emerge for government, and if governments are to endure, they need the authority to do what is necessary to meet the new challenges they must face. Constitutions are intended to endure through the ages, but if they are too rigid and fixed, they may constrain governmental authority in a way detrimental to government's ability to govern effectively. When the demands of public management require government to exercise a power the constitution does not allow it to have, something must give. Either the constitution must be changed or ignored, or it must be followed, with the problems government needs to address left to tear at the fabric of the polity. Constitutions are important, but they are not so important that a strict adherence to them takes precedence over the well-being of the polity. When time and circumstances demand it, constitutions must be changed or ignored, or states must find subtle and clever ways to "change" the document without appearing to change it.

There is, then, an inherent contradiction in the notion of constitutionalism. Constitutions must be presumed to endure through the ages and to establish and guide the law of the land. They resonate a political wisdom that should be followed for the welfare of the polity. But constitutions also need to be changed as times and circumstances demand. They are not straightjackets that hold captive the civil arrangements they constitute. It is important to maintain some appreciation for the eternal and authoritative character of constitutions, but in the end, the job of government is a human enterprise that necessitates the exercise of human judgment. It may be in constitutional systems that no one is above the law, but even here people proceed to govern each other through the artifice of the rule of law.

Questions about how the constitution should be changed and amended matter greatly. If it is easy to amend the constitution, if the supreme law of the land can be changed with ease and whimsy, there is not much point to having a constitution in the first place. If, on the other hand, it is too hard to amend the constitution, there might not be sufficient time to change the document to allow government to have the authority it needs to respond to the emergent problems it must address. One way to resolve this problem is to suppose that constitutions should not be complete legal systems unto themselves; instead, they should empower government to make law necessary to meet social needs and manage society effectively. If, however, the constitution merely establishes governmental institutions and empowers them to make any and all law that these institutions see fit, if, that is, it places no limitations upon the authority of government, it really doesn't do very much.

The holders of offices within the institutions established by the constitution may do whatever they wish, or whatever they think necessary, unconstrained by law. Governmental authority under these circumstances would be absolute. Of course, the constitution would still matter if it dictates how individuals who come to occupy the institutions of government are to be chosen. If *this* condition was left to those individuals occupying these institutions, say, after an initial strategy of staffing government, then the constitution would indeed be pointless.

So, constitutions, if they are to matter and still be able to endure, must do at least two things. First they must delineate the reach and limits of governmental authority, and second they must indicate how the institutions of government are to be staffed. The first condition empowers government to manage large-scale social problems within the polity; it introduces the law-making power of government. But constitutions should also limit this power and articulate civil liberties that protect citizen freedom from governmental intrusion. The second condition establishes the rules according to which people will come to hold offices in the institutions of government, that is, *public* offices. To these it is appropriate to introduce a third condition that viable constitutions must satisfy: they must dictate the rules governing how constitutions are to be amended.

The first condition is especially controversial because it confronts the centralization paradox, but it can be supposed that at some initial point of constitutional articulation and public ratification, the basic sentiments of the state's political culture will be acknowledged within the constitution. In liberal polities, this means that governmental authority must be sufficient to protect the basic rights and address the various coordination, collective action, and unintended consequence problems. The necessary authority is obviously indeterminate, but if constitutions simply declare broad grants of governmental authority to address problems, they effectively state, as we have seen, that governmental authority is absolute. If they fail to do this, on the other hand, they may need to be either amended or ignored at some future date as the centralization paradox works its will. One way to counter problems of this sort is to grant government broad authority to perform the functions and meet the challenges with which governments must deal, but also to put basic and unconditional constraints upon certain types of government activities through the constitutional articulation of appropriate civil liberties. In liberal polities, these will guarantee individuals a broad range of freedoms to operate autonomously, consistent with the opportunity of others to operate in this way as well.

Given the liberal commitment to individual liberty, and the necessary concessions about the important functions government must perform, this is not an altogether inappropriate compromise for liberal polities to make. The second condition, on the other hand, raises some curious problems in its own right. As noted already, in liberal polities, public offices should be open to everyone; this is a fundamental condition of respect for personal freedom. But governmental offices are also important slots, and it is necessary to recall here the importance of getting qualified and capable people into such jobs. Government must resolve large-scale social problems of various and indeterminate sorts. To do this, it will require a variety of different abilities and expertise, and it will need to be open to adding additional experts in the future as the management of public affairs places new demands upon government. So, the appropriate talent and expertise are important factors in determining who should be awarded at least certain kinds of governmental jobs.

This thought generates two important questions. First, who decides which individuals have the appropriate talent and expertise to fill governmental slots, and second, should a liberal polity provide citizens with training and education in governmental service in order to make them eligible for governmental slots in the event that they elect to pursue this career option? The first question asks about who should measure the mastery of the masters, and put this way, it is all but impossible to answer. Only the masters themselves can measure their own mastery. So it might seem that the masters should simply appoint themselves to governmental posts. But one might still wonder about what kinds of experts, what kind of talent, and what kind of education is necessary for governmental service. Which masters should be permitted into the governmental process? The second question stumbles upon problems suggested by these questions. If it is decided that education and training for governmental service really is necessary, what kind of education, and what sort of training, is appropriate? If citizens don't know the type of mastery necessary for government, they will be unable to determine how to train the masters they need.

Perhaps this predicament can be overcome by stipulating that the first institution of government should be established with the authority to answer questions of this sort. This institution would be charged with making decisions about the kinds of problems that need governmental management and the kinds of masters that are appropriate for this purpose. The constitution could authorize this initial institution to create supplementary institutions to address the managerial needs of the polity as conceived by the initial institution. Since this implies that the initial institution must have the authority to set *public policy*—to identify ends to be achieved by government and to set the means by which these ends will be achieved—it can be called it a *legislature*, since this is the traditional role of legislative bodies.

Of course, with the introduction of a legislature to be established by the constitution, staffing problems simply recur. How should the legislature be staffed, and what expertise is necessary for legislators to have? These questions need to be asked against the background awareness that public offices should be open to all. Since it seems impossible to put any definitive answers to these questions abstractly, it might be best to structure the constitution in a manner that leaves these issues to the citizens of the polity themselves. If the citizenry is sensitive at all to the needs and concerns of the polity, their collective will could be employed to staff the initial institution. This participatory element of constitutional government might even seem required by the liberal commitment to freedom. A concern for freedom would seem to necessitate citizen input into the process by which citizens are governed. This means that citizens should be eligible to hold slots in the legislature, but they should also be permitted to have some input into who eventually is awarded a place in the legislature.

This indicates a need for elections, and if elections are to matter, they will need to be competitive. There is little point to an election if the outcome is a foregone conclusion. When elections are competitive, the electorate is able to compare the qualifications of candidates seeking a place in the legislature and evaluate their views about the policy options the legislature should pursue. To institutionalize this selection process, elections can be mandated by the constitution, and specific times and circumstances under which elections will be held can be officially established.

But competitive elections are only the first step in resolving problems about how to staff the legislature. Since these are important governmental slots, it is necessary to make sure that they will attract capable people. In a decentralized social system where individual talents and abilities are purchased in a market arrangement, this means that legislative slots must offer people those things they are taught to want. It would violate the liberal commitment to freedom to draft some individuals considered appropriately talented and require them to enter government service. So government must compete with all other social services and occupations for the most talented and capable people. This might mean attaching hefty monetary compensation to legislative slots, but it might also involve attaching esteem and honor to these slots in order to make them attractive and assure that they do not become at the same time a terrible drain on the wealth of the general public who must ultimately pay for governmental workers.

This seems to be a plausible first step in building a constitution. It is difficult to build respect and esteem for legislative service into the constitution, but it is possible to encourage the development of a culture that displays and encourages a view of legislative service as an honorable profession, and reasonably attractive monetary compensation can be constitutionally established. The first requirement of constitutional architecture, then, would seem to involve fashioning a constitution that establishes legislative slots to be filled by competitive elections and that attaches desirable rewards to these slots so that reasonably bright and accomplished individuals are attracted to them. The citizens themselves (a status to be determined officially by constitutional stipulation but informed by the liberal commitment to freedom) are then constitutionally mandated to examine the candidates for legislative slots, review and consider candidate thoughts on how they think they should proceed in office, and decide between them by means of a vote. This would also build an element of democracy into the political system if citizen involvement in the electoral process constitutes sufficient public participation in politics to qualify the system as democratic—an issue to which we shall return below. While this is hardly a direct democracy, competitive elections do provide the citizenry with the opportunity to participate in the process by which it is governed.

A political system of this sort is ordinarily described as a *representative democracy* to distinguish it from direct democracy. In a representative democracy, the people themselves are not responsible for policy formation, but through the electoral process, they have the opportunity to review the activities of their representatives and to vote accordingly if they are unhappy with their behavior. If legislative offices are attractive enough and if elections are genuinely competitive, capable individuals who happen to think that some legislative activities are inappropriate may well decide to attempt gaining a seat in the legislature. Thus the electoral process should facilitate public debate on legislative policy through a campaign process associated with public elections.

Other problems and issues surround the formation of a legislature, and these also require constitutional articulation. How large should the legislature be? How should representation be apportioned? Should all citizens vote for all legislative slots, or should legislative slots be elected by jurisdictional subunits of the polity? If jurisdictional subunits are decided upon, how big should they be, and how can representational equality be guaranteed so that citizen input into the governmental process will be relatively equal, as required by liberal morality? These are important technical matters that require a constitutional remedy, but it is perhaps best to put them aside for present purposes in order to consider if there are other institutional requirements a constitution should address.

Legislatures set policy and enact it officially by means of the legislative process. But difficult problems remain. If the polity is large, the problems it must address are likely to be complex, and there is no reason to think that legislators will have all the knowledge, information, and expertise to successfully address all of them. Further, someone must implement the policy shaped and articulated by the legislature. If legislators themselves were required to perform this function, there would probably be little time for them to do anything else. A legislature with the ability to manage and oversee all the real, potential, and emerging problems in a large polity would have to be huge. And the bigger the legislature gets, the more difficult it will be for it to get anything done. It looks, then, like some governmental functions will need to be left to others. For the sake of efficiency, it seems best to leave it to the legislature to establish and staff certain auxiliary governmental institutions whose specific purpose is to address and manage the social problems identified as in need of centralized management.

But how should all this be implemented? By what process do these auxiliary governmental institutions come into being, and how do citizens know that they are doing what the legislature has asked them to do? In traditional political terms, the authority to make law is only one dimension of sovereignty; the sovereign must also be able to enforce the law it makes. Legislatures need help in making sure that the policy it sets is dutifully executed, and the laws it makes duly enforced. If legislatures pass laws necessary to guarantee that the basic rights are respected throughout the polity, it is also necessary to see to it that these laws are obeyed and honored by the general public. These laws, in other words, need to be enforced, and in traditional political terms, this has been understood to mean that an *executive* office is necessary to authoritatively enforce the laws passed by legislatures, for it would be too much to require legislatures to do this themselves.

Moreover, some managerial structure is required in order to organize and oversee the various auxiliary institutions the legislature must establish in order to manage the large-scale social problems government needs to address. The legislature could undertake this function, but as governments develop both in terms of size and complexity—thanks to the centralization paradox—the job of governmental management will become increasingly time consuming. In order to avoid overburdening the legislature with this work, which would limit the time the legislature can spend considering the kinds of functions government needs to perform and the direction that public policy should take, it makes some sense to lodge this responsibility in the executive office as well. This seems like a reasonable division of governmental labor; the legislature will spend its time engaged in the legislative process (articulating law and policy) and leave the execution of these laws and policies to an executive office.

The framers of the U.S. Constitution decided to place these separate functions of government in separate institutions, with the Congress performing the legislative function and the president performing the executive function.

By constitutional design, this was intended to check against the abuse of governmental authority by designing a natural antagonism in government. Each branch of government should ideally perform its functions in a manner that keeps an eye on the other branch and checks the possibility that the other branch will abuse its power. Given the size and complexity of the United States and the logic of the centralization paradox, this seems in retrospect like a wise decision. Independent of any concern for checking the abuse of power residing in one institution, this division of labor seems necessary if government is to work efficiently in a complex and troubled political setting. Yet it is a decidedly cumbersome process, and while it has worked reasonably well to date, it is also a recipe for governmental *deadlock*. If each branch frustrates the efforts of the other, how can government get anything done?

The problem of deadlock might be defeated by building the executive function into the legislature and permitting the legislature to hold the executive accountable, creating, in effect, a *parliamentary system* in which one legislator or minister (a prime minister) assumes the executive function. This has the advantage of efficiency even if it expands the potential for legislative abuse. If, however, legislative posts are elected by the people (if, that is, the legislature serves at the pleasure of the citizenry), there is an evident democratic check on legislative abuse.

But there is another way to guard against legislative abuse. Constitutions, once again, are paramount law, and they can both constrain and empower governmental institutions by articulating the bounds of governmental authority. But how can the citizenry (or for that matter, public officials) tell whether some legislative action is really authorized by the Constitution? How can one tell whether a governmental institution is constitutionally authorized to make certain policy or whether this policy falls into a prohibited zone where government is not constitutionally authorized to act? Consider, for example, the Constitution of the United States. Some of the rules contained in the Constitution are clear and rather exact. To serve as president, for example, the Constitution states that a person must be a natural-born American of at least thirty-five years of age.[8] It also prohibits the legislature from issuing bills of attainder and from making *ex post facto* laws.[9] These rules are reasonably clear, and it should be evident how to follow them, as well as when they have not been followed. But other rules are less clear, and their ambiguity raises certain difficulties. The Constitution authorizes Congress to regulate commerce with foreign states, Indian tribes, and among the several states.[10] But what does "regulate" mean, and what is "commerce"? And how should one interpret the phrase "among the several states"? The First Amendment to the Constitution is also explicit: "Congress shall make no law" that restricts, among other things, free speech. But what is free speech? Or, more to the point, what speech should be held to be free? Should deliberately false advertising be considered speech not to be regulated by government? Is a protest demonstration a form of speech?

The legislature or the executive could be empowered to settle these questions, but if this strategy is built into the constitution, the document would allow these institutions to determine their own authority and to decide for themselves the appropriate limits to this authority. This again introduces the possibility of the abuse of their constitutional authority. An alternative possibility is to lodge the function of interpreting the Constitution and declaring its meaning as law—something called the *judicial function*—in another institution of government. Since the responsibility for settling legal disputes in the Anglo-American political tradition is situated in courts of law, it might be good to establish a judicial institution, a Supreme Court, with the definitive authority to declare the meaning of the Constitution and hence to decide the proper realm of authority of the legislative and executive functions under the Constitution. There may be no particular reason to follow political tradition here, of course, but the judicial function in a complex political system is likely to take a good deal of time and require a good deal of expertise in its own right. Therefore, establishing a separate judicial branch of government again seems like a reasonable division of labor, though of course staffing problems again arise. How can the citizenry be sure that individuals who gain slots in the judiciary will have the expertise necessary to do the job well?

As most Americans know, the Constitution places the judicial function in a third institution of government, the Supreme Court. But it does not explicitly empower the Court to act as the authoritative interpreter of the Constitution. And as most Americans also well know, the Supreme Court does act as the final authority on the meaning of the Constitution by exercising the authority of *judicial review*—that is, the authority to hear cases and controversies involving the actions of governmental officials (either legislative or executive) and declaring upon whether they are authorized by the Constitution or whether they exceed the constitutional authority of the offices in question. But the Court came by this authority as a matter of historical circumstance rather than as a matter of constitutional design.[11]

Few Americans complain about the Court's authority of judicial review. It has the salutary consequence of requiring the other institutions of government to play by constitutional rules, as the Court understands them, and thus it restrains the authority of the legislature and the executive at least in principle. But it also makes the Supreme Court an extraordinarily powerful institution of government. It may be good to have a court sit to restrain the actions of the legislature and executive, but who restrains the power of the court? In the American context, it is customary for judges to acknowledge that they must restrain themselves—or practice *judicial self-restraint*—but if this is carried to extremes, the court abdicates its responsibility to keep the other institutions within the confines of the Constitution. If, however, the court actively works to guarantee that these other institutions play by constitutional rules, *as the court understands them*, it may unwittingly frustrate the ability of government to respond to the problems it needs to manage. Once again, government needs the authority to govern, and constitutions, if they are to endure, cannot become straightjackets that frustrate the governmental process. Interpretive institutions like the Supreme Court, then, face tough duty. They must enforce appropriate constitutional limitations upon governmental institutions, but they must also permit these institutions to exercise the authority they need to govern. The latter concern naturally tends to swallow the former concern, but if government is to do the work required of it, this cannot be viewed as such a bad thing.

But this is also a source of possible political tension. Government exists, under liberal political morality, to police and protect basic rights. But of course the great irony in this is that sometimes government must limit or restrict these rights in order to manage large-scale social problems and maintain a roughly equal liberty for all citizens of the polity. If at least some of these basic rights are articulated in the constitution in the form of civil liberties, their meaning is likely to become a matter of public dispute. When, if at all, and under what circumstances can government set aside the rights of some in the name of the public good? And what exactly is one allowed to do in the name of, say, the free exercise of religion, an obvious candidate for a basic right? These disputes need an authoritative resolution, and hopefully one that will promote rather than retard equal liberty throughout the polity. If disputes of this sort are defined as legal, it will fall to the judiciary to resolve them. But how can the citizenry be sure that the courts will do a good job of this? To leave this matter to the democratic process would reintroduce the problem of majority tyranny. But if the matter is left to the courts, it might result in a form of minority tyranny. If the judiciary is charged with interpreting the constitution and the civil liberties that help define the liberal ideal of freedom that is to be built into the constitution, what political or legal recourse does the citizenry have to address possible abuses of the judicial function by the court?

Constitutional architecture, it seems, is tricky business. It is no doubt a good idea to constrain the authority of government by means of a constitution, but a constitution that comes to operate as a straightjacket and constrains government to the point that it is unable to function is hardly worth the paper it is printed on. Before George Orwell wrote *1984*, he published a short fairy tale called *Animal Farm*. The story, among other things, is a lovely treatment of the perils of constitutional government. The animals on Orwell's imagined farm rebelled against the authority of the farmer, threw him out, and established their own egalitarian governmental system complete with a constitution stating the fundamental political principles they would live by. But the pigs, under the leadership of one character named Napoleon, managed to take totalitarian control of the farm nonetheless and to assure their legitimacy by manipulating and rewriting the constitution to suit their needs.

As with *1984*, *Animal Farm* can be read as a warning about what may well befall states that lose sight of their own political culture. The animals on the farm were easily manipulated because they failed to understand, or even remember, the principles written in their own constitution. Orwell's story is a chilling warning to polities that think constitutions can guarantee that government will not abuse its authority. People, including government officials, are not easily restrained by words on parchment. They can be restrained only by a citizenry that remains familiar with the principles upon which its government is founded and that remains clear on the purposes this government is established to address. Constitutions can be useful things, but there is no substitute for a politically astute citizenry if things are to go well in the polity.

DEMOCRACY

Given the problems inherent in constitutionalism, perhaps it would be better to opt for a different form of government. Liberal morality also suggests that some form of democracy might be appropriate for liberal polities. The right to freedom guarantees individuals a maximum amount of control over their lives consistent with an equal amount of freedom for others. But citizens of any polity must also be subject to the authority of their government. Although the point is a matter of considerable contention among political philosophers, it is commonly supposed that citizens have an obligation to obey their governments. If government is to be effective in managing public affairs and protecting basic rights, a high degree of citizen acceptance of government is necessary, and the practical expression of this acceptance (or the acknowledgement of the government's legitimacy) is to obey the laws and lawful commands of government.

But how is the acceptance of governmental authority reconcilable with the ideal of freedom? If some people are subject to the commands of others, that is, if citizens are subject to the commands of their governors, it would seem that governors will enjoy a freedom not available to citizens. This is inconsistent, on its face, with the ideal of equal freedom. One might respond to this by noting that governors are also subject, as citizens, to the laws they make.

But even so, those individuals who hold political office, even in a representative democratic system, and enjoy the authority to make law still seem to possess a freedom, viz, making and changing the law (even within constitutional parameters), that others don't have. So it looks as if the ideal of equal freedom must be something of a fiction, and the polity must be divided into two groups: sovereigns and subjects.

One response to this dilemma can be presented in terms of a democratic form of government. Democracy lodges sovereignty in the people— something that is generally referred to as *popular sovereignty*. If everyone in the polity is permitted, even encouraged, to participate in the governmental process—if, that is, everyone participates in the lawmaking process—then everyone in the polity qualifies as both sovereign and subject, and citizens are required to obey only those laws they legislate for themselves.[12] So, democratic government recognizes and respects the ideal of freedom, and this makes it an appropriate form of government according to liberal morality.

Democratic theory, however, must confront the issue of citizenship mentioned earlier. It is certainly too strong to say that everyone in the state should be permitted to participate in the democratic process. Should citizenship status be granted to newborn infants, children, the mentally infirm, or resident aliens? If democratic participation is restricted to citizens of the polity, who should count as a citizen? Definitions of citizenship can be quite restrictive. In the formative years of the United States, only white male property holders over the age of twenty-one were allowed to participate in the democratic process. By today's standards, this is intolerably restrictive, but it hardly bothered the most egalitarian liberals of the eighteenth century. Still, the equal freedom condition suggests that all people that make their home in the polity should be accorded the status of citizenship once they reach the age of adulthood—whatever that is understood to be.

The standard is admittedly arbitrary. If the adulthood requirement is necessary to guarantee that only able and astute individuals capable of understanding the responsibility that comes with citizenship are entitled to participate in the democratic process, then virtually any interpretation of adulthood is bound to be inadequate. There are probably many fifteen-year-old people who can exercise the wisdom and responsibility necessary for citizenship, and there are probably many fifty-year-olds who cannot do so. But some line must be drawn, and consequently, some capable individuals will be excluded, and some incapable ones will be included.

Additionally, the problem of resident aliens remains. Citizenship is another boundary that defines the political realm; it distinguishes those considered members of the polity for purposes of political participation from those who are not members in the requisite sense. Polities have the right to decide who should be entitled to membership and who should not; this too is a condition of communal self-determination. It too is a political function. If everyone who happens to be physically in the polity on election day is permitted to vote, how can a polity be sure that the outcome of the vote is an accurate expression of the public will. Imagine Canadians driving to American cities on election day to participate in American elections. Or, on a more parochial scale, imagine New Yorkers driving to New Jersey to vote in that state's statewide elections. The obvious strategy for dealing with such problems is to place restrictions on voter participation by placing conditions on citizenship. But these conditions are also likely to be imperfect, and some individuals may be denied the right of political participation even though they reside in the state and otherwise function as residents.

Democracy, particularly direct democracy, is different from constitutional government. In constitutional government, the constitution defines and limits the authority of the state. In democratic government, there are no limits on governmental authority; the will of the people, not the law of the constitution, is supreme. This reintroduces the problem of majority tyranny. Constitutions may protect minorities against the majority will, but in democracies, the will of the majority rules. Is this reason to be suspicious of democracy, or to think that constitutionalism is preferable, under liberal morality, to democracy? By way of answering this, it is necessary to look more carefully at the ideal of democracy.

Most Americans are accustomed to thinking that democracy involves, and even requires, citizen participation in terms of voting. Voting is commonly advertised as a citizen's civic duty. But there is a great deal more to democracy, ideally conceived, than just voting. Democracy requires citizen involvement in three key aspects of the governmental process: agenda setting, discussion and deliberation, and decision making.

Constitutionalism as discussed above and seen through the prism of liberal morality contains a democratic dimension. Offices are open to all, and the central institutions of the government established by the constitution are composed of elected offices. The citizens of the polity, in a representative system, elect the individuals who will do the formative work of government, making and implementing public policy. This, once again, is a form of representative democracy constrained by constitutional principles. But constitutionalism of this sort permits only a terribly thin form of democracy. The most ideal and classic form of democracy—the ideal of direct democracy mentioned earlier—is characterized by a vastly more expansive form of citizen participation.

In direct democracy, citizens determine for themselves the policy directions their government will take. If they do not implement these decisions themselves, their participation directs the actions of those individuals holding the offices charged with implementing the public will. But how should the public will be determined?

Imagine that an elite group is charged with studying the problems that government must address and then making select recommendations to the people. These elites would, in effect, set the ends of government and then simply ask the citizens to ratify them. Under this scenario, an element of meritocracy is smuggled into the democratic process; the citizens have no greater responsibility than responding to elite decisions. In effect, the elites set the agenda to which the citizens must respond. This constrains the democratic process at the outset; citizen concerns and interests are excluded from the public forum, and the context of political debate is fixed for them by the political elites. The spirit of democracy can be restored, however, by opening the political agenda to all citizens, or by allowing all citizens access to the agenda process. The interests and concerns of the citizenry at large will receive full expression only if all citizens are permitted, even encouraged, to introduce and recommend policy proposals to the polity as a whole.

Access to the political agenda is crucial to a viable democracy and crucial to the ideal of equal freedom. Everyone should have the opportunity to place policy proposals before the public. If some are excluded from this process, they are denied an opportunity that others have. Additionally, their ideas and insights are excluded, at the outset, from political consideration, and something vital and important may fail to reach the public forum. But access to the agenda of political decision making is only the initial phase of full democratic government. The second phase, discussion and deliberation, goes to the heart of the democratic process.

Democratic deliberation is at its best when all citizens are permitted to weigh into the colloquy that ideally takes place in the public forum. Once items are placed on the political agenda, democracy really gets under way. Now citizens have something to talk about, think about, ruminate upon, and decide on. Democratic deliberation is best regarded as a process of communal self-education. The deliberative process is characterized by extended discussion and debate, and all citizens should be allowed to express themselves, articulate their thoughts, and present their concerns to the people. Everyone gives everyone else something to think about. This makes two important contributions to the overall effectiveness of democratic government: First, it facilitates the presentation of expert and intelligent views on particular issues identified in the agenda-setting process as problematic. Experts of various stripes are allowed to explain and defend their ideas and thoughts in the public space, thus enriching the general level of understanding throughout the polity. Second, the kinds of interests that might be involved with regard to any policy issue are expanded, thus extending discussion beyond the private interests and desires of some individuals, who might happen to have a personal stake in the outcome, and toward a more expanded sense of the public interest.

Both contributions of democratic deliberation are of the first importance for a self-governing polity. Centralized management of large-scale social problems becomes an increasingly technical affair as the problems that government must address and manage become increasingly subtle and complex. Folk wisdom, prejudicial views, and ideological orientation are not very helpful when it comes to managing the complex and challenging problems that modern polities must face. If democracy is going to work, the citizenry must have some way to educate itself. Citizens must have access to good advice, necessary knowledge, and essential background information, or democracy will either result in disaster or evolve into some form of *meritocracy*.

But the second contribution that deliberation makes to the democratic process is of equal, if not even greater importance. Viable democracies need some way to cultivate a sense of the *public interest* or *general welfare*—some understanding of what is in the best interest of the polity as a whole. Think of the health of an organism like the human body. Imagine that Jones has a poor heart and needs a particular medicine to keep his heart functioning effectively. Imagine further that the required medicine will damage Jones's liver over time, but without it he will surely die. Should Jones take the medicine knowing that it will harm his liver? Since his heart will likely stop without it and Jones will die, it looks like taking the medicine is in his best interest, assuming that his overriding goal is to keep living and not simply to die with a healthy liver.

Suppose, however, that Jones's decision is to be made democratically by the various organs of his body. His heart, no doubt, would vote for taking the medicine; without it, the heart will stop working—not an attractive prospect for the heart, one can suppose. The liver, however, may just decide to vote against taking the medicine. It may understand that without the medicine the heart will cease to function and the resultant death will put an end to the liver as well. But the liver may reason that Jones is going to die at some undetermined future time anyway. So, while it doesn't really know how much time it has left, it would like to spend its remaining days in a healthy state and not suffer the ill effects of the medicine. The private interests of the heart and the liver split here, and if a vote were taken without democratic deliberation, they would certainly cancel each other out.

In the democratic process, however, other organs would be permitted to contribute to the deliberative process, and they might do so in either of two ways. The lungs, brain, and stomach, for example, might each express their own private interests, and the ensuing election might do little more than display the collective expression of the various private interests that constitute the organism. But the lungs, brain, and stomach might not have clear and distinct private interests that guide their thinking about whether to take the medicine, and so they might ask about what would be in the best interest of the organism as a whole. Or they might have discernible private interests but still think it most important to decide the matter by considering the best interest of the organism as a whole. By expanding discussion and deliberation to include all organs of the body, it is more likely that a general concern for the best interest of the organism will emerge and that the private interests of immediately affected parties will not prevail over the best interest of the organism.

The analogy between a human body and the body politic should be apparent enough. The difference, of course, is that in the polity, the parts that constitute it really can discuss the best interests of the whole and reach some consensus on the direction the polity should go. Democracy is possible for polities, not for bodies, but both can be considered organisms, after a fashion, with a determinable sense of overall well-being. Without deliberative discussion, no sense of the public interest can develop, for the public interest is not discovered but created. It is an understanding reached through the process of deliberation, a process that expands public awareness of the polity and public thinking about what is best for the polity.

All this might appear slightly naive to more cynical democratic spirits. It could be argued that modern polities are just too diverse to expect much in the way of a merger of thinking on the public interest. Group antagonisms are likely to pose insurmountable barriers to the kind of coming together suggested by this review of democratic deliberation. Even if this is correct in practice, however (that is, even if democratic processes simply exhibit a contest between private interests in conflict), democratic deliberation still plays an important educative role in addition to the expansion of relevant knowledge already mentioned. For open deliberation and public discussion also have the salutary effect of making citizens more present to each other, reducing the apparent strangeness that might separate citizens in a highly pluralistic polity, and perhaps encouraging a mutual understanding and acceptance that will facilitate the ends of toleration so important to pluralist polities.

Decision making, the final crucial aspect of the democratic process that needs to be considered, becomes reasonably straightforward and mechanical in the wake of democratic deliberation. At some point, deliberation must end, at least with regard to particular policy proposals, and the public will needs to be expressed. It is time to vote. Deliberation may not yield unanimity of view, but it should generate consensus. Opinions, thoughts, and viewpoints are likely to change during the deliberative process, but at some point they should also harden. After sufficient time to deliberate, minds should be made up, and as deliberation forms and shapes the public will, it is time for this will to officially declare itself. This is the job of elections; this is the time when citizens act to declare where they stand on policy issues. This is the time when the issue is settled and contention is set aside.

Can democratic government overcome the problem of majority tyranny, or is it objectionable precisely because it cannot? If democratic government operates ideally, the problem of majority tyranny should not arise; that is, if some sense of the public interest emerges from the process of democratic deliberation, the resultant vote should not be regarded as a majority imposing its will upon a minority. The majority displays the dominant view about what is in the best interest of the whole after considerable discussion. This can hardly be considered an attempt by some preestablished dominant majority to impose its wishes on defenseless minorities. Even if the struggle and strife of political discourse fails to create a unanimity of view, it still can bring the body politic together and reinforce the sense in which citizens are all on the same side—fellow members in the collective political enterprise of making things go well, or as well as possible, for everyone. Disgruntlement and disagreement can also breed a form of unity, as people inspired by the democratic ideal see themselves as fellow citizens who happen to disagree on certain policy matters (and perhaps to agree on others) rather than as alien strangers whose interests and well-being lie in irreconcilable opposition to one another. Democracy as ideally conceived, in short, can do much to facilitate political unity by reinforcing fundamental political boundaries.

But the logistical and time problems that direct democracies face as they grow in size and complexity are difficult, if not impossible, to overcome. If everyone in the polity is allowed access to the agenda, it is likely that it will grow in size to the point of being unmanageable. The age of computers can overcome some of the logistical difficulties, but it is important in direct democracy that everyone be allowed to speak and that everyone else be required to listen. As we shall see shortly, democracy in its most ideal form is simply impossible in the United States. Compromises must be made, but compromises quickly defeat the virtues associated with direct democracy.[13]

CONCLUSION

By way of summary, it would seem that both constitutional government and direct democracy are institutional forms of government reconcilable, in principle, with the requirements of liberal morality and thus suitable for polities with liberal political cultures. Is one preferable to the other? Americans have obviously developed a commitment to constitutional government, although the United States also salts aspects of representative democracy into the mix. But constitutional government is still not democratic in nature, and it is worth noting a crucial difference. Democratic government demands much of its citizenry; in particular, it demands extended political involvement and participation. Democracy—whether it be direct or representative—can't work if the people do not participate; it fails in varying degrees as political participation wanes in the electorate. This is a danger for constitutional government as well, of course, insofar as it relies upon open and competitive elections to fill important governmental slots, but it is particularly damning for democratic government.

Because the form of constitutional government reconcilable with liberal political culture will most likely need to rely upon a representative system, constitutional government frees people up from the demands of political participation associated with direct democracy. Some participation is still essential, of course, but under constitutional government, people are free to lead their own lives and to opt out of political participation if they wish. They need only elect their leaders; they need not lead themselves. Democratic government, however, depends upon political participation; from the democratic point of view, people are not really free if they only elect their leaders. To be free, they must govern themselves; otherwise they are subject to the authority of others, and it matters little if these authorities are elected or not. Yet if one thinks democracy does not bring freedom but rather enslavement to political involvement, then constitutional government may seem more attractive. Under constitutional government, one is free not to engage in politics and to leave political matters to others who might happen to care about such things. One is free from the need to care about them in order to care about other things that might matter more. One need not spend one's nights talking about public policy; one can spend one's nights writing poetry or playing the oboe instead. But of course the job of government must still get done, and therefore some people must decide to take up public service. This again makes it important for polities that avail themselves of a constitutional system to find effective ways to attract people to government work.

This does not settle the issue between constitutional and democratic government, of course. As we have seen, there is something to be said both for and against both institutional systems. But perhaps it is not terribly important to worry about which form is more suited to liberal political cultures. There are telling reasons to think that both institutional forms may be inadequate for the contemporary needs of liberal polities, and these reasons might influence one's views about the institutional form of government that is most appropriate for these polities. This, in any event, is the issue to be explored in the chapter to follow.

NOTES

1. For more on the subject of authority and its relation to politics, see E. D. Watt, *Authority* (New York: St. Martin's Press, 1982) and Richard E. Flathman, *The Practice of Political Authority* (Chicago: University of Chicago Pres, 1980).

2. Aristotle, *Politics*, Bk. III.

3. Cf. Robert Dahl, *Democracy and Its Critics* (New Haven, CT: Yale University Press, 1989).

4. This point will be examined and discussed more thoroughly in chapter 7.

5. Aristotle, *Politics*, Bk. IV.

6. Cf. Robert Dahl, *A Preface to Democratic Theory* (Chicago: University of Chicago Press, 1956).

7. U.S. Constitution, Art. VI, cl. 2.

8. U.S. Constitution, Art. II, sec. 1, cl. 4.

9. U.S. Constitution, Art. I, sec. 9, cl. 3.

10. U.S. Constitution, Art. I, sec. 8, cl. 3.

11. *Marbury v. Madison*, 5 U.S. 137 (1803).

12. The political thought of the Swiss thinker Rousseau is of particular importance in the development of this notion. See Jean-Jacques Rousseau, *The Social Contract*, trans. Maurice Cranston (Baltimore, MD: Penguin Books, 1968).

13. These concerns are discussed in greater detail in chapter 7.

Chapter Six

The Bureaucratic Phenomenon

Experience tends universally to show that the purely bureaucratic type of administrative organization—that is, the monocratic variety of bureaucracy—is, from a purely technical point of view, capable of attaining the highest degree of efficiency and is in this sense formally the most rational known means of carrying out imperative control over human beings.

Max Weber

Bureaucratic power . . . implies the reign of law and order, but at the same time, government without the participation of the governed.

Michael Crozier

The job of government building is not complete even after a liberal polity has selected between constitutionalism and democracy. Regardless of the choice that is made at this point, more work remains to be done in order to construct a viable government. If a fairly sizeable polity is anticipated, a decision to go with constitutionalism makes a degree of sense, but even if this choice is made, it is still not possible for legislatures to manage social problems without considerable help. The need for auxiliary institutions to support legislative efforts remains. Nor is this need obviated if the legislative power is placed in the general citizenry and democratic processes are adopted. Auxiliary institutions will still be necessary to help the people gather the information that is crucial to decision making and to explore the ramifications of possible policy options. Similarly, government will need an executive institution to implement and enforce policy decisions. If the executive office is headed by a single individual, this person cannot be expected to execute all public policy and to enforce all the laws alone. In a large polity, this is a monumental undertaking.

Policy-making institutions need information to make wise policy, and implementing institutions need functionaries to put these policies into effect. Government needs eyes and ears, and it also needs foot soldiers to do the actual work. Management implies organization and is impossible without it. Organization, the coordination of expertise, is essential if government in a complex world is to police basic rights and promote public well-being. The institutional challenge of managing large-scale social problems thus necessitates the introduction of what can be called the *bureaucratic phenomenon* into the process of thinking about politics. Bureaucracy is antithetical to democratic participation in government, and the more democratic one wants the polity to be, the more reliance upon bureaucratic management is bound to be troubling. In fact, bureaucracy may be thoroughly antithetical to liberal political culture itself, a possibility explored in subsequent chapters. But government that must manage a large and complex polity and address the challenging problems this polity must face is ineffective without it. If large-scale social problems are to be managed effectively, the polity will need to develop a substantial bureaucracy to do the job.

THE INTERNAL ORDER OF BUREAUCRACY

When John F. Kennedy became president of the United States, he faced a significant problem that his government had to address. A few years earlier in 1957, the Soviet Union had put in orbit around the planet a man-made satellite called Sputnik. The Soviet success signaled more than the fact that the Soviet Union was ahead of the United States in missile technology, a fact that seemed by itself to pose a considerable threat to American security in the emerging nuclear age. It also signaled that America's chief ideological opponent in the post–World War II era had managed to gain something like "achievement bragging rights," and Americans did not relish the possibility that Soviet accomplishments exceeded American achievements, suggesting perhaps that the Soviet system of politics and way of life might be superior to American politics and American ways.

Thanks to Kennedy's call to arms, the space race was on. Kennedy vowed that the United States would land a person on the moon before the Soviets could, and he urged his fellow Americans to embrace the space race and support his cause. But how would the United States manage the extraordinary accomplishment of transporting a person to the moon and winning the space race? Did Kennedy turn to America—that nation of tinkerers, inventors, and entrepreneurial spirits—and say, "Go get 'em, my fellow Americans!"? Did he send Americans into their garages to use their independent initiative and cleverness, confident that they would work away, in the fashion of Wilbur and

Orville Wright, Ben Franklin, and Thomas Edison, as independent inquirers, and then sit back and wait for "good ole American know-how" to prevail against the centralized and monolithic Soviet space program? Of course not. He put the project in the hands of a (centralized and monolithic) governmental agency—the National Aeronautics and Space Administration (NASA)—and left the challenge to it.

Putting a person on the moon was obviously a complex problem, and by turning to NASA, Kennedy made the only logical move open to him. It thus fell to NASA to coalesce and organize the expertise necessary to meet the large-scale challenge posed by the space race. This is what government does, and what it must do, in order to govern effectively when social problems reach even a modest level of technical, logistical, economic, and social complexity. It is what governments have always done when faced with large-scale social problems. The president as chief executive is required to enforce the laws of the land. But the president does not walk the streets looking for criminals to arrest. Instead, the president oversees the formation of organizations with law enforcement powers that amass the knowledge and implement the manpower necessary to do the job. As commander-in-chief of the armed forces, the president of the United States is charged with fighting the wars (presumably declared by Congress) that might be considered necessary for national security. But this does not mean that the president fights these wars personally or all alone. Instead, it is the job of the president to oversee the armed forces and make sure that they are trained in the art and technology of warfare.

All this implies centralization, for management requires centralization. And at the center of centralization is the bureaucratic phenomenon. But then just what is bureaucracy? The term formally suggests government by bureaus, but what is a bureau? How do they work? And are they consistent with the liberal political morality that anchors the idea of politics in the American mold? In the process of putting some answers to these questions, some of the central tensions within the political life of the United States will be uncovered. And the resolution of these tensions, it is important to emphasize, will do much to shape the nature of the political future of the country. Can bureaucracy work as a dutiful servant within a liberal political culture, or does it pose a threat of considerable significance to that culture and its ability to endure?

The bureaucratic phenomenon is complex, for bureaucracies are more than just institutional structures. They contain their own independent cultures that influence the ontological horizons of both the agents who hold positions within them and the general constituency they serve. These cultures emerge from the logic inherent in the general structures that typify the bureaucratic phenomenon. They also have a transformative power that tends to divide the population subject to bureaucratic operation into two separate groups: the managers and the managed. The most effective avenue from which to approach an understanding of bureaucratic culture is to imagine a bureaucracy as an institution designed to manage, control, and resolve large-scale problems and challenges as efficiently as possible. That is, the best way to recognize and evaluate the emergent bureaucratic culture is to look initially at the logic that pervades the bureaucratic phenomenon.[1]

Bureaucracies are mechanisms established for specific purposes. As social problems or programs become more complex, the challenge of coalescing the expertise necessary to address them effectively becomes more daunting. Imagine, for example, the types of experts needed to put someone on the moon. Obviously rocket scientists are necessary, but so too are biologists, chemists, astronomers, mathematicians, engineers, and so forth. In fact, even the most knowledgeable individual would be hard pressed at the outset of the process to know exactly all the various experts that will be required to get the job done satisfactorily. As the challenge is explored and analyzed, new dimensions to the challenge will become apparent, and new experts will need to be brought into the mix. It must also be kept in mind that bureaucracies in liberal polities emerge within a socioeconomic culture already in place and must operate according to the basic rules of this culture. Bureaucracies are composed of social roles—important functional slots, or jobs—that must be filled with people with the appropriate expertise. Because liberal polities like the United States are committed to decentralized strategies for staffing social roles, the bureaucracies in these polities must also purchase the talents of its citizens in order to get capable people into required slots, and therefore bureaucracies need to have budgets appropriate to this end. This means they will also need accountants, managers, and purchasing agents, to mention but a few operational functions that expand the range of experts that bureaucracies require to operate effectively.

Imagine now that something like the basic components of a space administration charged with putting a person on the moon have been identified. Even with this modest beginning, it should be clear that the number of individuals required to get the job done is going to be quite large, and one can expect the number to grow as things get under way. How should all these people proceed in order to get their job done? Suppose they decide to proceed democratically. Let everyone involved make suggestions about what to do first, debate and discuss the various suggestions and proposals, and then vote on each one. Perhaps this method of operation would eventually get the job done, but it would certainly take a great amount of time. And if this method could succeed at all, it would certainly do so only with great difficulty. Is it really necessary for rocket scientists to have input, say, on the biological problems associated with thinking about how to construct the technology that human beings require to live outside the earth's atmosphere?

Or suppose they proceed in a decentralized manner allowing the various fields of expertise to resolve their own problems in their own way. Is it reasonable to be confident that the technologies these various groups develop will work together or that the various components of the enterprise will fit together in a workable package? Decentralized operations are necessary up to a point, but someone needs to have some overview of the entire operation in order to make sure that all elements of the project are compatible, and this necessitates a considerable amount of centralized management and control. Division of labor is an essential feature of bureaucracies asked to perform complex tasks and resolve complicated problems, but to make this division of labor effective, there must be some centralized control that guarantees organizational efficiency and effective coordination of the various tasks that need to be performed. Imagine an army without leaders that is asked to fight a war. Could an army composed only of privates hope to fight efficiently?

The centralized management necessary for bureaucratic efficiency requires hierarchical organization, and hierarchical organization entails layers of authority understandable in terms of superiors and subordinates. The military provides an apt illustration of the hierarchical character of bureaucracies. Everyone in the military has a rank that indicates his or her position within the hierarchy. To be effective, the military must be confident that rank is honored by all members of the bureaucracy. If the general gives an order, it falls to those receiving the order to do as they are commanded and to pass the command down to those units properly charged with putting it into effect. Like any bureaucracy, the military depends upon the expertise of its commanding officers and the loyalty of its subordinates. Everyone needs to understand her role in the organization, and everyone needs to meet her organizational responsibilities. Only in this manner can the organization function as a single unit to achieve the objective put to it.

Bureaucratic hierarchy makes possible the integration of two key elements of bureaucratic management: expertise and information. Put in the most straightforward terms, bureaucratic decision makers—those superiors charged with exercising the expertise required to put the operational structure of the organization into effect and direct it toward the realization of its goal(s)—must pass their instructions down to functionaries who implement decisions. Along the way, marching orders may be embellished and given practical expression; general orders will receive more precise formulation by middle-range bureaucrats and be passed further down the hierarchy. But decision makers also need information in order to make their decisions. By virtue of their position, they are rather isolated and depend almost completely upon the information that comes to them from lower levels of the organization.

Information management is a key challenge of bureaucratic operation. Consider, for example, the intelligence problem associated with formulating U.S. foreign policy. Good foreign policy demands good intelligence, and to get good intelligence, the United States needs a variety of sources of information around the world. In effect, the United States needs a complex system of global eyes and ears. Some information can be gathered by technological means. During the cold war, the United States relied heavily upon sophisticated technology to gather information about Soviet military capability. Other information, however, must be gathered by people working diligently and often clandestinely to snoop around and uncover various tidbits of information. Since good information is crucial, redundancy of information gathering is important in order to have a good check on the validity of what seems to be going on. But as a result, American intelligence agencies are likely to gather huge amounts of information. How can all this information be processed in an effective and efficient manner? Should American intelligence agencies just gather all the information they can and then dump it on the desk of the president at the end of the day? This obviously makes little sense, for it would overburden the president terribly.

Processing and synthesizing information and passing information along to superiors thus become important functions of bureaucracies. Bureaucracies invariably need information in order to perform the functions required of them, but they also gather more information than can be easily synthesized by agency superiors. So decisions about what is important and what isn't important need to be made as the information gathered works its way up the chain of command, and a sufficient number of intervening levels of bureaucratic organization must be established in order to guarantee the effective transmission of information to appropriate decision makers. While this is a necessary feature of bureaucratic efficiency and effectiveness, it is also, ironically, an unavoidable aspect of bureaucratic inefficiency. Bureaucratic agencies will stumble, for example, either if crucial information fails to reach decision makers in sufficient time for them to make good use of it or if crucial information is not recognized as such at intermediate levels in the organization and is put aside, overlooked, lost, or discarded. Following the disaster that struck American shores on September 11, 2001, the American intelligence community came under critical attack for not discovering the plans of the terrorists and alerting the polity to the danger. In response, members of the intelligence community and government officials suggested that, in fact, the United States might have had the necessary information but was unable to process it effectively in sufficient time. Given the complexity of information management in this particular dimension of bureaucratic operations, this is an altogether understandable probability.

Information management explains one reason why bureaucracies develop multiple layers of superiors and subordinates. This provides one reason why bureaucracies seem invariably to be such large organizations, but there are other reasons why bureaucracies grow in size and complexity. Bureaucratic size is also influenced by the size and nature of the function a given bureaucracy is asked to perform; the larger the task, the larger the bureaucracy. The more complex the task, the larger the bureaucracy. But bureaucracies can grow and develop additional layers of authority even if their tasks remain the same, and this is another source of irony within the bureaucratic phenomenon. It is important to understand why and how this happens, for it reveals something of the paradoxical character of bureaucracies.

Bureaucracies are necessary for government in the complex polities of today because they are efficient, but it is the very demand for efficiency that tends to make them rather inefficient—hence their paradoxical character. In some bureaucratic enterprises, the chain of command sharpens the orders that go down to subordinates, and by the time the orders reach the level of the foot soldier, it is reasonably clear what the lower subordinates are supposed to do. This makes bureaucratic oversight of these lower subordinates reasonably unproblematic. But this is not always the case, and decision makers need to be confident that their decisions are being implemented effectively, if in fact they are being implemented at all. When lower subordinates have a great deal of discretion in their job performance, problems of bureaucratic oversight arise. How can decision makers know or be reasonably confident that subordinates are doing what they are supposed to do?

Bureaucracies differ in their operational effectiveness depending upon the nature of the function they perform. Sometimes subordinates have important expertise not duplicated elsewhere in the organization, and it is up to them to figure out how best to perform the tasks required of them. When this is the case, as it frequently is in colleges and universities for example, superiors must trust to the efficiency of their subordinates. But superiors are never very comfortable with this; it is a potential source of agency inefficiency. To combat this problem, bureaucratic superiors will do their best to find ways to monitor and measure the work of their subordinates.

This is a necessary feature of bureaucratic efficiency, but it is also—*and at the same time*—a source of bureaucratic inefficiency. Superiors must be confident that subordinates are doing what they are expected to do rather than sleeping at their desks or in the fields. Consider, for example, the way city police departments differ from the military. In the military, it is relatively easy for superiors to monitor the activities of subordinates, and correspondingly, the job performance expected of the subordinates is generally rather clear. Privates do what their sergeants tell them to do; they have little discretion to decide for themselves what they should do. Police departments are different. Police officers on the streets walking a beat or driving around in a squad car are typically on their own. Their sergeant is not looking over their shoulder. While training and regimen are used to enable officers to conduct themselves according to departmental policy, police officers must still exercise tremendous discretion while on the job and away from the stationhouse.[2] How do superiors know that street-level officers are doing the job expected of them rather than sleeping under a bridge or taking extended donut breaks?

The slothful behavior of subordinates is a key source of bureaucratic inefficiency, and to cope with this problem, bureaucracies need to develop strategies that encourage subordinates to be as productive as possible. Bureaucracies are structurally designed to promote this end. Hiring is typically based upon merit, understood in terms of ability and expertise. People do not get jobs in bureaucracies, at least ideally, because they happen to be the manager's wayward nephew. Similarly, retention and promotion decisions are based upon job performance. Excellence at a given position, along with dedication to the ends and mechanics of the agency, is crucial if an individual is to work up the bureaucratic hierarchy. Slothful behavior, if found out, will likely lead to dismissal, but even if things don't come to this, job performance reports will reflect this slothful behavior, and promotion will be unlikely. So bureaucrats have self-interested incentives for performing well on the job and for being as productive and dedicated to the ends of the agency as possible. Bureaucrats are rewarded with the things people learn to want in decentralized polities (money, prestige, etc.), and this guarantees that they will want to move upward in the bureaucratic hierarchy because bureaucracies are deliberately structured to reward capable workers in this way, thus encouraging effective job performance.

Of course, job performance must be measured in some way, and this must be done by superiors. Official performance reports may be used; for example, college deans may ask their faculty to indicate how many articles they have published during the academic year, how many students they have instructed, how many college committees they have served on, and so forth. Sometimes performance standards are controversial. Imagine a police department that expects its officers to write at least one traffic citation per shift because its chief is confident that in the course of a day's work an officer will see at least one traffic violation. Superiors may be suspicious that officers who don't write at least one citation aren't working very hard at their job or are exercising their discretion over their time unwisely or against departmental policy. But if word of this policy leaks out to the general population, the public might become irritated because the police department enforces a quota system, forcing officers to write citations for modest or questionable violations in order to meet their quota. The public is unlikely to have any sympathy for the fact that department superiors aren't trying to harass the public but instead are trying to be certain that their officers are doing their job.

The careful monitoring of subordinates is time consuming and complicated. Performance standards are important, but someone must review them and check on their reliability. This is the only way a bureaucracy can be confident that workers are doing their job. But the job of managerial oversight takes time and effort from superiors, and the expenditure of the time required burdens their job. How many subordinates can a superior monitor? This depends in large measure on the nature of the agency involved, but all agencies have an interest in working to make subordinate oversight as thorough as possible in order to guarantee that subordinates are being efficient. So, the more superiors an agency has, the easier it is to monitor the activities of subordinates.

The oversight problem reproduces itself at each level of the bureaucratic hierarchy. Imagine an agency with street-level operatives whose job is to perform the services they are told to do by agency decision makers. Decision makers will want to know that the street-level bureaucrats are doing their job and doing it efficiently. The best way to achieve this end is to introduce an intermediate level of managers just above the street-level operatives whose job will be to monitor the efficiency of their subordinates. But then who is going to monitor *their* efficiency? Who will check to see if they are doing the job expected of them? It looks like another managerial layer is necessary to oversee the initial managers. And so it goes! Bureaucracies can continue to grow and expand even if their basic functions remain the same, because they will tend to add managers to make sure that even immediate supervisors are satisfactorily supervised. Imagine a crew from the city's water bureau working away, one person digging a ditch while two others watch. This looks like a waste of time and manpower; that is, it looks terribly inefficient. But what is happening in this scenario is happening *because* the agency is trying to be efficient. One person is required to dig the ditch; another is required to make sure the first person really digs the ditch as ordered and does so efficiently and doesn't take too many coffee breaks. And another is required to make sure that the supervisor, whose job is to make sure the first person is being efficient, is doing this efficiently and not sneaking away with the first person for an extended lunch hour. Given the logic of bureaucratic management, it is a wonder that there are only three people at work on the ditch!

There is one final method of promoting bureau efficiency worth mentioning. Sometimes bureaucracy is criticized for being burdened with "red tape," that is, with all kinds of rules that seem at times to frustrate members of the public who find interaction with bureaucrats irritating, time consuming, and unnecessarily complicated. But management by rule, and agent rule following, are crucial features of the bureaucratic phenomenon. Rules provide standardized ways for dealing with agency problems and structuring bureaucratic roles. They tell subordinates how their job should be done, and as job performance becomes more routinized, rules can be formulated to further standardize worker behavior.

So, paradoxically, the bureaucratic commitment to efficiency actually begets inefficiency. To make matters worse, there is no ready method or standard of measure to evaluate bureaucratic efficiency accurately. Corporations resemble bureaucracies in many ways; they are institutions that rely heavily on management techniques and the organization of talent and expertise in order to achieve a specific goal, usually the production of some commodity or the performance of some needed service. But unlike bureaucracies, corporations exist and operate within the context of a market economy. They sell their services or products in an open market environment, and this enables them to construct an effective measure of their efficiency. All they need to do is measure their overhead—the cost of producing and marketing some commodity or of performing and providing some service—against their income (the total amount of money they make selling the commodity they produce or the service they perform). If one subtracts overhead from income, one gets a raw number (the profit margin) that measures corporate efficiency. Discounting market fluctuations, a corporation operates more efficiently over the course of a year if its profit margin is greater than the previous year, and it is less efficient if its profit margin decreases over the same period.

To become more efficient, corporations need to find ways to increase their net profits, either by raising their income or by lowering their overhead. Bureaucracies, however, do not have the luxury of functioning in a market environment. They do not have the opportunity to measure their income against their overhead because they have no income. As governmental agencies, they draw their financing from the public treasury. Most Americans know that NASA managed to land a man on the moon in just eight years after President Kennedy signaled the beginning of the "space race," while the Soviet Union never managed to accomplish this extraordinary feat. But there is simply no objective standard that can be applied to determine whether the agency did its job efficiently, that is, whether it managed to achieve its goal in the fastest possible time while spending the least amount of money required to get the job done. In defense of bureaucratic operation, it can be argued that increased oversight is worth the cost because it guarantees that an agency will achieve its goals quickly with limited wasted time; oversight is presumed to guard against inefficient or wasteful work habits on the part of agency operatives. But things would go better if operatives worked hard on their own without the need of rigid oversight.

One way to promote this end is to make bureaucratic activities more routine and to develop formal rules to govern how agents perform their jobs. Reliance upon formal rules promotes bureaucratic efficiency in several ways. As job performance becomes more routine, agent discretion and uncertainty in how their job is to be done can be eliminated by the formulation of rules of operation. Coordination between the various offices of the bureaucracy also becomes clearer and more straightforward if rules govern interagency coordination. Agency contact with clients is also streamlined if this contact is governed by rules. This may also eliminate the possibility of favoritism and influence peddling between agents and clients. Finally, rules governing the permissible and impermissible spending of agency money protects against wasteful agency operation. So, bureaucracies tend to, over time, become laden with rules.

But there is a paradox lurking here as well. Rules undoubtedly contribute to bureaucratic efficiency. But they also tend to eliminate agency flexibility and frequently irritate clients/constituents who find the agencies with which they interact overwhelmed with rules that send them from one line to another in search of someone who can help them resolve their problems. The result is the appearance of bureaucratic red tape, and from the standpoint of clients, a sense of bureaucratic inefficiency is likely to emerge. Bureaucratic reliance upon rules also reduces agent discretion and dampens originality and creativity in job performance that may actually promote bureaucratic efficiency.

Despite these efficiency problems, it would be a mistake to conclude that bureaucracy is inefficient or wasteful. Without bureaucracy, it would not be possible for government to perform the functions required of it. Social complexity necessitates bureaucratic management; or perhaps it is better to say that bureaucratic management is the price a polity must pay for the social, economic, and technical complexity that modern polities have created for themselves. Insofar as this complexity is itself a result of decentralization, the centralization paradox is again evident. The more decentralized a polity becomes, the more centralization is required to manage the problems created by decentralized activity. This is, it can be supposed, a mixed blessing, and one that exacerbates the management dilemma noted earlier. But regardless of whether one sees the glass as half full or half empty, it should be admitted that the bureaucratic phenomenon is an unavoidable fact of life in modern polities.[3]

It is easy to complain about bureaucratic inefficiency, particularly for those familiar with the advantages that corporations have in measuring their own efficiency. But complaining doesn't do much good, and telling bureaucracies they must learn to do more with less doesn't help much. If bureaucracies are given less money, they may simply end up doing a poorer job of providing the services people need from them. If this is the result, the polity as a whole suffers because it invites dangers that it might well prefer to avoid. This, too, is a feature of the paradox that haunts the bureaucratic phenomenon. But this is not an end to the difficulties introduced by the bureaucratic phenomenon, a fact that becomes apparent when focus is shifted away from bureaucratic structures and toward what can be called the bureaucratic mentality.

THE BUREAUCRATIC MENTALITY

If bureaucracies were staffed with robots programmed to perform the functions required of them, they might operate reasonably well. But bureaucracies are staffed with people, and these people often have their own agendas that can color bureaucratic operation, exacerbate bureaucratic inefficiency, and encourage bureaucracies to grow in size and undertake additional but perhaps unnecessary functions.

To understand this point, it is necessary to emphasize yet again the way that presumptively decentralized polities get able people into important social roles: liberal polities typically attract capable individuals to these slots by purchasing their talents and abilities. To achieve this end, they must entice people into competing for important slots by offering them things they want, and to do this, they need to encourage people to want the things the polity promises as a payoff for working in a socially useful fashion. Given the psychology of liberal political cultures, some sense of self-interest must be promoted in order to get people to serve the public interest. The things people are taught to want in the United States have already been introduced; not surprisingly, they are wealth, power, and esteem. So, if bureaucracies are to attract capable people, they must offer them opportunities to achieve these goods, and this is accomplished in a variety of ways.

It is relatively easy for bureaucracy to offer prospective bureaucrats power because power is built into the nature of the bureaucratic structure. The further one moves up the bureaucratic hierarchy, the more power one gains. The more subordinates one has under one's direction and control, the more power one is able to exercise. Therefore, there is an obvious incentive for subordinates to work hard and do a good job, since advancement within the hierarchy is conditional upon job performance. Superiors will want to expand their power by increasing agency size in order to have more subordinates under their control and larger budgets to manage. This contributes to bureaucratic growth, regardless of whether this growth is needed to increase agency effectiveness, and another source of inefficiency is introduced.

Esteem is also relatively easy for bureaucracies to supply to their agents. It is a consequence of hierarchical position within the agency. Esteem can be readily understood in reputational terms; the more power one is perceived to have in the agency and the more capable and effective one's job performance, the stronger one's reputation tends to be. And the stronger one's reputation, the greater one's esteem. So the desire for greater esteem also tends to drive subordinates to work hard and move up the bureaucratic ladder. This increases bureaucratic efficiency since hard workers are likely to perform their jobs better than slackers. But the quest for esteem, like the pursuit of power, also contributes to bureaucratic inefficiency. Since superiors will feel better about themselves if they have many subordinates, there is a tendency to increase the number of subordinates immediately under one's authority. And people pushing upward will put pressure on superiors to make new slots for them higher up in the agency.

The upward push also tends to encourage bureaucracies to expand their functions. Agents pursuing upward mobility will work to initiate new bureaucratic functions by finding new goals or objectives the agency can pursue. This encourages the adoption of new functions for the agency to pursue. Bureaucracies don't want to die, but they can die if their function is no longer needed or if they reach the goal they were designed to achieve. NASA managed to put a man on the moon; it achieved its operational goal. But it is still with us because it managed to persuade funding sources (i.e., the federal Congress) that there are important new goals it should be permitted to pursue. It managed successfully to find new goals and in the process expand its purpose from the limited goal of putting a person on the moon to the more nebulous and inexhaustible goal of space exploration.

When intra-agency pressure to develop new goals and expand functions is linked with the centralization paradox, one sees the peculiar dilemma that the bureaucratic phenomenon poses for modern polities. By way of illustration, consider the operation of the Federal Bureau of Investigation (FBI). The FBI was initially established to combat the problem of organized crime in America. Organized crime extended beyond the jurisdictional boundaries of state and local police departments. These departments lacked the coordination and resources necessary to deal effectively with what was increasingly recognized as a national, and not an exclusively local, problem. And the FBI eventually managed to bring organized crime under relative control. But driven by a particularly zealous bureau chief, it also began to identify new dimensions of crime that required the attention of a national police force. In fact, it managed to persuade its funding source (again the federal Congress) that a national police force was necessary in order to investigate the possibility that there were other law enforcement problems out there that needed to be addressed. Since no one knows for sure what kinds of criminal activities might be dreamed up by individuals acting to pursue their interests in ways possibly detrimental to society, the FBI could claim license to hunt for criminal activity even if this activity didn't actually exist. Searching for possible problems caused by decentralized human activity thus became an important agency function in its own right.

The FBI has been successful in finding new functions to perform, and it has been joined by other national bureaucratic police agencies, like Alcohol, Tobacco, and Firearms, in pursuing the possibility of additional law enforcement problems. Ironically, even if criminal activity ceased—an obviously remote possibility—the likelihood that someone is up to something illicit somewhere inspires agency dedication to discover criminal activity. All this is exacerbated by the fact that criminal elements don't usually advertise themselves but try instead to proceed with their business in the most clandestine fashion possible. Knowing this, the lack of any obvious indication of criminal activity fails to convince anyone that some illicit criminal activity isn't taking place. And this is reason for national police agencies to continue hunting around in search of criminal activity.

It is probably not too fanciful to suppose that the pursuit of money and wealth is a primary, if not the primary, incentive to pursue a career in bureaucratic service. While wealth is not built into the nature of bureaucracy like power and esteem, it typically becomes an important tool with which to encourage effective agency leadership and to inspire subordinates to work hard in order to move up the hierarchy. The higher one moves in the agency, the greater one's compensation. Since bureaus compete in a market economy with corporations and professions that often provide their functionaries with excellent salaries, they too must offer high salaries to attract capable people. In many universities, for example, the faculty in the business, medical, and law schools make more than faculty working in the arts and sciences. Market forces make this an inevitable feature of academic life. So the market itself naturally drives up bureaucratic salaries, thus increasing the dilemma of bureaucratic inefficiency.

The great wealth, power, and esteem that come with positions in the higher reaches of an agency often have funny and deleterious implications for the bureaucratic mentality. The expanded sense of self-importance that bureau leaders develop may encourage them to make more work for subordinates than is really necessary for bureau operation. At present, for example, the university where I teach is demanding that faculty develop assessment strategies in order to measure faculty teaching effectiveness. The general faculty response is to insist that this is both foolish and unnecessary. Faculty already assess student learning by giving examinations, assigning papers, and grading all this work. The final grade in a class is an assessment of student learning. But we are now told that this is not what the university has in mind. The administration thinks faculty need to determine basic learning goals and then find ways to measure success in reaching these goals. So it seems that students will be required to take additional tests, fill out questionnaires in addition to class evaluations, and submit to administrative interviews in order to see if they have learned anything. Since it seems unlikely that this will reveal anything not already in evidence by student cumulative grade point averages, the exercise seems rather pointless. But it is a good illustration of bureaucracy at work—superiors looking for ways to "professionalize" (read complicate) bureau performance.

BUREAUCRATIC CULTURE

The bureaucratic phenomenon with the accompanying bureaucratic mentality raises some crucial difficulties that polities need to confront if they are to endure. The inevitable trend toward centralization that follows from increased decentralization accelerates with the development of bureaucracy because bureaucracies naturally tend toward greater centralization as bureaucratic leaders look to expand their wealth, power, and esteem by searching for more functions for their agencies to perform and as bureaucratic leaders work to convince legislatures that more centralization is required in order to manage new or increasingly complex social problems. Insofar as centralization introduces greater governmental control of the social environment, it would seem to threaten the freedom of individuals to live their lives as they wish. If centralized management of social problems is inevitable, it also brings with it a greater regulation and control of social life that seems antithetical to freedom as this notion has traditionally been understood within liberal political cultures. The managerial dilemma—the tendency for complex polities to generate more management than they really need—thus becomes an increasing problem in complex polities.

To make matters worse, increased centralization places growing pressure on a polity's economic system. While bureaucracies are necessary for government in an era of great social complexity, they are still not productive in the economic sense of the term unless the state opts to pursue social production by means of a thoroughly centralized, or government controlled and regulated, economic system. Movement in this direction would require the elimination of the free market and hence of the reliance upon market mechanisms for the distribution of social goods, resources, offices, and opportunities. This pushes toward a socialist economic system in which the state manages the general spectrum of economic activity. But *socialism* is generally considered distasteful in states committed to decentralized economic systems, for both moral and economic reasons. Not only do managed economic systems jeopardize the freedom of individuals to live their lives as they wish, but they also tend to be terribly inefficient, partly for reasons already on display in the problems that haunt bureaucratic efficiency, and partly because they inhibit the independent effort, creativity, and initiative of the polity's population. This, in any event, is a standard criticism of socialist economic systems, and regardless of its general accuracy, it displays rather effectively the cultural opposition to socialist economic strategies in political cultures with a historic commitment to decentralized economic activity.

In those polities committed to decentralized economic systems, bureaucratic nonproductivity burdens the overall economic system because bureaucracies chew up social wealth without producing any in return. The productive elements of society must therefore produce more in order to generate the wealth required to support the growing bureaucracy. If social wealth does not grow at a rate at least equal to the growth of the bureaucracy, social wealth will need to be redirected from the general public toward the bureaucracy, and in a political culture where it is commonly believed that "a penny earned is a penny got," this will not sit well with the general citizenry. If it is not possible for modern polities to function effectively without bureaucracy, it also becomes increasingly difficult for them to function effectively with increased bureaucratic centralization. Citizens need the services government supplies, but they do not always want to pay for them. At some point, something must give.

There are few, if any, happy solutions to this problem. One way to deal with it is to understand the problem as just another large-scale social problem that government must learn to manage. Doing so might involve establishing a bureau or agency to police centralization and monitor governmental efficiency for purposes of educating decision makers on governmental need and governmental waste. This is the response one would expect from anyone committed to the need for centralization, but it risks exacerbating the disease rather than providing a cure. One more agency triggers the bureaucratic phenomenon yet again, inspires centralized governmental growth, and chews up the very resources it was intended to protect without much guarantee that it will succeed in making government generally more efficient.

Another way to deal with the problem is to limit the amount of money government has to work with. This move is on display in the many tax revolts America has recently witnessed in many states, particularly those with initiative and referendum systems that enable the electorate to amend state constitutions by popular vote. This is the type of move likely to be popular with people who prefer a decentralized political arrangement. But it, too, is not without its problems. Agencies have ways of fighting back. When their funding is limited, they can elect to curtail important social services or to under-fulfill their functions to the point that the electorate, or their specific constituency, feels the pinch. Nor need this be a conscious choice by agency superiors; it may instead be the natural response of agencies feeling too underfunded to do their job effectively. The result in either case is a reduction of necessary or important services that works to the detriment of the general well-being of the polity or to particular elements of the polity.

This, however, may not be the greatest problem associated with telling government agencies that they must do more with less. If a polity commits to live with a considerable degree of decentralization, it has no way to track and monitor the possibly deleterious consequences that decentralization might create. It has been noted already that the eighteenth-century faith in an invisible hand steering social growth and assuring social well-being is rather naive. People just don't know enough about the consequences of what they are doing to be confident that decentralization will assure that things will go well. Humankind may already have done something to so disrupt or distort some aspect of the ecosystem, for example, that the damage is irreversible. Some polities may already have set in motion problems, yet to be discerned, that will eventually erode their social fabric, if not discovered and addressed, and send them into economic, environmental, or social collapse. This is not a risk that polities should elect to run naively or cavalierly.

These difficulties are familiar enough to many Americans, and the discussion of this chapter may be understood (perhaps profitably) to bring a particular perspective to some of the key issues that currently crowd the agenda of much contemporary political discussion in the United States. But intractable and troubling though these difficulties might be, they are not the ones that require careful thought and analysis from anyone interested in thinking seriously about politics. They are only symptomatic of more pressing problems that matter greatly for a thorough understanding of politics and that need to be pulled into the light of day and made clearer. These deeper issues go to the heart of efforts to get clear on how to draw a proper balance between centralization and decentralization in the political life of the polity, and how to balance the ideals and demands of liberal political culture with political necessity.

The elaboration of these deeper issues begins with the recognition that bureaucracy brings into being its own distinctive culture. It was argued at the outset that liberal political culture has both an ontological and a normative component. These components are basic and perhaps natural features of cultures in general. The way people see and understand the world is deeply and necessarily linked to the way they evaluate and appraise the world. Cultural values and ideals both fit and reflect the standard conceptualizations of the world at home in that culture and detail the general conception of the way things are supposed to work. So, to understand bureaucratic culture, it is necessary to unpack it in a manner that brings attention to its ontological and normative elements.

The most formative ontological element of bureaucratic culture is the institution. That is, the institution—the edifice that constitutes the bureaucracy—is the primary social unit. The institution has as its end the management or control of the function it has been established to address. People take on the identity of bureaucrats or agents within the institution in the eyes of bureaucratic culture. They are woven together within the institution in order to guarantee that the institution functions effectively. Thus a secondary and derivative ontological feature of bureaucratic culture is organization. Agency identity is further fixed by the organizational role one plays within the institution; one is what one does, so to speak. One's sense of pride and esteem is correspondingly linked to the way one performs one's job, along with the importance one attaches to the performance of that job for the overall success of the institution.

This introduces another derivative feature of bureaucratic culture. People see themselves within bureaucratic institutions as parts of a larger whole—as parts of the institution itself. They are particular types of functionaries within the institution, and this sets their sense of self. The institution, in other words, is a collective of workers, none of whom is entirely identical with the institution itself. There is a familiar saying in the sports kingdom that nicely displays this way of seeing: "There is no *I* in *team*." Athletes playing team sports are expected to dedicate their skills and their efforts to the overall success of the team. Bureaucratic institutions are teams in this same sense, and the bureaucratic culture works to cultivate the same sense of commitment to the institution and to perceive oneself as a functionary in the overall enterprise of the institution.

The institutional commitment to management introduces another derivative feature of bureaucratic culture. Bureaucratic institutions, once again, are hierarchical; this is dictated by the need for efficient management. But it also means that bureaucrats will see themselves as functional elements falling someplace within the overall agency hierarchy. Thus personal identity is fixed not only by the function one performs within an agency but also by the station or place one occupies in the hierarchy. Put cryptically, one can say that people become identical with their titles, and titles locate people within their organizations. Linguistic practices within bureaucracies sometimes aptly display this sort of hierarchical worldview. It is commonplace, for example, for people associated with a bureaucracy to refer to superiors by title rather than by name. In universities, the faculty say things like, "The Dean said we cannot hire another position," instead of, "Jane Smith, who has the final say, said we cannot hire another position," and so forth. Titles, in short, fix identities—sometimes both inside and outside the institution. Bureaucrats become their roles, so to speak; they define themselves and their coworkers accordingly and expect others to do so as well—and others do so, again both inside and outside the institution, with telling frequency.

A distinctive set of norms accompanies the ontological elements of bureaucratic culture and defines and informs the normative schemes of those who become immersed in this culture. Chief among these is the ideal of authoritativeness that differentiates roles and job descriptions within bureaus. Bureaucracies are a microcosm of the functional ends of government. If it makes sense to understand civil association in terms of the societal need to coalesce existing expertise in the polity and bring it to bear on large-scale social problems in order to adequately address and resolve these problems, then bureaucracy is the mechanism that polities must use to achieve this end. Bureaucracies blend various talents and abilities into a working system capable of effective social management. Within any given agency, decision makers will need to be experts on the various aspects of the function of the organization, and some will need to be experts on the managerial requirements of the agency itself. This dependency upon expertise requires agencies to place great weight on the authoritativeness of those experts they depend upon. Agents are considered authoritative with regard to the jobs they are expected to perform, and bureaus reward authoritativeness by means of advancement and promotion.

Acknowledgment of agent authoritativeness lends credibility to the orders of decision makers within a given agency. Lieutenants who have faith in the knowledge and ability of their generals are likely to carry out their orders with the confidence that they are doing what they should. Correspondingly, bureaucratic chains of command are strained if the rank and file have little faith in the authoritativeness of the decision makers.

But the presumption of bureaucratic authoritativeness also affects agency relations both with its specific constituency and with the general public. A sense of authoritativeness generates faith in the public at large that all is well, that government is in control, and that things will be okay. Increasingly bureaucratized societies exhibit a sense of the omniscient "they" who are in charge and who will address and resolve social problems when and if they arise. If a particularly terrifying crime is committed and people worry about their safety, police agencies swing into action and present an authoritative image. *They* will catch the culprit and protect the people, *they* are authorities on these matters, and *they* will take charge. Correspondingly, the public is often left with a sense of frustration and impotence when confronted with bureaucratic authoritativeness. The public need only sit back and relax, or at most provide the kind of information to government agencies that will be helpful. But the *authorities* will solve the problem, and the public ought not get involved—they are likely only to make things worse.

The norm of bureaucratic authoritativeness penetrates all elements of highly bureaucratized polities, and the more bureaucratized a polity becomes, the more one should expect a pervasive sense of professionalism to be on display. Society is now imagined to include a collection of professionals who are there to solve problems and who assume the responsibility for doing so. Of course professionalism is a necessary and inevitable social response to complexity, and something one should expect even in more decentralized social arrangements. If the drain in the kitchen sink is clogged, call a plumber; if the car isn't running well, take it to a mechanic. Most people lack the exceptional range of talents and abilities to meet all their needs themselves. Professionalism is a natural extension of the social division of labor that emerges as things become more complex and technical as polities develop. But bureaucratic professionalism takes this phenomenon a step further by removing political problems and issues from public view and placing them within the jurisdiction and province of declared experts on the subject. There is little left for the citizenry as a whole to do but watch; bureaucratic politics is a spectator sport.

As the norm of authoritativeness implies, knowledge is power both within bureaucracies and within highly bureaucratized polities. The need to cultivate and maintain an aura of authoritativeness inclines bureaus to operate according to a norm of secrecy.[4] Decision makers do not advertise all the knowledge they have or pass along all the information they may have gathered. Sometimes agency effectiveness is tied to the norm of secrecy. The police don't tell the public all they know about a particular crime because doing so might make their job harder. But even if this is not the case, agencies are apt to act in great secrecy. Because knowledge is power, it is guarded jealously. And because authoritative professionals may cultivate a language and subculture of their own that characterizes what they do, others are closed out and unable to clearly understand the nature of the practice they pursue. Authoritativeness breeds organizational and institutional secrecy, and this secrecy breeds distance and a sense of aloofness within the agency and between the agency and its public.

Authoritativeness, of course, is built into the hierarchical structure of bureaucracy, and when these two features are taken together, a second basic norm of bureaucratic culture comes into view. By virtue of their hierarchical structure and their differentiation of knowledge within this structure, bureaucracies tend to be authoritarian and inegalitarian institutions. The notions of "superior" and "subordinate," along with the logic of the chain of command, establish social relations within bureaucracies. If agent identity is fixed by the agent's role within the institution, then agent self-perceptions will be measured by the place one holds within the agency. Bureaucrats live in a world of superiors and subordinates, and they invariably see themselves and others in these terms.

There is, moreover, a certain coldness about a culture that buys the talents and abilities of the population by attracting labor with the promise of rewarding people with the things it teaches and encourages them to want. Competition is necessary, of course, to get capable people in important slots, but as we have seen, this may have a deleterious effect on the losers of the competition. Some will be the losers in the great social competition for those things Americans learn to want: power, money and wealth, and esteem. The invariable result is likely to be a significantly lowered self-image in the losers and an extremely magnified self-image in those who perceive themselves as winners. But bureaucratic culture adds to this phenomenon by introducing another source of social inequality. Subordinates who have little chance of further advancement may lack self-esteem, while superiors who have reached what they consider to be significant goals will feel themselves superior in a sense that reaches one's attitude about human worth itself and thus transcends the boundaries of job performance.

In effect, bureaucracy introduces the outline of a new class system based upon talent and ability. Inspired by the sense of professionalism introduced above, bureaucrats become a new form of social elite, and within this universe of elites there are additional class divisions to be found. Bureaucratic culture is hardly the only source of inegalitarianism to be found in modern liberal polities. The corporatism that has emerged with advanced capitalism introduces elites of its own that parallel bureaucratic elites, and not merely in economic terms. Corporate leaders constitute a new elite in their own right (a group of superior beings, so to speak), and given the manifold interconnections between the corporate world and the bureaucratic phenomenon, elites frequently serve in both roles and move with considerable ease between corporations and bureaucracies. This emergent class of elites constitutes something like a new aristocracy that has germinated within liberal polities and that stands apart from the social plebes that serve in subordinate capacities in both the corporate world and the bureaucratic phenomenon.

This brings us at last to the third and final norm of bureaucratic culture that needs to be introduced and considered: the norm of rationality. The great virtue of bureaucracy, it will be recalled, is efficiency—and never mind for the moment the kinds of inefficiencies to which bureaucracies give birth in the name of efficiency. Bureaucratic management can boast of being the most rational method of addressing and resolving large-scale social problems.[5] And when compared with a decentralized strategy for dealing with complex social problems, it quickly becomes evident that the weight of reason is on this side of the equation. An agency that runs smoothly (that is, an agency where all agents function effectively under capable managerial supervision and do their respective jobs) is invariably the most efficient mechanism imaginable for dealing with social problems and serving the large-scale needs of the polity. Bureaucracy is, in an important sense, the instantiation of rational methods of problem solving within the polity. And within bureaucratic culture, it is recognized, advertised, and eulogized as such.

This commitment to rational organization and efficient problem solving encourages bureaucrats to value the bureaucratic enterprise and their specific roles within it. Good privates march where their commanding officers tell them to march, and good captains carry out the orders of their generals faithfully and diligently. This is not just a military characteristic; it is the end product of valuing rational management and bureaucratic efficiency. The bureaucratic reliance upon formal rules again contributes to this process. Good bureaucrats follow the rules of the agency, and not only because this is a good way to keep superiors off their backs. They do so because the norm of rational management, once internalized, dictates that they should. This is their job, their role, their part of the larger enterprise to which they contribute. When attached to the norm of rational management, rule following becomes the central *modus operandi* of middle-level managers and subordinates within bureaucratic agencies. Rules are followed because this is how things get done; rules are followed because this is how bureaucratic management works. Rules are followed because it is the rational thing for bureaucrats to do. Rules are followed because this is the path to efficiency. Rules are followed because the norm of rational management requires it.

CONCLUSION

This, in brief, is what the bureaucratic phenomenon looks like. Social complexity and the various challenges and problems introduced into the polity by virtue of size and the consequences of decentralization make this phenomenon a practical necessity in the modern world. Bureaucracy is perhaps an inevitable response to the problems created by decentralization, but it is more than just the practical form that centralization takes. It is this, of course, but it also inspires and facilitates greater centralization in its own right. Bureaucracy, this is to say, begets bureaucracy, and as it does so, it spreads and nurtures bureaucratic culture throughout the polity. Bureaucratic necessity is thus on a collision course with liberal ideals. So understanding politics in those complex polities that make tremendous demands upon their government requires that one think about the nature and likely consequences of this collision. This is the issue to which we shall turn in the remaining chapters.

NOTES

1. For a comprehensive analysis of the bureaucratic phenomenon, see Anthony Downs, *Inside Bureaucracy* (Boston: Little, Brown & Co., 1967).

2. Cf. William K. Muir, *Police: Streetcorner Politicians* (Chicago: University of Chicago Press, 1977).

3. For a discussion of the inevitable growth of bureaucracy in the Unite States, see Peter Woll, *American Bureaucracy* (New York: W. W. Norton & Co., 1963).

4. Cf. Max Weber, *The Theory of Social and Economic Organization*, ed. Talcott Parsons, trans. A. M. Henderson and Talcott Parsons (New York: The Free Press, 1964).

5. Ibid., 329–41.

Chapter Seven

Requiem for Democracy

In politics as in architecture, form must follow function at least to some degree. Government must be structured in a manner that enables it to perform the tasks and fulfill the challenges it exists to confront. But government should also fit the political culture in which it operates. Ideally, government should be a reflection, or perhaps a manifestation, of the political ideals that animate the polity. Problems arise when political ideals become inconsistent with the demands of political necessity, or when the form of government required by the political culture is no longer capable of meeting the practical needs of the polity. When this happens, something must give, and an inquiry into the nature of politics is important in order to understand what must give and why.

The inevitability of centralization, driven as it is by the centralization paradox, means that bureaucratic structures are necessary for modern states if they are to meet the practical challenges they face. And this introduces a crucial question. Is the bureaucratic phenomenon consistent with the governmental ideals associated with liberal political culture? Put more prosaically, this question asks if the apparently inevitable reliance upon bureaucratic management is reconcilable with the ideals of liberal morality. This issue introduces the subject of the present chapter.

LIBERALISM AND DEMOCRACY

It looks, on its face, like the bureaucratic phenomenon is inconsistent with those governmental institutions recommended by liberal political culture. The

177

liberal emphasis upon freedom suggests that decentralized and perhaps even localized government institutions are preferable in a liberal polity, but the centralization paradox pushes in the opposite direction. And centralization receives another push from the bureaucratic phenomenon, which by its nature drives in the direction of greater centralization. Bureaucratization of the polity involves the centralized management of social problems and government by professionals with the expertise necessary to manage these problems. But this is hardly consistent with democratic governmental decision making. If liberalism requires some form of democratic involvement in the political process (either via direct or representative democracy), then there would seem to be a natural and troubling tension between liberal political culture and the bureaucratic phenomenon.

Liberals believe political authority is antithetical to the ideal of individual freedom. Liberal individualism introduces a morality that champions personal independence and autonomy. In its minimalist or libertarian form, liberalism reluctantly admits that just enough political authority must be tolerated to assure the polity that each citizen is maximally responsible for her own life. Built into this conviction, it will be recalled, is the belief that individuals are their own authorities on how their lives should go, that independent persons are best able to decide for themselves what matters to them and how they should live their lives. If persons are best able to decide for themselves how their lives should go, they should be allowed to do so. They should be permitted the freedom to make key decisions about what they will do with their lives, who they will be or become, and what direction and form the narrative of their lives will take.

The liberal case for some form of democracy follows from this set of claims. Because persons are conceptualized as autonomous agents, they should also be considered to be their own authorities on what is best for them. Nobody can claim special knowledge that entitles them to decide what others should do with their lives. Everyone should be allowed to decide these matters for themselves.

When people find themselves in associations, on the other hand, they will invariably face decisions about how the association should be governed or managed—questions about the policy directions it should adopt, the rules that govern member participation, and so forth. These are decisions that affect all members of the association and influence the way their collective lives will go. How, then, should decisions like these—let us call them *collective decisions*—be made? One way to decide this matter is to let association elites make key decisions about the operation of the association. But this is not a strategy that will appeal to liberals because it supposes that there are some elites within the association that know better than the rest of the membership how the lives of the members should go, at least insofar as these lives are affected by member involvement in the association. If people are autonomous, the liberal argument goes, they should be permitted to have a voice in any and all decisions that affect them. Association elites may provide information and even insight on what they consider the proper course of conduct for the association, but if the association is to meet the conditions of liberal morality, they cannot dictate to others in a way that allows the elites to have authoritative control of the collective decision-making process. Everyone should have equal input into this process; that is, collective decisions within associations should be made *democratically*.

If one adds to this argument a premise stating that the polity is an association faced with making important collective decisions affecting the way the lives of its citizens will go, it follows that in a liberal polity these decisions should be made democratically. This concludes the argument for the view that democracy is the most appropriate form of government for liberal polities.[1] The argument suggests that the proper response to bureaucratic management in liberal polities is to insist upon more democracy, not less. Democratic involvement becomes crucial in such a political setting in order to cultivate public control of emergent bureaucratic institutions.

This argument has a powerful simplicity about it, and anyone committed to the basic ideals of liberal political culture is sure to find it attractive. Nevertheless, it is important to submit the argument to careful scrutiny in order to see if it can stand the test of critical review and thus qualify as compelling. Does the argument apply to the conditions it is intended to address in a practical and viable way? Is it germane given the conditions within which it is presumed to operate?

DEMOCRACY: THE FUTURE OF AN ILLUSION

People whose worldview is largely fixed by liberal political culture are likely to find nothing wrong with the liberal argument for democracy, but even committed liberals may have some reservations about the practical pertinence of the argument in complex modern polities like the United States. So perhaps it is best to begin a critical review of this argument by thinking first about the question of pertinence.

By now it should be apparent that democracy is a many-splendored thing. The purest form of democracy, once again, is direct democracy. Recall that under direct democracy all citizens are entitled to equal participation in the democratic process. This should be understood to mean that all citizens are entitled to maximal involvement in the basic elements of the democratic process: agenda setting, discussion and deliberation, and decision making. The maximal involvement condition thus requires the adoption of a direct democracy as the proper form of government for a liberal polity. But for reasons already encountered, it seems that direct democracy is the least pertinent form of democracy for large and complex modern polities—liberal or otherwise. It will be helpful, at this point, to develop the reasons that lead to this conclusion a bit more thoroughly.

Democracy in its ideal form has three great enemies: size, time, and expertise. The larger and more complex the polity, the more these enemies of democracy require compromises that push in a direction away from direct democracy and toward a more compromised democracy. This introduces another crucial question. How far can a polity slide away from the ideal of direct democracy and still continue to qualify as a democracy in any sense? The answer to this question, it would seem, is fixed by the liberal argument for democracy. How many qualifications can be made to the ideal of direct democracy and still leave one confident that all citizens have viable input into the decisions that affect or influence how their lives will go? To answer this question it is necessary to consider the modifications to democracy mandated by size, time, and expertise and then to consider whether these modifications compromise the liberal ideals that support the case for democracy.

Size and time are related problems in a direct democracy. The smaller the size of the polity's population, the more time each citizen will have to discuss and deliberate upon collective decisions. The more time there is for this deliberation, the more likely it is that the polity will reach some general consensus on how things should go. Direct democracy works best in small groups, at least from a logistical standpoint. But large groups encounter obvious problems. If everyone has equal access to the agenda, it is possible, and indeed quite likely, that the agenda will become so large that it would take an eternity to get through it, even if discussion and deliberation was held to a minimum. But ideally, discussion and deliberation should not be held to a minimum; all citizens should be allowed sufficient time to explain their views, ask questions, and explore the possible implications of some policy proposal. Expanding the amount of time allowed for discussion and deliberation, however, simply burdens the democratic process beyond all reasonable measure.

It is perhaps worth emphasizing that the problems introduced by size and time cannot be overcome by technological developments. The population of the United States is now around three hundred million, a size that makes the notion of a workable direct democracy in the polity seem laughable. Suppose, however, we think smaller. Is direct democracy possible in a city of the size of, say, five hundred thousand citizens? Well, imagine that all citizens of the city were limited to putting but one proposal on the agenda. It isn't likely that everyone would bother to do this, but suppose that half the population does want to put something there, leaving the city with 250,000 proposals to consider. Suppose further that discussion and deliberation time was restricted to ten minutes for each citizen for *all* proposals on the ballot. If everyone took their allotted time, it would take 2,500,000 minutes for discussion and deliberation, or 41,667 hours, or 1,736 days. That works out to 4.75 years, and that's working around the clock!

To make matters worse, ten minutes per person to discuss 250,000 proposals seems ridiculous; in fact, allowing only ten minutes to discuss one policy proposal seems overly restrictive. What can one say in ten minutes that both informs others and responds to the views being expressed by the 499,999 other citizens? The ten-minute restriction makes a mockery of discussion and deliberation. But so too does the limitation placed upon access to the agenda. Why should citizens be allowed to introduce only one policy proposal?

Of course, these numbers presume that everyone is taking turns speaking for ten minutes even if everyone else isn't required to listen to what their fellow citizens have to say. But technology might permit us to streamline the process considerably. Suppose, for example, that everyone was able to place one item on the agenda by using a computer, logging onto www.government .com, and entering their proposal. Presumably this could be done in a few minutes; in fact, policy proposal submissions could be limited to just five minutes of computer time. Correspondingly, everyone could log on to www .government.com and take their allotted ten minutes to respond to the policy proposals they have reviewed and wish to comment on. Now all the information is available to all citizens, and they can access www.government.com at their leisure, review the proposals and discussions as they wish, and make their contributions accordingly, restricted only by the ten-minute requirement. Does this overcome the logistical problems created by size and time?

Imagine a dutiful citizen who wants to make sure she has had the opportunity to review and comment upon all the collective decisions that will affect her life. Suppose it takes one minute to read all the proposals and all discussion provided by fellow citizens. If 250,000 proposals are submitted, and if all of her fellow citizens have commented using their ten minutes, she would have 250,000 minutes of reading to do, taking her 4,167 hours, or 174 days! Several important compromises are still built into this scenario; the limitations upon discussion and deliberation are still significant, as is the limitation upon access to the agenda. But even so, it is absurd to suppose that a person could begin to spend 174 days working day and night on nothing but collective decision making. Even with technological streamlining, the challenges

posed by size and time are too onerous to make direct democracy viable in
even a modestly-sized polity.

It may be objected, of course, that there is no reason to insist that all citizens should bother to consult all the discussion and deliberation taking place
within the polity. Citizens can gather into small groups and discuss matters
among themselves, and perhaps this would be sufficient. But though it might
be sufficient, it is still a compromise. If citizens discuss matters only with a
select group, various viewpoints will remain locked within these groups, and
the polity itself will not be able to avail itself of all the disparate arguments,
positions, and points of view that should be considered before decisions are
made. It is an admittedly ideal characteristic of democracy that everyone has
a chance to be heard and that everyone has the opportunity to hear and consider the ideas of everyone else. But the more diverse and pluralist the polity
becomes, the more important this ideal becomes as well. All citizens should
be made aware of the disparate positions of different groups in order to give
these viewpoints the considered judgment they deserve by virtue of their
standing as a voice in the polity. So, the more compromises made in order to
lessen the time demands that direct democracy would make upon the citizenry, the further the polity moves away from democracy itself.

The burdens that size and time place upon democracy can be further complicated by noting a tension inherent in the liberal commitment to democracy.
When election time rolls around in the United States (i.e., when it is time for
decision making), Americans commonly hear lectures from political and
media sources about the importance of doing one's "civic duty" and voting.
Voting in the United States has become a rather modest activity requiring
only a moment of one's time. Voters take a few minutes out of their day to
go to the voting site, sequester themselves behind the protection provided by
the voting booth, and quickly register their preferences on the ballot supplied
to them. These anonymous decisions are then handed in, and the vote is presumably duly counted. The cost in time to the voter is arguably no more than
an hour at most.

But lectures about the importance of voting, particularly when they are
coupled with state efforts to make voting easier and less time consuming,
have the unhappy consequence of placing importance upon the wrong feature
of the democratic process. Insisting that voting, and voting alone, is a civic
duty minimizes the significance of both agenda setting and discussion and
deliberation. At best, this emphasis implicitly presumes that citizens already
know how they want to vote, that they already have an idea of what candidates and issues they want to support. The act of voting becomes a mere for-
mality that involves little more than finding sufficient time to formally
express one's choices.

In one sense, this merely illustrates the way democratic politics has been streamlined in the United States. Party labels and party affiliation streamline the electoral process, for example, by providing voters with a discernible indicator of what particular candidates stand for, the interests they represent, and the policies they support. If the Democratic Party represents and supports the interests of the working class, for example, then members of the working class can feel confident in voting for Democratic Party candidates, and additional worries about discussing issues and deliberating on policy proposals becomes unnecessary.

Things are hardly this simple, of course, even in localities where the party label still means something. In the United States, interparty politics tends to overshadow intraparty politics. But if political parties organize and streamline democratic politics by providing voters with recognizable labels and taking political discussion to the people through the campaign process, they also magnify the importance of intraparty political struggle.[2] In the early and formative days of party politics in the United States, intraparty struggle was a source of considerable democratic vitality. Party members would meet in local party caucuses to discuss issues, plan party platforms, and elect candidates for public office. In most states, however, the caucus system has given way to party primary elections, as the time burdens of the caucus system began to cause party members to wander away from participation in party politics.

Perhaps, then, there is a way to streamline the democratic process and make the demands of time and the challenges of size less destructive of the process. Perhaps it is possible to revitalize political parties and return to the caucus system, encouraging citizens to align with a party that articulates a general political philosophy that appeals to them, and lecturing them on the importance of becoming a participating member of their party's caucus. The caucus system still falls short of the democratic ideal, of course; deliberation and discourse now takes place largely between fellow travelers rather than between all members of the polity. But at least fellow travelers would have the opportunity to deliberate upon the position they would like to see their party take, and this is certainly preferable to a primary system in which party members merely select among the various candidates within the party who have presented themselves as contenders for public office.

But this seems overly optimistic and rather underestimates the problems posed by time and size. The old-style caucus system decayed for a reason, and part of this reason involves the time constraints it imposed upon party members. A great many Americans find their lives overly burdened, and time is an important yet terribly scarce resource. Those who work for a living find themselves facing the time demands of their job, and if they want to do their job well, get ahead in their profession, and generate the income necessary to support themselves and their families, they may find it necessary to put in long hours in order to assure that their careers go as they would like. What leisure time is available to people may be encumbered by family demands— taking the kids to softball practice, mowing the lawn, and so forth. Additional leisure time is reserved for those special activities and hobbies that enrich and embellish individual lives. If one loves to ski or play tennis, one will want to have time for these activities. If someone enjoys reading or watching a particular television show, she will want to make time for these things. No doubt people will also want to spend some enjoyable time in the company of friends, relatives, and neighbors. The way people elect to entertain them- selves matters to them and has a priority for how they want their lives to go.

Put simply, people generally find it easy to fill up their time and still wish for more. People treasure the time that is theirs and protect it accordingly. Imagine if the polity required citizens to spend two hours each day doing the business of the public, that is, engaging in political discourse, logging on to www.government.com and reading policy proposals, or attending a party caucus to discuss possible legislation and appropriate candidates for public office. No doubt some would find this an enjoyable and rewarding way to spend their time, but just as assuredly, others would not. While two hours out of the day looks like a modest commitment from the standpoint of the time demands made by direct democracy in large polities, it will seem terribly onerous to many people whose time is already at a premium. It is telling to recall the lectures Americans get about the importance of going to the polls and voting, just as it is telling to note how few Americans actually do this when election time rolls around. If only a modest number of Americans are willing to spend the time required to vote, who would want to spend two hours a day doing the business of the polity?

Imagine now that the familiar lectures about doing one's civic duty and voting are expanded to insist that doing the business of the polity is one's civic duty. No matter how one understands oneself, one cannot deny that one is a citizen, a member of the polity, and that duties and responsibilities come with this self-description just as a self-description of father or mother, bread- winner or worker, implies duties and responsibilities that encumber one's time. Such lectures will not only be met with skepticism; they may also be met with a legitimate liberal response. Part of being free, it could be argued, part of living in a free society, involves being free from having to do certain things, which might be necessary to sustain oneself, in order to be able to enjoy doing other things that one wants to do—things that matter to one and things that one has committed to do deliberately and voluntarily. If Jones must spend two hours doing the business of the polity, she is robbed of two hours that she could and otherwise would spend doing things that matter more to her. If she cannot do these things because she is required to engage in political discourse against her wishes, there is a sense in which she is enslaved by the very polity that presumably is dedicated to protecting and enhancing her freedom. If liberals cherish freedom, as indeed they do, they must also value the independence that people require in order to live their own lives as they wish. This would seem to mean that people—free people— should be permitted to participate in, or opt out of, political involvement as they wish!

In a free society (free in the sense that matters to liberals), civic engagement should be a matter of individual choice. Those who enjoy politics are free to pursue political involvement as they see fit; no one should be prohibited from political participation if they qualify as a citizen. But similarly, no one should be compelled to participate in civic matters if they prefer not to. In a liberal polity, the lives of the people belong to them, and the way they elect to live them is a matter of their own choosing. Nothing in the structure of liberal morality prohibits anyone from lecturing others on the importance of doing their civic duty, but there is also nothing in this morality to indicate that citizens are obligated to participate in the democratic process. People who recognize that their interests are at stake in this process may want to do so, but others who think their interests are effectively represented by others, who think that their involvement will make little political difference, or who put a low priority on participation given the other ways they have to spend their time will have little reason to take democratic participation seriously.

Perhaps, however, there is a way to defeat this argument. Suppose someone asks why people—free people—should be subject to collective decision making in the first place. Why should anyone have to participate in the life of the polity? These questions might seem to return us to the issue of anarchism with its attendant problems. Because people live in the company of others, they must take steps to resolve the various problems caused by the fact of human association and interaction. If individual lives are to go well, people need to organize with others in order to resolve problems that would otherwise trouble them and defeat their ability to live a good life. But once people do join with others in this way, they must adopt some method for making collective decisions. By joining with others, people bring the collective into being and introduce questions about how this collective will operate, how it will express its collective will, and how it will resolve the problems it encounters. The democratic process, the liberal argument for democracy contends, is the way to do this that most respects persons as autonomous beings. So, democracy should ideally prevail in liberal polities.

But democracy cannot function without citizen participation. If citizens elect not to participate, at least to some degree, in the political process, the process itself will collapse and nothing will get done. To be sure, this is highly unlikely, and for reasons that will seem rather obvious. It is invariably the case that *some* people will want to participate in the democratic process. Individual interests are often linked to the policies made and pursued by the polity. When interests are in opposition, collective decision making becomes a contest to determine which set of interests will prevail. Some citizens will certainly understand that their interests are best or properly realized by pursuing them through the process of collective decision making. These citizens will therefore have a clear interest in "capturing government" or working to amass sufficient support to capture and control the decision-making process.

Realizing this fact provides all citizens with a reason, albeit a prudential one, to participate in the democratic process. Citizens who fail to participate abdicate their ability to defend their interests when and if they come into competition with the interests of others. If citizens elect to opt out of the political process, they put their own interests at risk, and by so doing, they devalue their own freedom. For if others capture the collective decision-making process and frustrate the ability of some citizens to realize their own interests, those citizens who are now unable to pursue their own interests— that is, to live their lives as they wish—have, in an important sense, abdicated their own freedom. For freedom to be secure within a situation requiring collective decision making, all free individuals need to participate.

But this attempt to make a case for democratic participation gives rise to two further problems. First, it supposes that some citizens may have interests in opposition to others and that if these interests are realized, the interests of these others will be compromised. But this certainly isn't always the case. Many citizens may have modest interests that are largely, if not entirely, unaffected by the efforts of others to realize their own interests. If and when this is the case, the prudential argument breaks down, and so does the additional argument holding that individual freedom is diminished or devalued if people don't participate in the democratic process. If freedom is of value because it is the necessary means that enables autonomous beings to live their lives as they wish, these beings won't care much about being free to do things they don't want to do or have no interest in doing. Consequently, if they don't think their freedom to do as they wish is at risk, they won't care much about protecting their freedom to do things they don't care about doing.

It might seem that such a view is not very thoughtful. Since people don't know what future interests they may have, it would seem they should retain as much freedom of action as possible, and this means continuing to participate in the democratic process. But this argument quickly leads to a paradox. What sense does it make to avoid exercising one's freedom to do what one wants to do in order to protect the freedom to do otherwise in the future given the possibility that one might want opportunities in the future that one doesn't care for at present? If people did this, they could never make a decision about how to live their lives that would close off the ability to make alternative decisions in the future. If one's current interests are capable of being satisfied without participating in politics, and if the collective decision-making process is unlikely to change any of this, why bother to make the time commitment to participate in the democratic process? And why insist that one's freedom is jeopardized if one elects to opt out of this process?

Second, if one takes seriously the claim that the best way to protect one's interests, and hence one's freedom, is to participate in the democratic process, it becomes necessary to tighten the understanding of the type of democracy appropriate for liberal polities. The ability and opportunity to participate in collective decision making is hardly any guarantee that one's interests can be effectively defended. Recall again the problem of majority tyranny that troubles democratic government. If one is constantly or at least generally in the minority when it comes to decision making, what is the point of political participation? Losers in the decision-making process can claim with some justification that their freedom is devalued by democratic government. No doubt perpetual or habitual losers would prefer a constitutional system that places principled limits upon the kinds of things open to public decision making. That is, losers would prefer to have the range of democratic jurisdiction limited by authoritative legal mechanisms and would surely think this the best way to protect and defend their freedom.

KNOWLEDGE AND DEMOCRACY

So far, we have noticed that the problems of size and time require significant qualifications of the democratic ideal in large and complex polities, even if they are liberal polities. Perhaps suitable qualifications and compromises can be identified and established; perhaps, for example, the polity should opt for some form of representative democracy of the sort associated earlier with constitutionalism. But qualification and compromise move us rather far from the democratic ideal, and questions again arise about how many qualifications and compromises can be made consistent with the liberal argument for democracy. At some point, concessions to time and size may become so great that the point behind the liberal argument for democracy is lost, and the argument would work against the legitimacy of whatever governmental process results from all this qualification and compromise.

But the liberal argument for democracy is also suspect for other reasons.

If freedom matters to individuals, then the freedom to opt out of democratic participation should be respected. The pivotal premise of the argument supporting the conclusion that people should be permitted to have input into the decisions that affect them is not defeated by this point. But the premise states a permission only; it does not articulate a requirement. If people do not want to participate in the collective decision-making process, a commitment to freedom would seem to permit them to opt out. And there seems to be no good way to turn this permission into a responsibility. Insofar as democracy is terribly time consuming, one can expect at least some people (and perhaps a great many) to opt out, at least selectively, in order to reserve the time they require to do those things that matter to them more than participating in the democratic process. Yet the more people that opt out, the more democracy becomes something of a sham and the more the polity becomes a democracy in name only.

The problems of size and time, then, seem to defeat the ideal of democracy, and together they challenge the viability of the liberal argument for democracy. If liberals want democracy—*real* democracy—they had best reconfigure the polity in a manner that would allow for democracy. But this is hardly a practical possibility. The realities of size and complexity are already in place, brought about by the very decentralization that liberals have historically cherished. If it now seems that things look rather bleak for democracy, things are going to get worse, for the greatest enemy of democracy—expertise—has yet to be considered.

The discussion of bureaucracy emphasized the importance of knowledge and expertise in politics. The large-scale nature of the problems that government must address—their sheer scope resulting from the size and complexity of the polity—means that the centralized management of these problems will require huge bureaucratic structures. Bureaucratic institutions will invariably grow in size by virtue of their own internal dynamics. But in general, bureaucratic size is typically a function of the specialized and technical demands an institution must face. If one thinks of politics as the coalescing of expertise to manage large-scale social problems, that is, if one thinks of politics in terms of the *management* of social problems, then the need for expertise and for functionaries with the required knowledge is an essential feature of politics. But this need for knowledge and expertise is the greatest single challenge that a viable democracy must address.

Imagine a direct democracy operating without large bureaucratic institutions. Imagine, too, that the logistical problems introduced by the fact of size and the demands of time are largely settled. Citizens are devoted to democratic discussion and take an active interest in the welfare of the polity. But suppose as well that they face the problems that are typical of complex polities. Citizens must make decisions about energy policy, environmental policy, foreign policy, economic policy, public welfare policy, and so forth. These policy arenas introduce a great need for specialized knowledge in their own right, but they are also not unrelated. For example, foreign policy and environmental policy decisions will have an economic impact on the polity, economic policy decisions will obviously affect public welfare and health care policy, and so forth. Now, how will discussion and deliberation progress when it comes to the policy proposals in areas like these that shape the public agenda? What kind of expertise and informational background will citizens need in order to discuss these matters intelligently and vote on them wisely?

One way to resolve the problem raised by this question is to suppose that citizens will need to become experts on all these matters themselves. But this suggestion is hardly plausible. Citizens cannot be expected to become economists, atomic scientists, medical doctors, environmentalists, and so forth, in order to do the business of government effectively. In the United States, people don't even expect this of their representatives. The committee system in Congress, for example, permits an element of specialization in government. But while congressmen become reasonable experts on the matters addressed by the committees to which they belong, they hardly qualify as experts on other matters that government must address. If specialization is necessary for the Congress to do its job well, why should anyone expect anything less in a direct democracy?

If, however, citizens specialize in, say, two areas of governmental activity, the time demands upon them would still be extraordinary. Suppose Jones, a hardworking citizen, decides to specialize in health care policy and environmental policy. Jones must also earn a living, of course, and let us say that she works as an electrical engineer for eight hours a day. She must keep up in her own field and also keep up in both health care matters and environmental science. This is a demanding life for anyone, and if Jones wants to do her job well and also be a dutiful citizen, she will have very little time left for friends, family, and recreational interests. It is a positive feature of government that it manages sociopolitical problems for the citizenry and thus lifts the burden of self-government from the shoulders of the people. This allows people to live their lives as they wish and with relative confidence that the manifold problems of the public are well managed in the process. But direct democracy puts these burdens back upon the citizenry and in so doing restricts the individual's ability to go about living her life as she wishes.

It seems unlikely that Jones, or anyone else, would want for long to keep working at her job and also to stay current as an expert in the various sophisticated problems associated with shaping health care and environmental policy. The physical demand alone would surely prove overly burdensome as the years progress. Further, it is simply not feasible to suppose that Jones could manage to stay current in three complicated areas of inquiry. She would have to be something of an intellectual Hercules to pull this off; her work as an electrical engineer alone should be sufficient to keep her going almost full time. Even if Jones dropped one of her two governmental specialties, she would still be taxed beyond measure by her personal job and her political job.

It is perhaps telling to note that people don't really live their personal lives in this manner. Instead, they depend upon others for assistance and advice in the process of getting through life. Few people, if any, have the knowledge and expertise necessary to fully control their own lives and destinies. They do not go to medical school in order to address their medical problems, or go to law school in order to handle their legal problems. People do not become real estate agents in order to buy a house, car mechanics in order to fix their automobiles, accountants in order to manage their funds, or ministers in order to attend to their spiritual needs. They look to others for these services, and in turn, they provide others with some service as determined by the job and employment decisions they make. Individual lives are lived, this is to say, according to a division of labor. If liberal inclinations tend to encourage people to treasure a degree of independence and self-sufficiency, social reality works in a different direction. To say that people are social beings is to say, in an important sense, that they are also dependent beings. Society is a large mutual support system, a system of personal interdependency, and it is hard to imagine that it could be otherwise given the complexity and sophistication of the modern world.

If daily life invariably involves a division of labor, why shouldn't the government of the polity do so as well? Why does it make sense to rely upon a division of labor in the ordinary pursuits of life but reject such a division, in favor of full democratic participation, when it comes to government? People also have an important stake in making health care decisions, investment decisions, legal choices, and so forth, and it is because these things matter to people that they seek out and rely upon the advice and wisdom of recognized experts. Why should government not rely upon specialized wisdom and expertise as well? Why not abandon democracy in favor of a division of labor in which people knowledgeable in how to deal with the problems that government must address are empowered to deal with them? Why should the citizenry in general waste their time meddling in matters they don't fully understand in the name of democracy?

These questions anticipate a problem with the liberal argument for democracy. Recall that the argument depends importantly upon the idea that as autonomous beings, people are the unrivaled authorities on their own best interests. As appreciation for the division of labor associated with daily life indicates, however, this idea seems to be largely if not entirely false. People simply lack the expertise required for them to know what is best for them in all the various and complex areas of life, and someone would have to be an extraordinary thinker to be able to amass all the knowledge to qualify as really self-sufficient in the modern world. Instead, people ordinarily and unreflectively rely on the authority and input of others to make decisions about how their lives should go. People seek the advice of stockbrokers to help them with their investments; in fact, they may hand the responsibility for managing their portfolios over to the broker entirely. Decisions about one's health depend upon the insight and input of medical professionals. If someone is told her cholesterol is too high, she will likely follow her doctor's advice and alter her eating habits, get more exercise, or take the medicine her doctor prescribes. If someone is feeling depressed, he will likely visit a psychologist and put his troubles in more professional hands. In fact, reliance upon professionals seems rapidly to be becoming a characteristic feature of modern life, and self-reliance a casualty of an ever-expanding division of labor. Caring for one's self increasingly involves putting one's welfare in the hands of others.

Perhaps, however, all this overestimates the individual's dependency upon others. The doctor may tell Jones that she needs to lower her cholesterol, but the decision to do so is still her own. And she can ignore this advice if she decides to do so. A broker may tell Smith to put more money in bonds and stay away from the stock market, but the decision to do so remains with Smith. All these so-called experts do is help people make decisions about the best way to achieve desired ends, but the ends chosen belong to the people themselves. But this reply is misguided on a couple of counts. It depends upon the ability to distinguish ends from means, and on the corresponding claim that it is permissible to have help in choosing the means to achieve desired ends provided the ends chosen are of one's own choosing. But the ends people have, or are likely to have, are both rather straightforward and fairly pedestrian, and it is not terribly hard to give a reasonably accurate, albeit formal, account of them.

Imagine someone decides that she wants to live happily—hardly an uncommon or extraordinary ultimate end. How should she go about doing this? How does a person go about living happily? Happiness, it should be noted, is very much a social construction. Few people today think they would be happy living the life of a knights-errant or a commander in the legions of imperial Rome. Nor is this simply a concession to the absence of imagination in the average American. Contemporary society does not present these options to people; instead, people learn rather quickly that the path to a happy life runs through the realm of existing social possibilities. The socially determined conditions of happiness have been noticed already. People learn to want wealth and money, power, and respect and esteem and to seek these things as means to the end of a happy life. This is a large generality, to be sure, and not everyone is going to be so motivated or so thoroughly self-directed. Nonetheless, a decentralized society that relies upon market mechanisms to get able people into important slots must encourage people to want these things, or something like them, in order to get them to contribute profitably to social life.

If the understanding of what it means to be happy, along with the accompanying wish to be happy, is a social construct, so too is the corresponding view of how best to realize the desired happiness. People learn to want to be thin, to be as attractive as possible, to desire wealth, to cultivate the esteem of others, and to amass the power they can because these are the mechanisms that enable them to realize the end of happiness. These are not separable means to the end of happiness; they are features of happiness. And to live life as a quest for their accumulation is to live a life devoted to happiness. What has become of individual autonomy in all this? What has become of the liberal desire to assure that the lives people live are of their own devising, a product of their own voluntary choosing?

So there is reason to be suspicious of the liberal claim that people know best what is good for them, or that they are the best judge of their own interests, and so forth. Our sense of what is good for us is itself a social construct, and if we rebel against this construct, we are perhaps properly considered a self-destructive personality. It is not personal self-destruction that really matters, however, because insofar as people stray from or rebel against this social construction, they also become socially dysfunctional in the sense that they fail to contribute their share to the collective enterprise of living together. They don't do their part, and if too many people fail to do their part, social life itself—whether it is liberal or whether it is inspired by different cultural influences—is correspondingly endangered.

Still, there is some room left for the liberal devotion to personal autonomy in all this. To say that our lives are our own within a suitably modified liberalism should be understood to mean that our *futures* are importantly our own and are circumscribed only by the nature of or the limits upon our talents and ability, along with the abilities of the competition we encounter along the life path we have chosen. Not everyone can go to law or medical school, but from a social perspective, this is a good thing. A society composed of only doctors and lawyers could hardly function well; the complex and sophisticated polities of today require a wide range of talents and abilities, and they require that these talents and abilities be developed in a wide variety of ways. To be sure, modern society needs doctors and lawyers, but it also needs engineers, scientists, police officers, masons, plumbers, electricians, entertainers, car mechanics, and so forth.

Personal goals are adjustable within certain general constraints, and individual lives are invariably sagas of continuing adjustments. Few people chart a path for themselves and steadfastly stick with it because, as the old song goes, "time and chance happen to us all." We control matters as best we can, but it is time and chance, and not prior social determination, that most affects our lives.[3] In liberal polities, people are free to work out the direction their lives will take for themselves within the social context in which they find themselves and of which they are a part. Contra Plato's vision in the *Republic*, people in liberal polities should not be told what to do in life or how to contribute to the social whole. They must take the social world in which they live as it is, but within this context, they will enjoy the freedom to make of their lives what they will, limited only by their own native ability and personal dedication to the task at hand. Although we are socially determined beings, liberal culture still allows individuals a degree of wiggle room to chart their lives for themselves. Given the deep and deeply important sense in which people are, after all, social beings, this still gives reasonable, even admirable, expression to the liberal notion of autonomy and provides room for the considerable importance liberals place upon the ideal of freedom.

CONSTITUTIONAL DEMOCRACY?

What has all this to do with the problems that the need for specialized knowledge raises for a viable democracy? Two key points should be stressed in response to this question. First, the classic liberal argument for democracy no longer seems viable in the highly technological and complicated societies liberalism has helped inspire. People can no longer reasonably be said to know what is best for them. Perhaps this has always been a myth, but it certainly makes little sense in the complex, interdependent social condition on display in modern polities. Second, this is hardly reason to abandon, at least entirely, the liberal emphasis upon individual autonomy and the concern for equal freedom that it inspires. It is, to be sure, reason to be more modest about protestations in favor of individual autonomy. Human beings are (and always have been) social beings, and this means that they are (and always have been) interdependent and dependent beings.[4] But there is still a good amount of space here for decentralized polities to leave room to individual discretion when it comes to determining how one's life will go, what people will do to contribute to the lives of others, and how they will develop and refine the talents and abilities they happen to have.

These conclusions have important implications for thinking about politics. If it is time to let go of the idea that direct democracy, or even significant citizen input into the political process, is a political good, it might seem that this only means that constitutionalism and/or some form of representative democracy is the best form of government for polities whose political cultures are shaped by the liberal tradition. There is, this is to say, no reason at this point to admit that some form of meritocracy is the only viable form of government for liberal polities. But the problem posed by the need for knowledge and expertise in the management of social life, and the concurrent demands of centralization, have similar implications for these two forms of government as well.

Constitutional government is automatically suspect if it is supposed that the constitution places principled restraints upon government power and authority and thus provides an institutional safeguard against the abuse of power. The notion of limited government is simply inconsistent with the first law of politics: governments need the power necessary to govern. In an increasingly complex and sophisticated social environment, it is simply not possible to know what kind of limits are appropriate for government. People cannot know what the future holds, what problems will arise that need a bureaucratic response, or what dangers human beings will create for one another under decentralized conditions. The social factors that drive the centralization paradox cannot be foreseen or known in advance. Consequently, constitutions that limit the power of government will likely turn out to be recipes for disaster if they are not either ignored or carefully finessed by means of clever constitutional interpretation.

One can still find solace in a constitution that articulates certain civil liberties crucial to the practical construction of the ideals of a polity's political culture, of course, but even here things are hardly simple or straightforward. In the United States, for example, the liberal political culture supports the idea that persons should be free from the prying eyes of the government and consequently that there are limits to what government can do when it comes to policing basic rights. But a polity that places limits on its government's ability to pry into personal lives is likely to be one that is hard pressed to police basic rights effectively and protect its citizenry against unscrupulous individuals. The Patriot Act, passed in the wake of the hysteria generated by the terrorist attacks of September 11, 2001, offers a salient example. The act significantly increased the government's information-gathering authority, but at the expense of several practical expressions of the civil liberties that protect citizens from government prying. Civil libertarians opposed the act vigorously, just as government officials defended it with equal vigor as something that was necessary to sustain domestic security. Perhaps sadly, very little public debate over the proper way to balance individual freedom from government scrutiny against the needs of domestic security was forthcoming in the wake of the passage of the act. In the end, it is a rather unhappy fact that the practical concern for security will probably tend to trump civil libertarian ideals, and it is difficult to see how it could be otherwise. Freedom from government doesn't count for much when and if people are vulnerable to violence from terrorists. And government controls the information about the nature and extent of the terrorist threat.

Of course constitutionalism still can have a modest organizational and structural role to play even in bureaucratic or meritocratic governments. An independent funding source is a good idea, for example, to maintain some control over bureaucratic spending, just as an independent agent is necessary to manage the various bureaus or agencies that do the actual work of government, guard against agency overlap of function, and organize agency workloads. And here an element of democracy—representative democracy— might be introduced back into the governmental equation by allowing for the popular election of the constitutionally established institutions that perform these functions, a conclusion reached above when the merits of constitutionalism were discussed.

But it would be a mistake to be overly sanguine about the extent to which a representative democracy would really qualify as democratic. The problem of knowledge and expertise remains; both knowledge and expertise work as a trump against the effective oversight efforts of a legislature. Imagine, for example, that a representative democracy is constitutionally structured to run as follows. First, the citizenry elects representatives based upon the policy positions of the candidates, with simple majorities determining the outcome of the contested elections. Second, representatives presume the election is a majority endorsement of their policy positions and thus feel justified in heading to the seat of government for the purpose of putting their policy objectives into effect. Underneath the college of representatives stands a bureaucratic system charged first with gathering information about what is happening within the specific fields the various bureaucratic agencies are established to service, and second with implementing the policy decisions made by the college of representatives that apply to the specific field an agency services. So information goes up to the representatives of the people; the representatives then evaluate this information and respond to it and make policy decisions in light of the policy desires of the victorious majority. These decisions, in turn, are to be dutifully implemented by the appropriate bureaucratic agency.

If this system sounds familiar, it should; it is a rather streamlined description of the idealized, textbook account of the workings of American government. But consider how the knowledge trump is likely to affect all this. Direct democracy is troubled, once again, by the fact that the people can't be experts on all the matters and issues they must decide upon as citizens. They must rely upon the input of experts in order to have the information needed to make an informed decision. But the input and information they receive will dictate the decision they make. How could it be otherwise? Knowledge, in politics as elsewhere, is power, and the control of knowledge involves the exercise of power. Experts can realize their desired decision outcomes simply by the way they control and present the information needed for the decision to be made.

If the knowledge trump works to co-opt the viability of direct democracy, why won't it do the same when it comes to representative democracy? The answer, of course, is that in all probability it will. It is important to say "in all probability" here because representatives may themselves become experts in the fields of government that become their specialty. As noticed previously, for example, the committee system permits congressmembers to specialize in the Congress of the United States. But this probably offers very little in the way of solace. Even though representatives may become experts in certain fields of government, they remain reliant upon the federal bureaucracy for the data and information they must use in the policy formation process. The Congress cannot duplicate the research and expertise of the federal bureaucracy without reproducing the bureaucracy itself. Consequently, Congress, and even the president, are as hostage to the bureaucratic system as the people would be under a direct democracy. People in the upper reaches of government have little choice, at some point, but to believe what they are told, and what they are told will dictate, in the end, what they will do. If decision making falls to the people's representatives in a representative democracy, decisions are also made, for all practical purposes, below the level of representation, where and when government must rely upon a bureaucratic system to get things done.

It could be argued, however, that the knowledge trump can be trumped itself if it is possible to find a way to rely upon overlapping and competing sources of knowledge. But reliance upon competing sources of information— literally competing experts—is more likely a recipe for frustration and stagnation in government rather than a check against the knowledge trump. Suppose Smith doesn't like the recommendation of her doctor that she have an operation in order to resolve some medical problem. She decides to seek a second opinion. The second doctor tells her the operation isn't necessary, but to address her condition she must give up doing some activity that she very much enjoys. She elects to seek a third opinion. Her third doctor tells her that her condition can be addressed effectively without the operation and that she won't need to give up the activity she enjoys. Suppose further that each doctor evaluates her medical condition, offers reasons explaining why the offered evaluation is correct, and defends this evaluation against the recommendations of the others. Who should Smith believe?

Situations like this—situations of expert disagreement—are not uncommon; they are important testimony not only to the fallibility of experts, but also to the fact that people don't know everything. Sometimes all people have to go on are best guesses, and best guesses can differ from expert to expert. But although this may be true and important to understand, it doesn't help Smith decide what she should do. Smith now suffers from a kind of information gridlock. On one hand, she is unable to decide which of the experts she has consulted is right. To be able to decide this, she would need to be a super expert on the medical condition that troubles her; she would need to know more about it than the doctors she has consulted. But if she were such a super expert, she wouldn't have needed to consult a doctor in the first place. On the other hand, at this point Smith no longer needs to worry only about which of the three doctors she has consulted has made the correct assessment of her condition. She now needs to worry whether any of the three is actually on target. Competing experts tend to undermine their own authoritativeness; in the face of considerable disagreement, why should anyone believe any of the claims made by the so-called experts?

Expertise, and the authority it generates, ultimately depends upon the faith of those subject to it. If this faith is warranted, it is because of the past successes that some expert has had in handling the problems that people need to have handled. So Smith might elect to follow the advice of the doctor she has the greatest faith in, given her previous track record with this doctor. Or she may elect to make the choice she most favors for nonmedical reasons. If she doesn't particularly want the operation, and if she certainly doesn't want to give up the activity from which she derives considerable enjoyment, then she might just decide to go with the advice of the third doctor. If there are no good grounds to distinguish between the three recommendations, why not make her choice the one she prefers for nonmedical reasons? Or she may just be paralyzed, unable to make a choice because she now has too much information. In the face of contrary and conflicting information, she has no way of knowing what she should do, and so she might as well do nothing.

The paralyzing effect of competing knowledges will work this way in both direct and representative democracies as well, again frustrating the viable operation of democratic processes within large and complex polities. The paralysis brought on by competing knowledges can be mollified, however, if it is built into the bureaucratic process itself. Agencies receptive to competing knowledges can work out the conflicts within the confines of their own hierarchical structures, and experts working together can make best guesses concerning the most desirable or useful course of conduct. The uncertainty produced by competing knowledges, incomplete knowledge, and controversial knowledge is not foreign to experts working in complex areas and who are accustomed to admitting the limitation of their knowledge. Within the bureaucratic structure, experts can bring the available knowledge to bear on a given problem in the best way possible, and agency decision makers will then be faced with making what looks like the best decision possible given the available and accepted knowledge of the day. This, too, is part of the division of labor that increasingly characterizes social life in a complex and only dimly understood world.

Perhaps, however, this discussion makes too much of the importance of knowledge and expertise in the governmental process. People might be happy to concede that there are many areas of governmental decision making that require familiarity with varieties of technical scientific, economic, and sociological knowledge. When people face decision making in these fields, it might be admitted, things default in favor of the special knowledge of the appropriate experts built into the bureaucratic process. But not all areas that require governmental decision making are like this; some may very well require special information but not specialized knowledge of some sort. Foreign policy decisions, for example, may depend upon specific information about what other countries are up to, but if people know this, they can proceed to make foreign policy decisions without any additional economic, sociological, or scientific training. So here, it might seem, there is room for viable democratic procedures; here representatives of the people, if not the citizens themselves, can make viable and effective policy decisions.

Suppose we beg the question of whether decision making in, say, the foreign policy arena actually does require specialized training and specific expertise. It probably does, but the question is arguable. It is not a question we need argue here, however, because even if reasonable policy decisions could be made by ordinary citizens without specialized training in foreign affairs, the knowledge trump is still present. Information, after all, is a form of knowledge, and it can be qualified, massaged, amended, and slanted to create in its recipients the kind of picture of what is happening that the sources of this information want to create. This is not to imply that information gatherers—necessary components of the decision-making process in any field of governmental activity—will deliberately distort or deceive in order to achieve their own specific agendas. Instead, it merely involves recognizing that information is never neutral or self-interpreting. Information gatherers will invariably form their own views of what is going on in the process of gathering information, and future information will be appraised as important or irrelevant based upon this general view.

As a result, information that gets reported to decision makers is likely, one might say very likely, to reflect the gatherer's own sense of what is happening in the world the gatherer is watching. The picture created by the information, in short, will be a product of the way the information gatherer has come to see the world she is charged with watching. This does not mean, of course, that information gatherers can control the decisions that are based upon the information they provide, but it does mean that decision makers will be responding to the world that the information gatherer sees. And if information gatherers understand the policy ends of decision makers, if they can anticipate the kinds of moves decision makers will likely make based upon the information they receive, then their influence over the decision-making process again becomes extraordinary. They can influence decision makers to do what they think best by presenting the information at their disposal in ways that make their favored policy option look like the clear or unrivaled choice. Nor is there anything deceitful or duplicitous in any of this. Information gatherers will almost certainly have their own sense of what should be done under specific circumstances, and given their view of what the circumstances happen to be, the information they present will very likely drive decision makers in the policy directions favored by information gatherers.

But it should be mentioned at this point that it would be equally misleading to suppose that the process of selective information reporting is never, or even rarely, deceitful or duplicitous, for this may take place more frequently than many people suppose. Information gatherers are also recognizable as bureaucrats, and the internal dynamic of the bureaucratic phenomenon is surely at work here. There is an old saying among people who have worked in the White House that one should never bring bad news to the president and should always bring good news instead. If presidents begin to associate an aide with bad news, they may elect to eliminate bad news by eliminating the messenger. If and when one's personal career is on the line, information gatherers and information presenters may have personal reasons for slanting the information in a way that favors their personal situation. This is not a good thing, by any means, but it also looks like an inevitable aspect of the bureaucratic phenomenon, regardless of whether it is providing information for independent democratic representatives or for decision makers within a specific agency.

THE PROBLEM OF POWER: A REPRISE

So then, it seems the future does not look good for democracy. The larger and more complex a polity becomes, the less viable real democratic proce-

dures become as well. The United States of the early twenty-first century
qualifies as a democracy in only the most nominal of senses if it is supposed
that the further a polity moves away from a spirited direct democracy the
further it moves away from being a democracy in any important sense. This
seems a gloomy conclusion, however, only if one also thinks that democracy—real democracy—is the form of government most appropriate for a liberal polity like the United States. This in turn suggests that the fate of
democracy in the contemporary world need not be considered all that gloomy
by diehard liberals, since there is little reason to insist that liberal polities
must be democratic in order to be faithful to liberal values and ideals.

As we have seen, it is hard to imagine modern social life in a way that does
not operate according to a division of labor in which everyone develops some
degree of expertise or ability that enables them to provide services needed by
others. This invites the admission of mutual interdependency and the corresponding surrender of the historic American fondness for self-sufficiency and
self-reliance. It invites the appreciation of the deep and abiding sense in
which people are social beings, that is, beings that are both shaped and influenced by, and dependent upon, the social world that surrounds them. Correspondingly, this encourages the abandonment of rustic and romantic
American images of strong and independent individuals (more about this to
follow) who are self-made and self-governed. But it does not necessitate the
rejection of the liberal emphasis upon the value and importance of personal
freedom, provided, of course, that people also understand themselves as
social beings whose life choices are presented to them by the social world to
which they belong.

If it is correct to think that the liberal idea of autonomy, and the liberal
values of freedom and equality, can be sustained within a social environment
that depends ultimately upon a division of labor, then liberal political culture
is not inconsistent, at least in principle, with a bureaucratic system of government. Bureaucratic government may not be the first choice of liberal polities,
but by now it should be apparent that social, technical, and economic necessity plays an important, if not determinative, role in dictating the form of
government appropriate for a given polity. Adherence to liberal ideals, particularly the liberal commitment to decentralized social systems, has allowed
socioeconomic conditions to develop and mature in a fashion that makes centralized social management a practical necessity. And size and complexity
dictate that centralized management will necessarily take the form of bureaucratic government.

There is, however, a traditional reason to worry about any government that
relies ultimately and necessarily upon a bureaucratic division of labor. *Power,
it might still be supposed, corrupts!* In fact, something of its corruptive char-

acter has already been noticed in the discussion of the bureaucratic mentality. So, is it possible to prevent bureaucracies from becoming independent little tyrannies even within a constitutional matrix? If power corrupts, why should anyone trust bureaucracies whose power seems unchecked even by constitutional structures and whose agents are not, for all practical purposes, really answerable to anyone? In the ordinary division of labor that characterizes ordinary life in decentralized modern polities, everyone is answerable ultimately to government. Only government is answerable to no one if democratic checks have no practical effect. So the problem of power is again before us.

But the response to the problem of power given previously still has force, even at this point. If people are well schooled in the basics of their political culture, they should be both willing and able to live by its norms because their vision of public life is set by its ideals. In a liberal polity, people can learn to respect one another as autonomous beings and to do their share to make sure that things will go well for their fellow citizens. In a polity where citizens are faithful to the norms and ideals of their political culture, and regardless of what else they happen to value, political power is capable of domestication, and there is then reason to trust those individuals who choose to live a life of public service. This, once again, is reason to cultivate one's political culture. But this is not easily done. Cultures are not static things; they are subject to transformation and alteration in their own right. So a final and crucial step in thinking about politics involves thinking about the way liberal political culture might be changed or transformed by the various forces that work against it. And this takes us to the final question that must be considered by anyone who wants to think seriously about politics.

NOTES

1. Cf. Robert Dahl, *Democracy and Its Critics* (New Haven, CT: Yale University Press, 1989) and Dahl, *Dilemmas of Pluralist Democracy* (New Haven, CT: Yale University Press, 1982).

2. Cf. E. E. Schattschneider, *The Semi-Sovereign People* (Hinsdale, IL: Dryden Press, 1960).

3. Cf. Jon Elster, *Sour Grapes* (Cambridge: Cambridge University Press, 1983).

4. Cf. Alasdair MacIntyre, *Dependent Rational Animals* (Chicago: Open Court, 1999).

Chapter Eight

Politics and the Future

He who controls the past controls the present, and he who controls the present controls the future.

George Orwell

Politics is about many things. First and foremost, it is about conceptual and normative boundaries and about personal and communal identity. To say this is to say that politics is about how people see and understand themselves and their social environment. This is the background against which political association must be understood if it is to be understood at all. A thorough understanding of this point is necessary if one is to further appreciate why politics is also about the values and institutions of civil association. Only against this background is it possible to grasp the important relationship between government and politics. Government simply is civil management—the self-conscious control of a civil arrangement bounded (at least in a just polity) by a common political culture and political history that enables citizens to live worthwhile lives together and to see that things go well, or as well as possible, for them.

Sometimes effective management is possible by letting things take their natural course and manage themselves, so to speak. This approach to the governmental process is particularly attractive in political cultures that place great value on the ability and opportunity of people to live their lives and contribute to the well-being of their community as they wish. These political cultures are committed, in principle, to a decentralized form of political association. Yet while the attractiveness of this management style should be apparent in polities with liberal political cultures, questions remain about its appropriateness. There is little reason today for citizens of complex and multifaceted polities to have much faith in the future if they rely exclusively upon decentralized management strategies, for the centralization paradox drives a tendency toward centralization. Decentralization is the great force that makes centralization, that is, the politically self-conscious management of civil life, necessary.

Civil society requires management for several reasons, but the need to manage can also be distilled down to a relatively simple idea: social life needs to be managed so that tomorrow goes at least as well, and hopefully better than, today. To put the point this way is to introduce one final thing that politics is about—politics is about the future. It is about making life go well, or at least as people would like to see it go, tomorrow and the day after; it's about making life's prospects attractive and exciting for those who will inherit a life in the polity. It's about passing along the strong commitment to civil association implicit in the political culture, and it's about helping continue the ongoing narrative of the polity that informs and influences the identity of those who belong to it. In an even more dramatic sense, it is about how human beings will manage to get along together, into the future, in their neighborhoods, their communities, their polities, and across the entire planet.

TOMORROW'S INHERITANCE

What might the future look like for citizens of the United States? How might future generations of Americans see and understand civil association? Will America's liberal inheritance continue to shape and direct life in the United States? It is, of course, impossible to answer these questions with any certainty; *fortuna*—that curious mixture of fortune and fate to which Machiavelli was so sensitive—has a way of making fools of us all. But thinking seriously about politics still requires one to speculate on them because what people do today will shape not just their tomorrows, but the tomorrows of generations to come. While it might be wise to concede that the future is not manageable, that decentralization is too entrenched and powerful to permit human beings to script their future for themselves, it also seems only prudent to try and shape the future in the best possible way. If Americans would like to see life's prospects get better for future generations (and whatever this turns out to mean), it is important to consider how today's decisions, commitments, and policies will likely shape what comes tomorrow.

The conclusions reached in the previous chapter will seem intolerably dire and pessimistic to many strong liberals who have become accustomed to thinking that democracy, in some form, is the ideal system of government for liberal cultures, if not for humankind in general. But size and complexity, the unanticipated but hardly unexpected consequences of decentralization, have created a condition in which democracy in the United States is possible only in the most nominal sense. This should not be understood to mean that Americans should give up on democracy as it has come to display itself in the country, although it does suggest that Americans might want to be self-consciously aware that democratic procedures do not stand for all that much in American politics. But liberal political culture can live without democracy, and rather easily at that, once the myth of radical individualism that has grown up around liberal politics in the American mold is abandoned and the mutual interdependence of modern social life is conceded—a concession, it is worth adding, that does not necessitate the deeper conclusion that individuals (and hence individualism) no longer matter much from a moral point of view. The lives that citizens of liberal political cultures elect to pursue are largely—though of course not entirely—still matters of their own choosing, but the choices available to them are configured by social reality and public necessity. To pursue a socially useful life is to engage in a lifestyle that contributes to the well-being and happiness of others. If people aim to make themselves happy by selecting a specific course in life, and hence by acting autonomously, they must also pursue a path in life that will similarly contribute to the happiness of others, for the available social roles provide us no real alternative.

Yet the seemingly inevitable dependence upon bureaucratic institutions and structures may still threaten liberal culture in more subtle and dangerous ways. If bureaucratic institutions are in principle compatible with liberal culture, it is less clear that the culture that accompanies them and that emerges from them (something identified above as bureaucratic culture) is also compatible with the ontology and morality of liberalism. Times change, and this can only mean that the human condition changes through time. To say, as I have, that the future is not itself entirely manageable is simply to admit that the forces at work in social life that control the phenomenon of social change are hardly understood, grasped, or fathomed. It is even probable that they are not understandable, graspable, or fathomable by poor beings such as ourselves. This perhaps tragic concession does not mean that we cannot try to understand the forces that determine the future, for if we do not try, we must certainly take what comes, and it is no doubt a central feature of modern human beings that they prefer to control their destiny rather than wait to take what comes. If politics is about controlling the future—managing tomorrow, in effect—then the effort to gain at least a partial understanding of what drives social and political change becomes necessary. This is a final, and yet terribly necessary, aspect of thinking about politics.

Many of the thinkers of the nineteenth century who concerned themselves with social and political thought set about to try and present a comprehensive theory of social change and political development. Of these, Karl Marx is perhaps the most familiar.[1] Marx supposed that history had a design of its own, and driven by economic forces, it was taking humankind toward its ultimate destiny. There is little need to worry about the extent to which Marx believed human beings had some degree of control over the realization of this destiny, but it is worth wondering, albeit briefly, about the claim that history has something in store for humankind. This social determinism is not overly popular today, partly because it presumes a historical purpose beyond human design that hardly seems believable, and partly because people today prefer to think that the future will be forged by conscious decisions made in the present. Still, Marx's monumental effort to understand the forces that drive social change and thus to spy on the machine that drives humankind toward its destiny demonstrates a point about looking toward the future that is worth keeping in mind. What people say about the future, what they say about the forces that drive social and political change, and what they say about how things might go in times to come may influence the history they seek to foretell. To comment upon the future is to affect the future.

Had Marx lived, worked, and written on Mars rather than in Germany and England, and had his worked never filtered down to this planet, our present might be very different than it now is. There is also irony in all this. People cannot hope to know beforehand how what they say about the future will affect this future; they cannot grasp the implications of their own ruminations. And this is perhaps reason to leave the future alone, reason to concede that the forces and variables that are at work shaping the future are too complex to tinker with. There is just too much to anticipate. Moreover, there is also that which cannot be anticipated—those things well beyond human control that threaten humankind with cataclysmic possibilities. Human beings hurtle precariously through space on this precious little orb without much of an ability to foresee when or if the planet will run into a gigantic piece of space junk that will obliterate life as we understand it on the planet. Human beings proceed along their way without knowing whether nature might produce some microcosmic bug that renders them deathly ill and that seems impervious to efforts to get it before it gets us. We continue going about our business, building, inventing, producing, and creating, without knowing precisely the unintended consequences of our efforts or whether our dumping, polluting, and tinkering might not at some point come back to haunt us.

None of this is intended to suggest that there is little or no reason to think about and worry about the future, but it does introduce some reason to appreciate the fragility, tenuousness, and mystery of the human condition. And it invites serious inquirers to approach ruminations—for they can be little more than this—on the future in a chastened and modest manner. In this spirit, it is no doubt best not to presume to predict, divine, imagine, or anticipate tomorrow and what life will be like then; this sort of thing can be left to futurists, palm readers, mystic seers, profiteers, and charlatans of differing stripes. Critical reflection on the future requires one to look at the present to see if it is possible to discern any deep conflicts or tensions there that might be festering within the polity that need, at some point, some sort of resolution or reconciliation that will impact the future. And it may already be apparent that such a tension is implicit in the preceding discussion. For there does seem to be a conflict lurking within the account of American political culture as it has been developed above. If bureaucracy as an institution does not seem inconsistent with liberal culture, if, that is, bureaucratic structures may service a liberal polity by providing the efficiency and expertise now required for managing such a large and complex polity without contradicting or compromising key liberal values, there is still reason to be suspicious about their presence in the liberal polity. While the structures themselves may seem relatively benign, they also generate their own culture, and this culture is not necessarily reconcilable or compatible with the liberal culture that it invades and may even transform.

RANDALL PATRICK McMURPHY V. DILBERT

For purposes of illustration and perhaps dramatization, it may be best to explore questions cautiously and metaphorically about what happens when bureaucratic culture bumps up against liberal political culture by looking for possible descriptions of what this clash of cultures might look like. In this light, I want to call to mind another novel that has enjoyed great popularity in the United States. Unlike *1984*, this novel was written in the United States in the early 1960s by a (then) young American writer who, unlike Orwell, was not terribly obsessed with political themes and issues, at least explicitly. While *1984* is aptly, perhaps even unavoidably, characterized as a political novel (whatever that means), Ken Kesey's wonderful *One Flew over the Cuckoo's Nest* is hardly ever considered a political work.[2] And there is little reason to suppose that Kesey intended or wanted to write a political novel, or a novel that took politics as a central theme—a Christ's tale perhaps, a political novel unlikely. Nonetheless, *One Flew* is one of the finest contemporary studies of American politics available.

For readers unfamiliar with the work, a brief account of Kesey's tale is in order. The story is set in Oregon's state mental institution in Salem, where the novel's irascible, yet curiously loveable, protagonist (one can hardly call him a hero in the classic sense), Randall Patrick McMurphy, has been incarcerated by the state to evaluate his mental condition. McMurphy has had a history of trouble with the law; in and out of jail, McMurphy seems a picture of social pathology. This brawling, boisterous, barrel-chested Irishman with a magnetic, even charismatic, personality is quick to fight, cheat, and tweak the nose of everyone in authority. He seems incapable of holding a job or having positive relationships with others. If society looked anything like Hobbes' famously imagined state of nature, a state where everyone is at war with everyone else, McMurphy would be right at home.[3] But he is tragically out of place in the vastly more social world of American society and seems destined to a life of incarceration, trouble, sex, fighting, gambling, and good times that can only end tragically in a world that has no real place for the likes of him. McMurphy is a self-confessed conman, working as best he can to advantage himself by taking advantage of others whenever possible.

McMurphy's confinement in the mental institution, it turns out, is his own doing. He thinks he has found a clever dodge that will get him out of his incarceration on a work farm and enable him to do "soft duty" in the mental institution until his time has been served. But McMurphy is destined never to leave the mental institution alive. While the story allows readers to continually flirt with the fact that after a fashion McMurphy can escape from his confinement at almost any time, he elects not to do so and to continue his struggle with his antagonist, Nurse Ratched—"Big Nurse," as she is called, in a way that invites obvious parallels with Orwell's Big Brother. But this is a struggle he cannot hope to win, a struggle he ends up not wanting to win. To understand this struggle, and why McMurphy is doomed once he sets foot in the institution, a bit more must be said about the sociopolitical circumstances Kesey encases this classic conflict within.

The mental ward Kesey describes is an institution in the classic bureaucratic sense. It contains distinctive authority figures whose position in the system is both hierarchical and premised upon the expertise of the persons holding the various positions. While the doctors in the story have the medical expertise that the institution relies upon, the real authority in this social microcosm is Big Nurse. She is in charge of the ward. She manages the daily affairs of the patients, maintains order, dispenses justice, and lovingly monitors the welfare of those who depend upon her to help them get from one day to the next. As one patient in the ward puts it, the hospital is a matriarchy. Unlike the brotherly care on display in Orwell's Oceania, Kesey's ward is governed by a more motherly figure who sees to the care and order of those in her charge.

The patient population, in turn, is composed of two groups: the Chronics and the Acutes. Since the inspiration for Kesey's tale came from his work in a California mental institution while he was in graduate school at Stanford, the presence of the Chronics is understandable enough; these poor devils suffer from any manner of debilitating psychological and physiological defects and are simply incapable of functioning at all in the outside world. They are representative of the sad sight one sees, and generally expects to see, in institutions of this sort. And if such institutions did not exist, the relatives of these poor souls would have to bear the burden of their care, or they would be left to pass away quietly, the disregarded and discarded mistakes of nature.

But Kesey well knew that there is no tale to tell about the Chronics; the tragedy of their lives is not of their own or anyone else's doing. There is just nothing to say about them, but the Acutes are a different matter. They are in the institution because they have either committed themselves or they have accepted the decision of others that they need to live an institutionalized life, at least for the time being. For the Acutes, life outside the institution, life in the social mainstream, is a frightening and overly challenging affair. If they are up to the challenge at all, the burden of meeting it is so great that they can find no joy, no pleasure, in life. They prefer the care, the structure, and the guidance of the institution; they accept the authority of Big Nurse happily because they cannot themselves exercise the authority necessary to meet their own responsibilities to themselves. They have surrendered authority over their own lives to Big Nurse, and as a result they enjoy a quiet, carefully monitored, docile existence in the voluntary ward of the institution, under the watchful and capable eye of Nurse Ratched.

Then comes McMurphy, invading the tranquility, security, and peace of the ward with his bluster and his own personal version of mayhem. If McMurphy had thought for a moment that he could walk into this setting and after a few days demonstrate that he is not insane, that he is as normal and sane as the next person, two minutes studying the culture of the ward should have cured him of the thought. But McMurphy never really does fathom his own situation, that is, until it is too late. All McMurphy needs to do is be himself, and he will stand out as the sociopath he is. And all McMurphy does is to be himself, and so his fate is sealed.

If McMurphy would pay a little more attention to his surroundings, he might notice that life inside the ward bears an uncanny resemblance to life outside the ward, life in the "real world," so to speak. In the ward, the Acutes live quiet, civil, and well-programmed lives. Their welfare is managed by institutional officers whose job is to provide for the needs of the patients. The patients, in turn, are free to turn to those matters that entertain them, while their activities are carefully monitored and policed by Big Nurse. All this resembles the division of labor that characterizes many aspects of modern American society, with the significant exception that the Acutes do not have to get up and go to work in the morning. Feeding and clothing themselves is not a part of their regimen; otherwise their lives look depressingly familiar.

They accept the care of the institution that is their home, but they have no role to play in the daily operation of the ward. And perhaps this is reason to rather envy the Acutes. Their time is entirely their own; their entertainment is constantly set for them; they are comfortable in one another's company. Like children at a daycare center, they play together; in fact, their lives are spent playing together. Absent McMurphy, the ward looks a little like life on a cruise ship or at a fancy resort in the Bahamas, although certainly less well appointed. The ward, in any event, is anything but a jail. It is a home, and the Acutes are there because they want to be, because they are convinced that this is the best life for them, because they are too timid, frightened, or overwhelmed to face life outside the ward. It is a life without care, without responsibility, and without worry. The ward is paternalism—or rather, maternalism—raised to an art form, and the mental institution is a bureaucracy dedicated to serving the needs of people who are convinced that they need to surrender the freedom needed to take charge of their lives in order to live well.

Yet the portrait of the ward that Kesey paints is decidedly and importantly ambiguous; if it looks like Heaven from one angle, it seems more like Hell from another. It is, readers are told, a type of combine, and as such, it is but an element of a much bigger combine—the social world outside the walls of the institution. A combine, of course, is a machine used by farmers that passes over a field and processes the grain growing there, leaving neatly packaged and harvested bundles where the wild grain once grew. As a verb, however, the word *combine* works to identify a process in which things are brought together in such a close relationship that their individual characters are lost and they are merged into a distinctive whole. So society, viewed as a combine, looks like a great whirling machine that stamps out individuality and processes individuals to fit together neatly as well-adjusted social units. Social life, this is to say, takes on the appearance of a processing mechanism that manufactures people to fit into the slots it needs to have filled. It is, to be sure, an apt metaphor for a bureaucratic culture, but at the same time, it indicates the considerable threat this culture poses for individual freedom and independence.

Would McMurphy take the time to notice, he would realize that he does not belong in the ward. He is not an Acute in the strict sense, of course; he is a prisoner. He is not there voluntarily and able to leave when his sentence is up. He has been committed, and thus his fate is placed in the hands of Big Nurse. But this is not the heart of his tragedy. His tragic flaw is that he cannot help but be himself, and the self he is has no use for authority, no use for bureaucracy, no use for order and tranquility. McMurphy thinks he is quite sane and thus able to live his life as he wishes, to be the kind of independent individual once championed by writers like Emerson and Thoreau—a self-formed, self-creating being able and willing to "march to the beat of a different drummer."[4] He soon finds himself at odds with Big Nurse, and their struggle quickly centers around the control of the Acutes. McMurphy brings fresh air into the ward. He has the temerity, but not the power, to challenge the combine. He challenges the authority of Big Nurse, he works to take money from the Acutes by gambling and declaring himself the "Bull Goose Loony" of the ward, he schemes and connives to have things his own way, he arranges fishing trips to the coast, he smuggles hookers into the ward, and he variously shatters the quiet and order of the institution with his own peculiar brand of *joie de vivre*. McMurphy's rejection of Nurse Ratched's authority becomes a rebellion as the Acutes begin to side with their newfound charismatic leader and question the authority of Big Nurse. Of course, McMurphy could not have done otherwise; he is just being himself. And from the standpoint of the institution, the self that he is is a sociopath. If readers look at McMurphy and see a normal and fun-loving, roguish Irishman, from the vantage point of Nurse Ratched and the institution, he is insane, and if we think of insanity as a type of abnormal asociality, as a form of sociopathology, then Nurse Ratched and the institution are quite correct—McMurphy *is* insane.

What should one make of McMurphy? Readers typically find him a lovable figure; they usually root for him in his struggle with Big Nurse and mourn him when he meets his inevitable fate. Like Winston Smith before him, and with whom he has so much in common, he is tamed by his adversary. But unlike Winston, he is not saved by the loving attention of Big Nurse; things are cruder in Kesey's asylum. Instead of suffering the "brainwashing" of Big Brother, he is eventually lobotomized at the command of Big Nurse and left a docile, breathing corpse.[5] He is beyond the cure of modern science but not beyond the power of the institution. The combine cannot tame McMurphy, but it has other ways to deal with him. But does his eventual death breathe life into the Acutes? Are they saved by his sacrifice, thus completing the Christ tale? Or will the Acutes eventually wander back to the ward, if they ever really manage to leave, and continue to live out tepid lives in the care of Big Nurse? Are the Acutes really salvageable? And is McMurphy really a Christ figure or an antisocial menace to the world around him whose fate is fixed by the social need for order, tranquility, and civility in life? Must not the combine prevail in the end?

If readers find McMurphy a willful and independent human being struggling against conformity, authority, and the management of the ward—a radical individual in the classic American sense—they must also concede that he *is* a sociopath. He cannot keep a job, he cannot live within the parameters of the law, he cannot get along with others, and he cannot contribute profitably to the society around him. McMurphy is ungovernable! If this is the trait that makes him attractive as a fictional character, it is also the trait that makes him a sociopath in real life. He is a lovely illustration of a person fit only for a thoroughly decentralized social condition. But he would not make a good neighbor, a good fellow colleague, or a good friend. A society of Randall Patrick McMurphys would be a realm of chaos. If he sought to bring the Acutes around to his way of life, to disrupt the life of the ward by provoking rebellion against Big Nurse, he would reduce the ward to chaos, confusion, and disorder. Why should readers find such a character admirable? Why root for him in his war with Big Nurse?

Before trying to answer these questions, it might be good to introduce another fictional character, someone quite different from McMurphy: the cartoon character Dilbert. Dilbert works, indeed Dilbert lives, in a structured, organized, and thoroughly managed environment. He daily confronts the idiocy of bureaucratized life, but he does not rebel against it. He shrugs and puts up with it instead, for there is no rebelling against it. Dilbert's world is in so many ways the world of contemporary America, and if the cartoon strip points out the absurdity, though not the horror, of the combine, it does so in a way that amplifies the resignation people often seem to have for their condition. This is the world that modern humankind has built for itself; it is the probably inevitable product of the economically, technologically, scientifically, and socially complicated world of mass production, material achievement, and social diversity that people living in places like the United States identify with the good life. It is not a place for a Randall Patrick McMurphy, perhaps not even for a Winston Smith, but it is a place that Dilbert can call home. For Dilbert is a character suited for a centralized world; he can find the silliness of this world without fighting against it. Dilbert gets along, as the saying goes, by going along. The humor the cartoon brings into our lives derives from our ability to see our own being in the characters that flow through the cartoon strip and to recognize with Dilbert the oddity that haunts the logic of management.

Dilbert possesses a great virtue lacking in the likes of McMurphy; he is at least governable. Dilbert has adjusted to a world that he finds just a little amusing and perhaps a little tragic at the same time. Dilbert prefers to smirk at the combine rather than go to war with it. This is the attitude of one who understands both that life in the combine has a price and that the price must be paid. He gets up every day and goes to work, he obeys the law, he is civil to his associates, and he approaches the social world around him with irony rather than anger. He does not set about to joust with windmills but takes social life as it is, does his job, and draws his pay. He is not a romantic character, but he is quite sane, quite normal, and by today's standards—the standards of a bureaucratized world—quite ordinary. He is, in a word that belongs to the jargon of psychology, *well adjusted.*

Dilbert and McMurphy are polar extremes. While Dilbert can find absurdity in his world, he looks upon it with amusement and does not war against it. McMurphy cannot do otherwise than war against a social condition that is inconsistent with his being. McMurphy makes a wonderfully tragic character; there is no place for him in a world like this. If his fight against Big Nurse ultimately becomes something of a selfish quest, a quest to free the Acutes from Big Nurse, it is nonetheless a fight he is condemned to fight; he cannot do otherwise. Readers can root for McMurphy, sympathize with his situation, and find solace in his willingness to stand up to the combine. Readers can only recognize Dilbert's consternation and smirk with him, or at him, as the case may be.

So it seems the effort to understand politics has unmasked yet another paradox. While readers typically and emphatically side with McMurphy in his struggle against the combine, Dilbert is not a character that elicits much in the way of sympathy or appreciation. Although many readers enjoy the cartoon strip, it is rare to find someone who thinks positively of Dilbert. But the workings of the centralization paradox have produced a social environment where Dilbert, not McMurphy, is at home, and where the likes of McMurphy can exist and flourish only in fiction. It is arguably no exaggeration to say that most Americans would prefer to have Dilbert for a neighbor rather than McMurphy. In real life, those readers who find something admirable about McMurphy would want to have little to do with this unmanageable reprobate. Why, then, do readers find Dilbert, the fictionalized portrayal of themselves and their neighbors, just a little pathetic while they also embrace McMurphy, the fictionalized portrayal of a classic sociopath, as something of a heroic individual?

AMERICA'S ROMANCE WITH THE ROMANTICIZED AMERICA

It is possible to put a satisfactory answer to this question by recalling the fundamentals of America's liberal political culture and by recognizing the way they are expressed within the American social setting. This can be accomplished rather nicely by looking at American popular culture. McMurphy belongs to this culture, of course, and so does Dilbert. But they are not alone, and when one looks for stories about what might be called the romanticized American, the radical individual fashioned in the American mold, one finds many cousins of McMurphy but very few relatives of Dilbert. Tales of heroic individuals have long haunted American fiction, tales about characters that seem larger than life and whose exploits both display those traits and values Americans admire and help shape public attitudes about admirable individual traits and political values. These characters once emerged from stories about the American frontier, where they were born and where they found a home. In some key instances, the fictive portrayal of rugged, independent, and free individuals parodied the lives of real Americans. Davy Crockett's exploits entertained and captivated eastern readers even while he lived among them. Kit Carson's fame in the East was driven by pamphlets dedicated to romanticizing his exploits in ways that far transcended his actual adventures. Nor did stories of heroic individuals pressing into the lawless frontier end with the conquering of the West. Instead, fictive writers continued to imagine and worship the frontier spirit by divorcing their characters from any pretense of reality and inventing new heroes for the American market. As the Old West that spawned so many visions of American heroes passed into history, legend merged with myth, and tales of individuals who managed to control events in a hostile, decentralized social environment continued to entertain a polity whose social reality no longer squared with its classic image.

The mythic American hero has now even found a home outside the Old West. He can be found in cities alive and well in the form of characters like Sam Spade and Mike Hammer, and even in the imagined future in a character like Johnathan E of *Rollerball* fame. Perhaps the finest presentation of the heroic American individual is not even set in America but in the Casablanca of World War II. There an American expatriate by the name of Richard Blain manages to control the Nazis, the Vichy French, an idealistic Czechoslovakian patriot, and a self-promoting crook, all on his way to guiding events and love in what looks like a hostile state of nature reminiscent of the Old West. But if the film *Casablanca* is one of the most enduring artistic portrayals of the mythic American, it hardly exhausts the genre.

Still, the Old West remains the proper home for such characters, and even when they are not present there, as in the case of Sam Spade and Richard Blain, the places in which these characters flourish remain states of nature. They cannot endure the combine; they have no place in an environment with authority, management, and organization. There is something ironic both about the actual characters that inspired the mythic American and about the continuing fictional portrayals of mythic Americans. Men like Crockett and Carson helped "tame" the West; that is, they were instrumental in "civilizing" the West, moving it from a lawless and hostile condition to one that is managed in a manner that makes life there hospitable, enjoyable, and livable for everyone. Their lives and labors were instrumental in transforming the Old West into the New West, a place with no place for those heroic individuals whose rugged independence helped domesticate it. As in the movie *Shane*, civilization has no place for the gunfighter. And characters with the spirit and independence of the romanticized and legendary gunfighters of the American West no longer have lives to live amid civilization. To imagine them there is to imagine Randall Patrick McMurphy locked in a death struggle with the combine—a struggle that can lead only to his own death.

But then what is it about the mythic American that captures the American imagination, and seems always to have captured the American imagination? Why should tales of this sort resonate so with the American psyche? And why should they continue to resonate with this psyche long after the anarchical environment in which they flourished has passed into history? In exploring these questions, it is important to remember the earlier comments on how political culture shapes identity, and also to appreciate how values are shaped by the existential conditions in which human beings find themselves. The values and ideals displayed by fictional figures like Richard Blain and Randall Patrick McMurphy are not just the norms of the Old West—in fact, they are probably not even the norms of the Old West—but the norms of the old liberalism that found fertile ground in America, particularly the America of the Old West. For the mythic American is a classic illustration of a free person, and when that character is kept alive in popular culture, the personification of what it means to be free becomes an illustration of what Americans learn to value in life.

By way of illustration, consider the myth that has come to surround Davy Crockett, one of the most legendary of America's frontiersmen. Alexis de Tocqueville met Crockett when he visited America and found him to be a boisterous, obnoxious, illiterate braggart—hardly the sort of character to inspire legends. But it is not the real Crockett that resonates with contemporary Americans. If it had not been for Walt Disney's fictional portrayal of Crockett in a television series of the 1950s, Crockett today would likely rate little more than a footnote in a history text on the saga of the American frontier. And it is the fictionalized Crockett of the Disney broadcast, and not the real Crockett, that provides such a lovely illustration of a romanticized albeit mythic American. In the Disney telecast, Crockett (played famously by Fess Parker) had a wife and children, but from the image of Crockett presented by the show, he was never home! Instead, he was off seeking adventure—fighting Indians, wrestling bears, floating down the Mississippi, and charging off to the Alamo, "where freedom was fighting another foe." What kind of a husband was this? What kind of a father was this? Today such a scoundrel would likely find himself faced with a quick divorce, hounded by the police for past-due child support, and roundly criticized as an irresponsible and lazy vagrant!

But this isn't the image Americans have of the fictionalized Davy Crockett. Instead, Americans are hardly troubled by his lack of role responsibility, preferring to find romance in his freedom. Even though he had encumbrances, the Crockett that Disney popularized was thoroughly unencumbered. His social attachments did not hold him back; he put them aside to challenge life to the fullest. He had the character traits necessary to meet whatever threat the lawless frontier, the savage natives, and even the autocratic Mexicans threw at him—Disney couldn't bring himself to show Crockett dying at the Alamo, leaving viewers with the everlasting image of Crockett holding off Mexican soldiers with the butt of his gun, the last freedom fighter standing. Clever, cunning, resourceful, independent, and imaginative, he was built for the frontier, built for the challenges of a life lived with uncertainty, difficulty, and struggle. These are the virtues of an individual capable of thriving, not just surviving, in a decentralized social condition. He was free by his own choosing, and he had the strength of character to make something of his freedom, to manage events, and to thrive in a lawless land.

If Crockett's freedom was total, if he was not encumbered by the annoyances of an appropriately social life that hold most people prisoner to their daily burdens like the ropes of the Lilliputians in *Gulliver's Travels*, his equality was also complete. There simply were no artificial inequalities present in the frontier, no maldistribution of social resources, no hierarchical authorities (or at least none that mattered), and no social organization (except ultimately the Mexican army) to chain him down. Everyone stood equal in the frontier, and those who excelled in the frontier did so because they had the attributes, the personal virtues associated with a strong character, that enabled them to do so. If some, like Crockett, triumphed in the frontier, it was because of their superior natures; only in the frontier could natural talent and ability prevail. In society, the weak, incompetent, and disgustingly evil can achieve their ends by gaining a power premised upon social inequalities, but not so in the frontier. That was a place for the virtuous, a place where virtue mattered. It was a place where individual initiative, industry, and effort mattered, and the heroic individuals of the frontier, as they are presented to the viewing audience, invariably put them to use for the general good of others and not for personal gain.

Free, independent, equal, and virtuous—these are the attributes of the liberal individual as this character has come to be displayed in America; they are the values and ideals that have emerged with and helped to shape the liberal tradition in America. In turn, they indicate the distinctive character of the personified images of the mythic American. (Readers familiar with the

Disney series may recall the simple folk wisdom that Disney's writers attrib-
uted to Crockett: "Make sure you're right; then go ahead.") It matters little
that these values and virtues were probably mythic even when the Old West
flourished, for they are the values and virtues that the Old East elected to
romanticize and mythologize in the legend of the Old West. In this sense, the
American self-image was formed in a romance with the West, and it is perhaps hardly surprising that the cowboy remains the standard image of the
free, independent, and self-reliant American. The American West proved fertile ground for America's mythic self-identity, and it took a firm and lasting
hold on the American consciousness.

Images of the mythic American, whether set in the frontier, in Casablanca,
in "the asphalt jungle," or elsewhere, do more than provide seemingly end-
less sources of entertainment for Americans who thirst for mythic representa-
tions. In fact, they have an important double effect on American culture, first
by reinforcing liberal values and ideals in the culture and second by helping
Americans cope with the fact that their lives are tragically different from the
lives lived by their mythic heroes. They offer Americans concrete images of
how life should be lived and of what a free and equal—that is to say, a decentralized—culture looks like. In this regard, they serve to publicize and popu-
larize what it means to be an American, understood ideally and against the
background of liberal political culture. Tales of the mythic American, in other
words, have a significant political message by virtue of the fact that they present Americans with images of ungovernable and apolitical characters, that is,
of free and independent individuals who have little use or need for government. Government can only impede and constrain such individuals, and
hence it seems only natural to be suspicious of an institution that is, in principle, a threat to the freedom and independence of the individual.

But tales of mythic Americans do more than propagate the Americanized
ideals of liberal political culture; they also provide important coping mechanisms that enable Americans to adjust to the fact that these values, these ideals, are increasingly out of place in the world that they helped mold and
shape. In the most immediate sense, stories about mythic Americans provide
a sort of escapism. If the daily life of most Americans is characterized by the
values and structures of a centralized society and if Americans still cling to
the visions born in a more decentralized era, then tales of decentralized conditions and perfectly free individuals help them endure. Americans can (and
do) root for Randall Patrick McMurphy as he challenges the combine and
struggles with Big Nurse in order to win freedom for the Acutes—to build
them back up to size so they can find the courage to confront the combine.
Americans can (and do) admire Richard Blain as the lone American in a foreign land and the lone character capable of controlling events in an uncertain

and hostile environment. This is good stuff for the national psyche, and for a moment, people can hold out the hope that the combine can be beaten, that centralization can be opposed, that the ideals of freedom and independence can really be lived. But Americans will neither root for nor admire poor Dilbert. And tales of the mythic American enable them to forget for a moment that the life of the typical American more closely approximates Dilbert's life than McMurphy's. While the social world of America is Dilbert's world, the American consciousness still clings to Crockett's mythologized frontier.

Yet this indicates only that social life in America is sadly inconsistent with the American consciousness. McMurphy cannot survive in Dilbert's social world, and as Kesey foreshadows in the opening pages of his story, the combine is simply too powerful for the independent individual. The virtues of the romanticized American individual are no longer appropriate for the realities of social life in America; they are the virtues and values that belong to an idealized vision of a frontier (qua, state of nature) that probably never really existed. McMurphy cannot defeat Big Nurse. It was never a fair fight; they were never equals. Seen from the perspective of a more centralized social order, McMurphy is just another Don Quixote—just as insane, just as anachronistic, and just as doomed. But seen from the perspective of more decentralized and more liberal times, McMurphy is another Davy Crockett, another Richard Blain, another heroic individual who will not surrender his freedom, admit his dependency on others, or concede the authority of the combine. The perspective that Americans adopt when they encounter fiction of this sort, the perspective cultivated by fiction that romanticizes America's mythic imagination, tells them much about who they are and about the psychic tension that has come to trouble their political identity. These stories help Americans reconcile their dreams, their visions, and their antique ideals and values with their political present. They bring these dreams and ideals back to life and validate them, if only for a moment.

POLITICS AND CULTURAL CHANGE

Cultures change, including political cultures. How does this happen? It could happen by means of a revolutionary moment, but this seems unlikely. It is somewhat fanciful to suppose that the ontology and normative posture of a culture can change dramatically and immediately as a consequence of one cataclysmic event. Ways of seeing and valuing do change, of course, but change is likely to be slow and evolutionary and to proceed in an almost indiscernible fashion. Change occurs in the process of dealing with conflict and contradiction in the polity. For change to occur, there must be some tension present in the polity that must be resolved through time. And it should now be apparent that there is a tension inherent in American political life that may well drive social and political change—a tension that has, in fact, already driven a degree of political change.

The tension that seems most likely to drive change in the American consciousness can be understood as a clash between the ontology and normative structure of liberal political culture and the ontology and normative structure of bureaucratic culture. The ways of seeing and doing that support a decentralized political system are diametrically opposed to the ways of seeing and doing at home in a centralized political system. If authority is necessary for modern social life, equality is in trouble. If management is unavoidable in modern society, freedom is in jeopardy. If organization is required to manage modern social problems, individual initiative and independence are largely out of place.

Romanticized images of individuals who belong to a different social world can perhaps do something to release the tension generated by this contradiction, but at some point—who can say exactly when—they will fail to satisfy and become fanciful and boring. At some point—and who can say exactly when—the dream of defeating the combine will become a nightmare. The combine will come to matter, and people will want to find a friendly image in the caring, nurturing visage of Big Nurse. Social life, in turn, will come to be seen not as a relationship among independent, self-interest-maximizing individuals, but as the interaction of social roles. Personal identity will be fixed not by one's presence as one person among others, but by what one does to contribute to social life, by one's place and role in the combine. Some will serve; others will be served. Some will be doctors, nurses, lawyers, electricians, or professors; others will be Acutes and push brooms, play poker, watch television, and clean bathrooms.

These ruminations anticipate, to be sure, the view that bureaucratic culture will erode liberal political culture and eventually replace it, that cultural change looks to be headed away from the ontology and normative structure of liberal political culture and toward something radically and significantly different—toward Dilbert's world. But they also imply that America is not there yet, that remnants of liberal political culture remain present in the American consciousness. If so, then perhaps it is not overly optimistic to suppose that something can be done about all of this, that what seems an inevitable transformation in American political culture can be forestalled if not altogether avoided. This thought—this hope, if seen from inside liberal culture—suggests a reason to return to Orwell's worries about political power.

The first point to be considered on this score is that bureaucratic culture looks little or nothing like the political world Orwell imagined in *1984*.

Orwell imagined a world where political culture atrophied, largely as a result of benign neglect, and nothing emerged to take its place. The result was a stagnant social condition in which nothing mattered to those who managed to gain power but its exercise, and the exercise of power required a victim. Deviance needed to be manufactured so that it could be cured. In Orwell's Oceania, the ruling elite sought to exercise power in a social environment where power was no longer necessary to maintain social order and stability. But once power became its own end, it had to be exercised; otherwise there was nothing for the ruling elite to do. Part (but only part) of the horror of the social world Orwell invents is that the proles are free but unable to make their freedom matter. They go about their sorry lives imprisoned not by the might of Big Brother but by the limitations inherent in their own ontological horizons.

This is not exactly parallel to the mental ward that Kesey imagined, but there are similarities. Big Nurse is not intent upon exercising power in a crude and brutal manner; it is not even fanciful to suppose that she really has the best interests, as she understands them, of the Acutes in mind. Unlike Big Brother, the loving visage of Big Nurse is no smoke screen. She understands the need for order to maintain stability in the ward. She holds two insights that are altogether typical of bureaucratic culture: (1) to go well, social life must be well-organized and carefully structured and monitored, and (2) the Acutes do not know what is best for them. Their well-being, their future, is in her hands. The future of Oceania is also in the hands of Big Brother, and it is, of course, control of the future that is the ultimate exercise of power in Orwell's world. But Big Nurse does not control the future in order to guarantee that she will be able to exercise power forever; she controls the future because she is the one with the knowledge to do so well. She knows what is best, and she needs power in order to make sure that those who lack this knowledge do not disrupt things and jeopardize the smooth flow of social life. While O'Brien describes a jealous and selfish concern with power in *1984*, Kesey has imagined a world where power is exercised for beneficent ends. To go on well, the ward (social life) must be managed according to the prevailing standards of rationality. The power on display in *One Flew* is not exercised because power has become an end in itself; it is exercised because power accompanies authority, and authority is the central virtue in a managed world.

The Acutes, however, are reminiscent of the proles in at least one crucial way. Like the proles, their ontological horizons are modest indeed. Their consciousness floats around their immediate lives and the activities of the moment. Until McMurphy disrupts their limited vision, they care little about life outside the ward, about the past, about the World Series, or about exercising any responsibility for themselves. The Acutes, like the proles, have become childlike; like children, but unlike the proles, they are happy because they are cared for. Like children, and like the proles, they are the limited spectators of the world around them. Like the proles, they are free; they could leave the ward if they elected to do so. But before McMurphy, they had no inclination to leave the ward; in fact, the world outside the ward frightened and confused them. They are refugees from the responsibility of self-care because self-care was beyond them, or at least they believed this self-care to be beyond them.

It would not be appropriate to say the Acutes lived in a condition of servitude any more than it would be appropriate to say that the proles lived in a condition of servitude. The Acutes did not serve anyone; instead, they were served. They differ from the proles in this regard because the proles received very little service from anyone. They simply endured, almost heroically, in conditions they were too stupid to recognize as horrible. The Acutes, on the other hand, were freed from the hardships of life by the service provided by Big Nurse. McMurphy does not try to restore their freedom; he tries only to make their freedom matter. He gives them the courage to return to a decentralized world, a world where they must manage to serve themselves. But Kesey's novel invariably leaves readers wondering how long the Acutes will be able to serve themselves. And this wondering spins around a crucial question: is the condition that makes the ward the only place where the Acutes can thrive a consequence of their own character defects (they are, after all, in a mental institution) or an aspect of a complex social being that makes the bureaucratic management of social life an unavoidable necessity?

Readers approaching the novel with the ontology and morality of liberal political culture in mind will want to insist that the Acutes do suffer from a defect of character, and one that is fixed by the selfless efforts of McMurphy. McMurphy, on this reading, sacrifices himself to save the Acutes and restore their strength of character. But McMurphy is also in a mental institution, and he is there because he could not manage life outside the ward. He too lacked the character necessary to survive in a social world that requires management, organization, and authority. He is an anachronism, a cowboy living in a place quite different from the Old West, and he can only fight the combine so long and so hard. Kesey conjures up the image of someone who has grown tired of the struggle and who has already managed to figure out that he has no hope of winning the struggle with Big Nurse and the combine. If he doesn't leave the ward when he learns that it is possible to escape, it is perhaps because he knows that there is no place for him to go. He has no reason to trade the ward inside for the one that awaits him outside. He is resigned to his last stand. Similarly, there is also no place for the Acutes to go. As the novel ends, some leave the ward—but for how long? Others simply transfer to a different ward, as if Big Nurse was the problem. So, what looks like a Christ's tale from one angle seems like a last hurrah for a dying culture from another.

SOCIAL CONSCIOUSNESS
AND SOCIAL REALITY

In *1984*, Big Brother controls the past in order to control social consciousness. In an environment where the past is continually changing, one cannot trust one's memory. Instead, one merely trusts the authoritative pronouncements of those individuals or institutions that occupy positions previously recognized and accepted as trustworthy. By controlling social consciousness, Big Brother is able to control social reality. This, once again, is the exercise of power raised to the level of art. But contemporary life is not exactly like this. No one controls the past in contemporary America, and therefore no one controls the present. If Orwell is right, this also means that no one controls the future. But a thoughtful reading of social conditions can yield some insight into the kinds of possibilities that the future has in store for Americans.

George Orwell, as a political thinker, seemed to fear that in his day, happiness was coming into conflict with freedom, and that if people had to choose between these two values, they would likely choose happiness. His writings might profitably be read as a fight against this choice and a warning cry about what making such a choice would probably mean. But Orwell's way of putting the issue might be overly simple. As bureaucratic culture erodes and replaces liberal political culture, as the social reality of the bureaucratic phenomenon begins to transform social consciousness, contemporary Americans are not confronted with a choice between freedom and happiness. The choice they confront is more subtle than this. The choice they confront is whether social reality should be permitted to determine social consciousness or whether social consciousness should make an effort to survive certain necessary transformations that must take place in social reality. If, however, the choice is not itself brought to consciousness, if Americans do not become aware of the fact that social reality is still in their own hands, at least to some degree, then social reality will determine social consciousness.

It is tempting to think that Kesey saw things in a manner similar to Orwell. It is tempting, that is, to suppose that Kesey thought the Acutes could choose happiness (the carefree, monitored, well-managed, and cared-for life of the ward) or freedom (the rough-and-tumble, decentralized, self-reliant life outside the ward). But freedom and happiness are more closely linked in individual consciousness than this. People who are happy with their situation will likely think themselves free. Freedom does not seem restricted if a person is prohibited from doing something she does not want to do anyway, and it seems fully realized if one is not prohibited from doing those things one wants to do. How one views one's opportunity set, the set of actions one is not prohibited from doing, is thus fundamental to ordinary reflections on freedom. By surrendering any concern about how to manage their lives, the Acutes qualified as free in their own minds. They could do the things that made them happy; consequently they believed themselves free. Their choice, insofar as they had one, was not between freedom and happiness, but about what things would make them happy. But this choice, insofar as it really was one, was heavily influenced by Big Nurse and her authoritative voice on what was in fact good for them. Their confessed inability to fend for themselves made them quite content to put their care in the hands of Big Nurse, and by way of a trade-off, Big Nurse provided a secure environment in which they could pursue those things in which they found happiness. The thought that they might be sacrificing their freedom thus never occurred to them, and could not occur to them given the way they understood freedom and its relation to happiness.

McMurphy changed all this simply by persuading the Acutes that they should want to do some things that Big Nurse didn't want them to do. Like ill-mannered children, they chafed against the authority of Big Nurse only when they were encouraged by a disruptive force to want to do things they previously had no interest in doing. Their rebellion was an attempt to reclaim some of the self-control they had voluntarily abandoned to Big Nurse. But they could not have their cake and eat it too; they could not find happiness in the structured environment provided by Big Nurse and also find happiness in doing those things inconsistent with this structure. A social system that faces this problem stands on the brink of suicide. If authoritative order is necessary for social survival, some aspects of self-control and self-determination must be conceded to the appropriate authority, and if it is not, then the order that is a precondition of happiness is jeopardized. So, while it might seem that McMurphy brought freedom to the ward, what he really brought was unhappiness and discord. At the novel's end, the Acutes are no longer happy with their situation, but it is far from clear that they can manage to survive in a different environment.

So it is not quite correct to think that the rise of the bureaucratic phenomenon means that the citizens of modern polities must choose between freedom and happiness. Understood within the liberal political tradition, the ideal of freedom identifies a decentralized social arrangement where individual choice and initiative are considered the proper route to personal happiness. But freedom of this sort is not the only route to happiness, and it may not even be the best route. Happiness can also be achieved by means of centralized management where social life is choreographed and structured in order to supply people with the things they want. In fact, this is guaranteed to assure personal happiness, because the things people learn to want are taught to them by the centralized order of the polity. Orwell seems at times to think that freedom is a good in its own right, an intrinsic good, and not just something that is good as a means to the end of happiness, an instrumental good. But freedom can be an intrinsic good only within the context of liberal political culture, and if a different cultural influence works to shape individual consciousness, one like bureaucratic culture that does not regard freedom as an intrinsic good, then this view of freedom will begin to sound quite strange and foreign.

All this implies that people whose consciousness is shaped by bureaucratic culture may consider themselves free by virtue of the fact that they are happy, that they can do the things they have learned to want to do. In the minds of individuals whose consciousness has come to be shaped by bureaucratic culture, they are free *because* they are happy; the two norms are no longer conceptually distinguishable. Therefore, order, structure, management, and organization need not, and with the full implementation of bureaucratic culture will not, intrude upon individual freedom, because the practical meaning of what it means to be free will have changed.

This is one plausible way to imagine how a transformation from liberal political culture to bureaucratic culture might take place. The transition, this is to say, need not involve the conscious abandonment of liberal ideals but their subtle co-optation. Liberal ideals can be transformed by the bureaucratic phenomenon in a manner that enables the words, complete with their normative significance, to endure (words like *freedom* and *equality*), but their meaning and significance will be reshaped by the new culture. The meaning of freedom, in other words, will be reconfigured according to the ontology and normative structure of the bureaucratic phenomenon. While the rhetoric of liberalism remains in place, the new culture that emerges is hardly liberal at all. Bureaucratic culture has simply assimilated liberal culture and transformed it by remaking liberal ideals in a manner consistent with bureaucratic ontology and bureaucratic morality. Freedom, in this transformed sense, is now easily reconcilable with authority and centralization and is no longer anathema to authority or centralized social management. Social consciousness is transformed by social reality without anyone noticing.

For those who still cling to genuine liberal sympathies, this is a dire situation. Is it also an inevitable one? Is it even an objectionable one? The answers to these questions are both complex and related. Suppose we start with the second question first. The difficulty posed by this question becomes apparent once one appreciates that there would seem to be no neutral or objective ground upon which to base an evaluation of the erosion of liberal political culture and a transformation to bureaucratic culture. These cultures themselves provide the perspective from which such normative judgments must be made and upon which they must be based. Philosophers sometimes try to get outside their own cultures and find a theoretical *terra firma* from which to make such judgments. But how can anyone know they have succeeded in this? If the ontology and normativity of one's culture shape one's way of seeing, what could one hope to see if one threw these things off? And what could it mean to throw them off? How could one really know that one had succeeded in doing so? Just as it seems impossible to see oneself from outside one's own skin, so too it seems impossible to conceptualize one's social world from outside the conceptual apparatus that configures one's way of seeing and understanding.

So it seems that an evaluation of the transition from liberal to bureaucratic culture will depend upon whether one's perspective is shaped by the old liberal view or the new bureaucratic view. If one sees things from the bureaucratic perspective, the question about the desirability of the transformation being considered is hardly problematic. The bureaucratic perspective guarantees that a cultural shift to a more bureaucratic, centralized, and authoritative social condition is both desirable and all to the good. Similarly, if one clings to a vestige of the old liberal view, the question about the desirability of the transformation is easily resolved. If one still sees individuals as independent beings of great moral value and as autonomous agents, one is likely to greet the transition to bureaucratic culture with both horror and anxiety.

What, then, about the question of the inevitability of the transformation? Seen from the perspective supplied by bureaucratic culture, this transformation may indeed seem inevitable. If social life in a complex, modern social setting is unimaginable without centralized management, then the transformation is sure to seem inevitable. But this is certainly no reason to view the transition with either horror or anxiety; instead, it might be reason to look favorably upon it. The German philosopher Hegel wrote about historical progress and imagined that reason would manifest itself in the world, and one might regard the transformation to bureaucratic culture in largely Hegelian terms.[6] Bureaucratic culture now fits the human condition, and seen from the bureaucratic perspective, this will be as inevitable as it is desirable.

But the liberal perspective suggests an alternative view about the inevitability of a social transformation to bureaucratic culture. If such a transformation is considered repugnant from the liberal perspective, there is reason to oppose it and not concede its inevitability. But liberals must still confront the centralization paradox, for it is this that drives the trend toward the bureaucratic phenomenon. Given the fact of decentralization, centralization is inevitable, and centralization remains a response to decentralization up to the point where it swallows decentralization completely, up to the point where all aspects of social life are completely managed by bureaucratic authorities. Given the account of the bureaucratic phenomenon offered above, moreover, it seems plausible to assume that centralization does become its own end under bureaucratic culture. When bureaucratic culture is fully in place, centralization is a goal in and of itself and not simply a response to decentralization. Once again, then, the specter of inevitability must confront the waning liberal spirit.

This is the challenge liberals must meet if they are to avoid a total transition to bureaucratic culture. Is it too late for liberals? Is bureaucratic culture already firmly in place in the United States? Perhaps not. If it were already in place, tales of mythic Americans would no longer resonate with the citizenry. Americans would find tales about Davy Crockett boring and outdated, they would regard characters like Richard Blain and Sam Spade as silly and misguided, and they would root for Big Nurse rather than Randall Patrick McMurphy in McMurphy's battle with the combine. If tales of mythic American heroes still resonate with Americans and work to provide them with an element of solace as they confront their Dilbert lives, then the ontology and morality of liberal culture must still be alive, at least to some degree, in the social consciousness of America. And this culture will continue to endure in the American consciousness until characters like Blain and McMurphy are no longer popularly regarded as heroic individuals but are seen instead as examples of an unhealthy social pathology.

So the issue of inevitability should still matter in American society because liberal culture is not yet dead, though it is surely dying. And here liberals are likely to take exception to Hegel and his way of thinking. They are unlikely to concede that the future is entirely beyond human control, that it is entirely structured and determined by historical or sociological forces over which human beings can exert no conscious control. This way of thinking is itself inconsistent with liberal culture, which concedes to human beings the freedom to participate at least to some degree in the shaping of their own future.

But how can liberals hope to domesticate the bureaucratic phenomenon given the necessity of the centralization paradox? How can liberals adapt to inevitable centralization in a way that does not also allow bureaucratic culture to replace liberal political culture? Here again Orwell's warning in *1984* seems relevant and to the point. Oceania became what it was because of the limited ontological horizons of the proles. Power became its own end in the hands of the inner party because no one in Oceania remembered or understood the ideals and convictions that defined them as the members of a polity. If liberal culture is to endure and survive the onslaught of the bureaucratic phenomenon, it will only be because the citizens of liberal cultures expand their ontological horizons and bring the ontology and morality of liberalism into clear view before them. People will need to understand who they are as liberal individuals and what the cultural boundaries are that correspondingly shape them and configure their identity; they must self-consciously keep their culture before them and understand what it demands of them. This, in the final analysis, is perhaps the most important reason one has for thinking about politics. Social reality will shape social consciousness if people do not make the conscious effort not to let this happen.

In practice, the effort to sustain a cultural consciousness against transformative change might be facilitated by focusing upon the notion of social justice, for the ends of social justice are themselves rooted in liberal political culture, and to worry about the justness of the liberal polity is to worry about how successful this polity is in living up to its own ideals. Thus a concern for social justice is an invitation to expand ontological horizons, and consequently an opportunity to breathe life back into liberal ideals. Still, thinking about politics requires a good deal of work and effort, and the problems that plague democracy are likely to replicate themselves here. It is much easier to come home from a hard day's work, flip on the television, crack open an adult beverage, and lose oneself in a ball game or vapid movie. It is much easier, in the modern age, to be a prole or an Acute than a committed liberal. But this means only that preserving liberal political culture may be unlikely; it does not mean that its transformation to bureaucratic culture is inevitable.

A EULOGY FOR LIBERAL POLITICAL CULTURE?

A eulogy can be either a commendation of something or the praising of someone or something that has passed away. It may be too early to eulogize liberal political culture in the latter sense. In the United States, the liberal tradition still provides crucial conceptual and normative boundaries that help Americans identify and understand themselves. And because of this, it is perhaps reasonable to eulogize liberal political culture in the former sense as an apt method of closure for a work dedicated to thinking about politics—and not just about government.

The liberal tradition in America has been a source of national strength and a foundation for national identity. Its very success has become the source of its greatest challenge, however, as the centralization paradox indicates. As a result of the emergence in America of the bureaucratic phenomenon, the fate of the liberal tradition now hangs in the balance, and along with it, the source of identity in which Americans have found great pride also hangs in the balance. If the liberal tradition withers and is replaced by bureaucratic culture, there will be no radical break with the language of the past. Freedom will not cease to be an issue, but freedom, as understood in the liberal tradition, will cease to exist. Equality will not cease to matter, but Americans will cease being equal. Rights will not cease to exist, but their meaning will be configured by the insights and requirements of bureaucratic authority. Government will not be transformed into Big Brother, but it will probably begin to look a bit like Big Nurse—or more like Big Nurse than it does now. And the process of government will become even more of a spectator sport than it now is rather than a participatory activity.

If this transformation is to be avoided, the citizenry will need to take a fresh look at politics and begin to recognize it as a complex subject in its own right. Citizens will need to see politics as something distinct from government and expand their collective ontological horizons to self-consciously comprehend their political culture. They will need to see themselves as fellow citizens committed to a common enterprise of living together, not just as Republicans or Democrats, liberals or conservatives, or lefties or righties. When it comes to thinking about politics, these disagreements don't matter much; there are weightier matters for citizens to focus on, reflect on, and argue about. But this becomes apparent only when people set aside these more commonplace squabbles and make an earnest effort to confront and understand the subject of politics. If politics thus understood does not become a vital part of the public discourse on how things might best go in America, it will soon be time to begin a different eulogy for liberalism.

NOTES

1. Marx was a terribly prolific writer, and there is no easy way to access the theoretical edifice he created. There are, however, a few excellent anthologies of his writings. Cf. David McLellan, *Karl Marx: Selected Writings* (Oxford: Oxford University Press, 1977) and Robert C. Tucker, *The Marx-Engels Reader* (New York: W. W. Norton & Co., 1972).

2. Ken Kesey, *One Flew over the Cuckoo's Nest* (New York: Signet, 1962).

3. Hobbes, *Leviathan*, Ch. 13.

4. See, for example, Ralph Waldo Emerson, "Self-Reliance," in *Emerson's Essays* (New York: Thomas Y. Crowell Co., 1926), 31–66; Henry David Thoreau, "Civil Disobedience," in *Civil Disobedience*, ed. Hugo Bedau, 27–48 (New York: Pegasus, 1969).

5. The fates of McMurphy and Winston Smith may not be so different after all, of course, although Winston's "lobotomy" is of a different sort than McMurphy's. But in

both cases, these characters lose their identity and their independence because the capacity think and function independently has been removed from them.

6. G. W. F. Hegel, *The Philosophy of Right*, trans. T. M. Knox (London: Oxford University Press, 1952). Hegel fashioned a new understanding of freedom in his political philosophy—one suited in its own way to the new bureaucratic world that he thought to be emerging. To be free, for Hegel, was to recognize that one was free because one was participating in the only rational way of proceeding in social life, viz, by serving the state as a functionary whose work was necessary to make collective life go well.

Selected Bibliography

Ackerman, Bruce. *Private Property and the Constitution.* New Haven, CT: Yale University Press, 1977.

Adams, Henry. *The Education of Henry Adams.* Boston: Houghton Mifflin, 1961.

Andrews, Lewis M., and Marvin Karlins. *Requiem for Democracy.* New York: Holt, Rinehart, & Winston, 1971.

Arendt, Hannah. *The Human Condition.* Garden City, NY: Doubleday Anchor, 1959.

Baier, Kurt, and Nicholas Rescher, eds. *Values and the Future.* New York: The Free Press, 1969.

Bailyn, Bernard. *The Ideological Origins of the American Revolution.* Cambridge, MA: Harvard University Press, 1967.

Barber, Benjamin. *The Conquest of Politics.* Princeton, NJ: Princeton University Press, 1988.

———. *Strong Democracy.* Berkeley: University of California Press, 1984.

Barry, Brian. *Political Argument.* New York: Routledge & Kegan Paul, 1965.

———. *Why Social Justice Matters.* Cambridge: Polity Press, 2005.

Bauman, Zygmunt. *Freedom.* Minneapolis: University of Minnesota Press, 1988.

Beard, Charles A. *An Economic Interpretation of the Constitution of the United States.* New York: The Free Press, 1941.

Benn, S. I., and R. S. Peters. *The Principles of Political Thought: Social Foundations of the Democratic State.* New York: The Free Press, 1959.

Berlin, Isaiah. *The Crooked Timber of Humanity.* Princeton, NJ: Princeton University Press, 1990.

Bickel, Alexander. *The Least Dangerous Branch.* Indianapolis, IN: Bobbs-Merrill Co., 1962.

Birch, Anthony H. *The Concepts and Theories of Modern Democracy.* New York: Routledge, 1993.

Blau, Peter M., and Marshall W. Meyer. *Bureaucracy in Modern Society.* 2nd ed. New York: Random House, 1971.

Boorstin, Daniel. *The Genius of American Politics.* Chicago: University of Chicago Press, 1953.

Burke, Edmund. *Reflections on the Revolution in France.* New York: Penguin Books, 1970.

Callan, Eamon. *Creating Citizens*. Oxford: Clarendon Press, 1997.

Campbell, Tom. *Justice*. Atlantic Highlands, NJ: Humanities Press International, 1988.

Carr, Craig L. *The Liberal Polity*. Houndsmills: Palgrave MacMillan, 2006.

———. *On Fairness*. Aldershot: Ashgate, 2000.

Cohen, Joshua, and Joel Rogers. *On Democracy: Toward a Transformation of American Society*. New York: Penguin, 1983.

Connolly, William E. *Political Theory and Modernity*. Oxford: Basil Blackwell, 1988.

Crick, Bernard. *In Defense of Politics*. 2nd ed. New York: Penguin, 1983.

Crozier, Michael. *The Bureaucratic Phenomenon*. Chicago: University of Chicago, 1973.

Dahl, Robert. *After the Revolution? Authority in a Good Society*. Rev. ed. New Haven, CT: Yale University Press, 1990.

———. *Democracy and Its Critics*. New Haven, CT: Yale University Press, 1989.

———. *Dilemmas of Pluralist Democracy*. New Haven, CT: Yale University Press, 1982.

———. *A Preface to Democratic Theory*. Chicago: University of Chicago Press, 1956.

Dolbeare, Kenneth M. *Political Change in the United States: A Framework for Analysis*. New York: McGraw-Hill, 1974.

Downs, Anthony. *Inside Bureaucracy*. Boston: Little, Brown, 1967.

Dunn, John. *Democracy: The Unfinished Journey*. Oxford: Oxford University Press, 1992.

Edelman, Martin. *Democratic Theories and the Constitution*. Albany: State University of New York Press, 1984.

Edelman, Murray. *The Symbolic Uses of Politics*. Urbana: University of Illinois Press, 1977.

Elster, Jon. *The Cement of Society*. Cambridge: Cambridge University Press, 1989.

Elster, Jon, and Rune Slagstad. *Constitutionalism and Democracy*. Cambridge: Cambridge University Press, 1988.

Ely, John Hart. *Democracy and Distrust*. Cambridge, MA: Harvard University Press, 1980.

Fishkin, James. *Democracy and Deliberation*. New Haven, CT: Yale University Press, 1991.

———. *Justice, Equal Opportunity, and the Family*. New Haven, CT: Yale University Press, 1983.

Flathman, Richard E. *The Practice of Political Authority*. Chicago: University of Chicago Press, 1980.

———. *The Practice of Rights*. Cambridge: Cambridge University Press, 1976.

Friedman, Lawrence M. *A History of American Law*. New York: Simon & Schuster, 1975.

Fuchs, Lawrence H. *The American Kaleidoscope*. Hanover, NH: Wesleyan University Press, 1990.

Gerston, Larry N., Cynthia Fraleigh, and Robert Schwab. *The Deregulated Society*. Pacific Grove, CA: Brooks/Cole Publishing Co., 1988.

Gitlin, Todd. *The Twilight of Common Dreams*. New York: Henry Holt & Co., 1995.

Gottfried, Paul Edward. *After Liberalism*. Princeton, NJ: Princeton University Press, 1999.

Gray, John. *Liberalism*. 2nd ed. Minneapolis: University of Minnesota Press, 1995.

Gutmann, Amy, and Dennis Thompson. *Democracy and Disagreement*. Cambridge, MA: Belknap Press, 1996.

Hall, Kermit L. *The Magic Mirror: Law in American History*. New York: Oxford University Press, 1989.

Hegel, G. W. F. *The Philosophy of Right*. Translated by T. M. Knox. London: Oxford University Press, 1952.

Higham, John. *Strangers in the Land*. New York: Atheneum, 1971.

Hofstadter, Richard. *The American Political Tradition and the Men Who Made It*. New York: Vintage Books, 1974.

Hohfeld, W. N. *Fundamental Legal Conceptions*. New Haven, CT: Yale University Press, 1919.

Huntington, Samuel P. *American Politics: The Promise of Disharmony*. Cambridge, MA: Belknap Press, 1981.

Ingle, Stephen. *George Orwell: A Political Life*. Manchester: Manchester University Press, 1993.

Johnson, Allan G. *Privilege, Power, and Difference*. New York: McGraw-Hill, 2001.

Kammen, Michael. *The Origins of the American Constitution: A Documentary History*. New York: Penguin, 1986.

Karst, Kenneth. *Law's Promise, Law's Expression*. New Haven, CT: Yale University Press, 1993.

Kesey, Ken. *One Flew over the Cuckoo's Nest*. New York: Signet, 1962.

Kymlicka, Will. *Multicultural Citizenship*. Oxford: Clarendon Press, 1994.

Lowi, Theodore J. *The End of Liberalism: Ideology, Policy, and the Crisis of Public Authority*. New York: W. W. Norton & Co., 1969.

Lustig, Jeffrey. *Corporate Liberalism*. Berkeley: University of California Press, 1982.

Machan, Tibor R., ed. *The Main Debates: Communism versus Capitalism*. New York: Random House, 1987.

McConnell, Grant. *Private Power and American Democracy*. New York: Vintage Books, 1970.

McLellan, David, ed. *Karl Marx: Selected Writings*. Oxford: Oxford University Press, 1972.

Miliband, Ralph. *The State in Capitalist Society: An Analysis of the Western System of Power*. New York: Basic Books, 1969.

Mill, John Stuart. *Utilitarianism, Liberty, and Representative Government*. New York: E. P. Dutton Co., 1951.

Miller, David. *On Nationality*. Oxford: Clarendon Press, 1995.

Muir, William K. *Police: Streetcorner Politicians*. Chicago: University of Chicago Press, 1977.

Newsinger, John. *Orwell's Politics*. London: MacMillan, 1999.

Nozick, Robert. *Anarchy, State, and Utopia*. New York: Basic Books, 1974.

Orwell, George. *1984*. New York: New American Library, 1961.

Parenti, Michael. *Democracy for the Few*. New York: St. Martin's Press, 1988.

Rawls, John. *A Theory of Justice*. Cambridge, MA: Belknap Press, 1971.

Regan, Richard J. *The Moral Dimensions of Politics*. New York: Oxford University Press, 1986.

Rogin, Michael Paul. *Fathers and Children: Andrew Jackson and the Subjugation of the American Indian*. New York: Vintage Books, 1976.

Rourke, Francis E. *Bureaucracy, Politics, and Public Policy*. Boston: Little, Brown, 1976.

Sandel, Michael. *Democracy's Discontent*. Cambridge, MA: Belknap Press, 1996.

Schattschneider, E. E. *The Semisovereign People*. Hinsdale, IL: Dryden Press, 1960.

————. *Two Hundred Million Americans in Search of a Government.* Hinsdale, IL: Dryden Press, 1969.

Self, Peter. *Political Theories of Modern Government: Its Role and Reform.* London: George Allen & Unwin, 1985.

Shapiro, Ian. *The State of Democratic Theory.* Princeton, NJ: Princeton University Press, 2003.

Shklar, Judith N. *American Citizenship.* Cambridge, MA: Harvard University Press, 1997.

Smith, Adam. *The Wealth of Nations.* Chicago: University of Chicago Press, 1976.

Smith, Rogers. *Civic Ideals.* New Haven, CT: Yale University Press, 1997.

Spinner, Jeff. *The Boundaries of Citizenship.* Baltimore: Johns Hopkins University Press, 1994.

Taylor, Michael. *Community, Anarchy and Liberty.* Cambridge: Cambridge University Press, 1982.

Tocqueville, Alexis de. *Democracy in America.* Edited by J. P. Mayer, translated by George Lawrence. Garden City, NY: Anchor Books, 1969.

Tucker, Robert C., ed. *The Marx-Engels Reader.* New York: W. W. Norton & Co., 1972.

Turner, Frederick Jackson. *The Frontier in American History.* New York: Dover Publications, 1996.

Walker, Samuel. *The Rights Revolution.* New York: Oxford University Press, 1998.

Walzer, Michael. *Spheres of Justice.* New York: Basic Books, 1983.

————. *What It Means to Be an American.* New York: Marsilio Publishers, 1996.

Watt, E. D. *Authority.* New York: St. Martin's Press, 1982.

Weber, Max. *The Theory of Social and Economic Organization.* Edited by Talcott Parsons, translated by A. M. Henderson and Talcott Parsons. New York: The Free Press, 1964.

White, Morton. *Social Thought in America: The Revolt against Formalism.* Boston: Beacon Press, 1966.

Wolfe, Alan. *One Nation, After All.* New York: Penguin Books, 1998.

Wolff, Robert Paul. *In Defense of Anarchism.* New York: Harper Torchbooks, 1970.

————. *The Poverty of Liberalism.* Boston: Beacon Press, 1968.

Woll, Peter. *American Bureaucracy.* New York: W. W. Norton & Co., 1963.

Young, Iris Marion. *Justice and the Politics of Difference.* Princeton, NJ: Princeton University Press, 1990.

Young, James P. *The Politics of Affluence.* Scranton, PA: Chandler Publishing Co., 1968.

Index

About the Author

Craig L. Carr obtained his Ph.D. from the University of Washington and is currently professor of political science at Portland State University, Portland, Oregon. His research interests include liberal theory, theories of freedom, justice theory, and democratic theory. He has published several books and numerous articles in the areas of political and legal philosophy, the history of political ideas, constitutional law, international law, and American party politics.